IMAGES AND REALITY IN INTERNATIONAL POLITICS

The Hebrew University of Jerusalem
The Leonard Davis Institute for International Relations

IMAGES AND REALITY IN INTERNATIONAL POLITICS

Edited by

NISSAN OREN

ST. MARTIN'S PRESS, New York
THE MAGNES PRESS, THE HEBREW UNIVERSITY, Jerusalem

© The Magnes Press, The Hebrew University, Jerusalem, 1984
All rights reserved. For information, write:
St. Martin's Press, Inc., 175 Fifth Avenue, New York, NY 10010
Printed in Israel
First published in the United States of America in 1984

ISBN 0-312- 40917-6

Library of Congress Cataloging in Publication Data
Main entry under title:

Images and reality in international politics.

Includes index.
1. International relations – Addresses, essays, lectures.
I. Oren, Nissan.
JX1391.I535 1984   327   83-40613
ISBN 0-312-40917-6

CONTENTS

Introduction		7
Edward N. Luttwak	Perceptions of Power in Retrospect	9
Michael Handel	On Diplomatic Surprise	20
Jonathan Wilkenfeld, Gerald W. Hopple, Paul J. Rossa	Bridging the Image-Reality Gap: An Empirical Perspective	34
Yehoshua Arieli	History as Reality Shaped by Images	57
J.H. Leurdijk	Images and Reality in International Politics: Security Perceptions in the Foreign Policy of the Netherlands	70
Davis B. Bobrow, John A. Kringen, Steve Chan	Change and the Chinese	81
J.W. Schneider, s.j.	The Interaction of Policy and Religion: The Vatican and the State of Israel	95
Frans A.M. Alting von Geusau	East-West Détente: Perceptions and Policies	105
Andrzej Korbonski	Image and Reality in International Relations: The Case of Eastern Europe	112
Kalevi J. Holsti	Détente as a Source of International Conflict	125
Abraham Ben-Zvi	Globalism vs. Localism: National Security Perceptions in American Foreign Policy	143
Shmuel Sandler	Presidential Strategies and Character: The Eisenhower and the Nixon Administrations	163
Michael Nacht	On Memories, Interests and Foreign Policy: The Case of Vietnam	184
Thomas C. Schelling	Alternate Sources of Middle East Conflict	206
Robert W. Tucker	The Middle East: The View from Washington	211
Nissan Oren	An Image: Israel as the "Holder" of the Regional Balance	238

CONTRIBUTORS

Edward N. Luttwak	Author and Political Analyst
Michael Handel	Senior Lecturer in International Relations, Hebrew University
Jonathan Wilkenfeld	Professor of Government, University of Maryland
Yehoshua Arieli	Professor of History, Hebrew University
J.H. Leurdijk	University of Amsterdam
Davis B. Bobrow	Professor of Government, University of Maryland
J.W. Schneider, s.j.	Professor of Religion, University of Tilburg
Frans A.M. Alting von Geusau	Professor of International Relations, University of Tilburg
Andrzej Korbonski	Professor of Political Science, UCLA
Kalevi J. Holsti	Professor of Political Science, University of British Columbia
Abraham Ben-Zvi	Senior Lecturer in Political Science, Tel Aviv University
Shmuel Sandler	Senior Lecturer in Political Science, Bar Ilan University
Michael Nacht	Professor of Government, J.F. Kennedy School of Government, Harvard University
Thomas C. Schelling	Professor of Economics, J.F. Kennedy School of Government, Harvard University
Robert W. Tucker	Professor of International Relations, Johns Hopkins University
Nissan Oren	Professor of International Relations, Hebrew University

Introduction

The way we perceive ourselves, the manner in which we are perceived by others, and finally, our own image of the way we think we are perceived — all constitute a fixed triangle within which our real lives evolve.

To be sure, there are great and meaningful differences between ourselves and our lives, on the one hand, and states and statecraft, on the other. This notwithstanding, the above triangulation retains a good measure of validity when applied to the international plane.

The discrepancy between what is real and concrete and what is imagined and perceived has been acknowledged from the beginnings of human consciousness. As we have become more verbal and our terminologies more refined, the problem has gradually been lifted from the plane of the intuitive and placed on the table of analysis. Although our understanding has grown immensely, the problem is far from being resolved.

Despite their respective intelligence services and data collectors, modern-day captains of politics perceive the world, other states, and particularly rival states as large abstractions. Unlike our individual lives, where perceptions of others are continuously readjusted by means of contacts and clashes which help reproduce reality, reality tests in international politics are less reliable as well as less frequent. It takes a war or an acute crisis between two states for them to concretize the reality of might and thus close the gap with the imaginary. And yet, are we not called upon to muster our misperceptions before the ultimate test?

This volume, which is a collective work, was designed to address some of the questions which arise out of the immense complexities of images as guides in international behavior. The undertaking remains necessarily modest compared to the overall objective. The problem has been attacked from various directions in an eclectic fashion. We have not blanketed the problem, as it were, but have rather undertaken several independent scrutinies carried out by practitioners as well as by professional intellectuals.

The contributions are arranged in three clusters. The first contains a number of essays addressed to general topics. The second cluster is made up of con-

7

tributions referring to various regional contexts. Finally, we include some views on the Middle East impasse. Thus, the general and the particular are admixed. Without any doubt, the representations made here are immensely fewer than relative themes which remain absent. This is the common fate of all compilations.

There is no sure way of measuring the durability of the insights which make up this volume. Putting it yet another way, some of the contributions are surely of greater relevance to the international scene than others. There is no way or established method of pre-judging the staying powers of an idea. The problem remains significant enough and its parameters broad enough for us to take our individual risks and hope that a contribution is made.

The design of the volume, its execution, its possible merits and certainly its failings are all to be attributed to the editor. The undertaking would not have become possible if not for the resources of the Leonard Davis Institute for International Relations, and the cooperation and inspiration of its staff and its associates.

Nissan Oren

Perceptions of Power in Retrospect

Edward N. Luttwak

Introduction

Over the last several years, it has been increasingly recognized that in addition to all the diverse arts and sciences that guide the conduct of military policy, a method is also needed to shape the outward manifestations of military power, for these are part of its "output."

Generalizing from the narrower ideas associated with the concept of deterrence, the conclusion has been reached that military power unrecognized (or discounted) by decision-makers abroad cannot fully achieve its purposes. Military capabilities that are not recognized, and thus fail to enter into the policy calculations of relevant decision-makers abroad, would still serve in the eventual conduct of warfare, but cannot support the ordinary conduct of foreign policy in the absence of hostilities.

To reassure or intimidate, to deter or coerce,[1] potential military capabilities must be manifest. Indeed, until the moment of actual combat, it is the manifestations alone that are operative; as far as the transactions of international politics are concerned, the underlying physical realities are irrelevant in themselves.

Research to date[2] has explored a variety of methodological approaches in the attempt to define the modalities whereby military power is manifest. The implicit goal of these efforts has been to define patterns of deployment, modes of operation and — to a lesser extent — guidelines for the development of equipment, which would all enhance the political "visibility" of American armed forces without the sacrifice of physical capability, at parity of cost.

It is obvious that the essential preliminary to the formulation of such specific techniques is the development of a general theory that can actually explain *how* power is manifest, to whom, and under what circumstances. In this quest for theory, various applications of current concepts in political science have been explored; there has also been some recourse to the psychology of perception. In addition, some studies have focused on institutional aspects of the problem, involving detailed analyses of the coverage of particular military phenomena in specific newspapers and periodicals.[3]

These efforts have yielded some partial theories of varying plausibility that still require testing. Purely intuitive approaches have also generated insights that cannot be formulated as refutable propositions but that have been widely recognized as new and valid. Nevertheless, it must be recognized that no general theory has emerged. Indeed, no such theory may be feasible at all in the absence of a whole structure of prior theories on cognition and decision processes.

This does not mean, however, that the "power perception" studies have been futile. As a direct consequence of the discussions and writings associated with these efforts, there has been a distinct increase in policy-makers' awareness of the problem. From the secretary of defense down to service echelons, it is now recognized that military forces cannot properly be evaluated exclusively in terms of their expected performance in the context of imaginary combat scenarios. Some attention is now also given to the continuing political effects of forces maintained and deployed.

In particular, it is now widely realized that the Soviet style of deployment tends to maximize visible capabilities as a by-product of its emphasis on initial combat capabilities. By contrast, the American preference for sustained capabilities achieves the opposite result. Similarly, the Soviet equipment preference for quantity rather than unit quality results in the manifestation of more visible power than the American preference for very high unit quality, resources expended being equal. In both cases, the traditional pattern of American preferences may have a compelling justification, but a recognition of their hidden political costs can still be of value.

As a result of this enhanced awareness of the problem, important military policy decisions now entail some consideration of the "power perception" dimension. It is possible to trace the influence of this new factor in the reorganization of the American army into sixteen divisions; in the implementation of the Nunn Amendment (ostensibly based on operational considerations alone); and, with less certainty, in the upward re-designation of U.S. navy warships. (For example, guided-missile "destroyer-leaders" are now designated as cruisers.)

A new dimension of the problem is examined in the following essay, in the attempt to lay the basis for a methodology applicable to a level of policy that has not yet been given much attention.

The Modern Geography of Military Power and the Classical Idea of the Balance of Power

For all the variety of their methodological approaches, all the "power perception" studies known to the present writer share a common subject: in each case, the military power in question is the totality of the capabilities of any given party, worldwide. Typically, when American and Soviet military capabilities are compared, all Soviet and American forces anywhere in the world are included in the evaluation, on the same footing and without geographic differentiation. The gross outlines of deployment distribution may be noted ("43 divisions on the Chinese border"), but the geographic distribution of forces is not incorporated in the comparison unless in a fairly specific "war-fighting" context. The presumption is that the comparison of the totality of forces is meaningful in a general sense, while their geographic distribution is valid only as an adjunct to specific comparisons focused on particular theaters of war.

This monolithic view of military power accurately reflects the patterns of data presentation that most analyses use and produce, the familiar side-by-side comparisons of Soviet and American inventories.[4] It also corresponds to the implicit framework of the classic idea of the balance of power, a far deeper influence on our understanding of these matters than our data-presentation habits. Formulated in the context of the European ascendancy, at a time when all non-European powers were exotic shadows irrelevant to European politics (except for the Ottoman Empire), and when colonial garrisons were always minuscule and could scarcely ever be recalled to Europe in useful time, the classic concept of the balance of power implicitly assumed that the totality of military capabilities would interact in the single European arena.[5] Hence men spoke of *the* balance of power as the single assay of relative strengths, military and not, implicitly meaning thereby the *European* balance of power.

To be sure, international relations at the peripheries of Europe did take place, and there was much experience of colonial conflict by the time the concept was formulated in its final form. Both naturally inspired some consideration of geographically limited balances also ("the balance of power in..."); but when European-style war and diplomacy began to expand toward the globalization that has now been fully attained, there should have been a parallel conceptual evolution to the notion of multiple, geographically limited, power balances, non-additive in the short run and each valid only in its own geographic context. It is not surprising, however, that this conceptual evolution failed to take place: core foreign policy ideas, established strategical notions, and even national self-images, were and still are anchored in the monolithic concept of the balance of power. The latter also favors elegant discourse on international politics based on the phraseology of eighteenth-century diplomatic comment; by contrast, acceptance of the new reality of separate, multiple, power balances would unavoidably require a clumsy phraseology qualified at each turn by geographic differentiation ("European-relevant American power viz. European-disposable Soviet power," etc.).

But in this case the price of verbal elegance is conceptual confusion, and this in turn is a potential source of policy error. Episodes such as the 1962 Cuban missile crisis render explicit the underlying conceptual distortions caused by the persistence of the monolithic view in a world of unevenly distributed military power, a world in which the tempo of crisis resolution may be much faster than the speed with which forces can be redeployed across the globe. Was the Soviet Union a "superpower" in 1962? In terms of the monolithic concept the answer would undoubtedly be affirmative. But in the "power zone" in which Cuba is located, the Soviet Union was distinctly inferior in all dimensions of capability except the strategic-nuclear. The conduct of American policy in the crisis made the issue of control of sea transit critical, and so it made the requisite naval capabilities critical also. In a surface-combatant deployment race conducted within the time frame of the crisis, it is certain that even the British navy would have out-deployed the Russians; the Soviet Union was certainly less than a "superpower" in the circumstances of the crisis. Today the Soviet navy is of course much better equipped than it was in 1962; at the same time, the strategic-nuclear capabilities of the Soviet Union have increased greatly from the limited and unreliable strike-back capability in place in 1962. And yet if the moves of the crisis were repeated in present circumstances, the outcome would be no different: (a) the values at stake would still be insufficient to justify the ultimate recourse to strategic-nuclear capabilities; (b) the strategic-nuclear balance would still prohibit Soviet countermoves in Europe to exploit circumstances geographically more favorable to the Russians; and (c) Soviet surface naval forces deployable in the Caribbean "power zone" would still be grossly inferior to those that the United States could deploy in the same area. Distance still counts.

The notion of separate balances manifest in separate "power zones" can coexist with the obviously global nature of strategic-nuclear capabilities because of the inhibitions that restrict the applicability of the latter. Diplomatic recourse to strategic-nuclear coercion requires the prior judgment that the issues at stake plausibly justify the risk of an eventual escalation to nuclear war.

The notion of separate "power zones" can also coexist with the reality of widely deployed tactical-nuclear weapons because of another set of inhibitions. It is clear that "power zones" are separated in the first place only because of the constraints that limit the long-range air mobility of armored forces, as well as the transfer speed of naval forces in general.[6] If, for example, light forces armed with tactical nuclear weapons were interchangeable with armor-mechanized forces for the purposes of crisis management in, say, the Middle East, then the mobility constraints would be much less restrictive in that particular case, and the Middle East would not constitute a separate "power zone" for the United States, at least as far as ground forces were concerned. Provided that access is made available at their destination, air-transportable light forces in moderate numbers can nowadays be delivered anywhere in the world by the United States, the Soviet Union and even some third parties. And if light forces were equipped with tactical nuclear weapons (which have a very high effectiveness "density"), they could then overpower much larger and much heavier forces deployed by an enemy in place.

But for the purposes of crisis management, the physical reality of tactical nuclear capabilities is nullified by the very powerful inhibitions that constrain the use of these weapons. It is now accepted that nuclear weapons cannot be used unless the values at stake in the crisis suffice to justify not only the direct military risks, but also the risk of a further escalation widely presumed to be capable of reaching the extreme of homeland-to-homeland nuclear attacks if any nuclear weapons are used anywhere, including against a non-nuclear state. This being so, the diplomatic value of coercion by means of tactical nuclear weapons is nullified as well.

Hence the global range of strategic nuclear weapons, and the unconstrained mobility of light forces made very powerful by their equipment of tactical nuclear weapons, are both insufficient to negate the effects of distance. For all the advances of modern transport, power still wanes as the distance from its geographic basing points increases. That is why separate "power zones" survive, each featuring its own peculiar balance of power which may differ very greatly from the theoretical abstraction of global comparisons.

Recognition of mobility constraints is incorporated into military planning and accepted as a prosaic aspect of its environment. And yet the obvious implications for the *political* aspects of military policy have not received sufficient attention. Even in the "power perception" studies the political significance of the separation of the "power zones" seems to have been missed. Yet it is apparent that, except for strategic-nuclear capabilities, almost all forms of military power are geographically conditioned; thus analyses of their manifestations must begin with the nature of this conditioning rather than with a search for universal modalities of perception and belief.

"Power Zones," Interest Clusters and the Maximization of the Political Utility of Military Power

In the course of informal interviews conducted for another purpose with respondents in Taiwan and Japan, a pattern of answers emerged that correlated quite closely with the answers given to identical questions by Israeli and West German respondents.

All respondents were of similar professional background, being senior civil officials for whom politico-military questions have a high degree of salience, or else senior officers.

The questions were simple and were ostensibly intended to elicit estimates of American and Soviet military power in terms of conventional categories, such as tactical-air squadrons (and number of aircraft), warships by classes, ground-force divisions (and number of troops), and so on. (As might have been expected, Taiwanese and Israeli respondents were consistently better informed than Japanese or West German respondents.)

In a second set of questions, geographically defined force-level estimates were elicited. In all cases it was carefully explained that no attempt was being made to test the quality of the national information available to these respondents in their official capacity. Immediate off-the-cuff answers were demanded and obtained, it being pointed out that this was only a memory test and not a test of professional knowledge.

The resulting data are not worthy of detailed tabulation. The unsurprising result was that respondents were far better informed of force levels in their own immediate areas than of force levels in their hemisphere as a whole, and better informed of hemispheric force levels than of global force-levels.

These results do not surprise because it is implicitly assumed that proximity correlates positively with improved knowledge, through access to local and direct information (including actual "perception," in the technical meaning of the word), just as the vision of the normally sighted is better closer at hand than further away.

But a third set of questions, which focused on the *sources* of information, revealed that the presumption was wrong. All respondents cited unofficial sources (and mainly the IISS *Military Balance*), which present overall global data much more intensively than they do data classified by areas of deployment, or even by hemispheres. In fact, as every analyst knows from his own experience, the very great majority of force-level data are stated in global terms, and the only geographically defined comparisons commonly seen are those of the NATO/Warsaw Pact, and especially the "Central Front," comparisons. This is true outside the United States also, since the ultimate source of military data of all sorts is in most cases the U.S. Department of Defense, with the intervening media also being American in most cases, except for the equally globalistic IISS. The privileged sources available to the respondents provided them with information that was either irrelevant in this context (i.e., PRC force levels in the case of the Taiwanese, Arab/Israeli comparisons in the case of the Israelis), or else of little consequence, with two exceptions: "Central Front" data for the West Germans and data on Soviet Far East naval deployments (and naval-air *operations*) for the Japanese.

Obviously, knowledge correlates with the *salience* of the object rather than with any particular cognitive advantage of adjacent subjects. Thus Israeli respondents were specifically knowledgeable of Soviet forces readily deployable into their own "power zone," and in particular of Soviet airborne forces (including considerable detail on lift capacities and transit facilities); they were also very much aware of current Soviet naval force levels, and also specifically Soviet naval "surge" capabilities. In parallel, these same respondents had detailed knowledge of the exact composition of the Sixth Fleet and of *its* surge capabilities. These respondents had a detailed appreciation of the basing and transit constraints imposed by host governments on the deployment of U.S. tactical-air forces into the East Mediterranean/Levant "power zone," but they had a much less precise idea of the full inventory of U.S. tactical-air forces; as for U.S. army and marine corps forces, there were fairly accurate estimates of U.S. *delivery* capabilities, but considerably less precise information on the overall array of U.S. army and marine forces.

Much the same pattern was in evidence in the answers of Taiwanese, Japanese and West German respondents. In each case, notions about the military power of the United States, and of its relative capabilities vis-à-vis the Soviet Union in different multilateral contexts, were made up by images of U.S. military forces weighted in a hierarchy of graduated deployability. Forces in place were given a full weighting, scarcely modified by any information on readiness; forces not regarded as *rapidly* deployable because of mobility, transit or political constraints seemed to have a weighting close to zero; and forces deliverable in various time frames were somewhere in between.

It appears therefore that a "short-crisis" (and "short-war") assumption has been implicitly incorporated into the perceptual frameworks of these respondents. Close scrutiny of the modalities of crisis and conflict in Europe and in the Far East does *not* necessarily support the implicit short-crisis/short-war assumption. It will be recalled, for example, that the 1961 Berlin crisis evolved over a period of months. In fact, it is only in the case of the Middle East that the historical record supports the implicit assumption shared by *all* the respondents. Right or wrong, what is of consequence here is that the respondents did apply a sharply graduated time-frame weighting to U.S. military forces.

Having thus already approached the question indirectly (in the hope of obtaining less premeditated answers), the questioners next asked the respondents a series of questions that explicitly tried to elicit their definition of *relevant* American power. Is American protection of great significance? (Yes, in all cases, of course.) How important is the actual military power that the United States now deploys for this protection? (Very important, in all cases.) Respondents rejected the suggestion that what really counted was the overall politico-economic strength of the United States; many respondents interpreted this suggestion in terms of a mobilization potential and, having done so, went on to discount its relevance in "modern" conditions (i.e., in short-crisis/short-war conditions). Next, the respondents were asked to identify the components of U.S. military power they thought most significant, less significant, and least significant. Their answers were a perfect match for the earlier set of questions that ostensibly tested their memory. In other words, knowledge *does* correlate with salience, and evaluations of American military power discriminate between forces in place, forces deemed to be readily deployable, and forces that could be deployed in a descending order of weighting.

When the notion of separate "power zones" is combined with this particular pattern of perceptions, a number of conclusions follow:

a. The overall military power of the United States manifest to all allies and clients is the sum of separate perceptions in different "power zones," in each of which the overall inventory of U.S. forces is weighted differently according to the degree of deployability to the zone in question.
b. In evaluating these perceptions as part of the peace-time "output" of U.S.

military forces, the allies and clients who do the "perceiving" are themselves of sharply different importance from the viewpoints of U.S. national
interests. Hence in evaluating manifest power and its worth, *two* sets of
weightings are needed: one attributed by the United States to the separate
"power zones," and the other attributed to U.S. forces judged to be relevant by local observers.

c. Unless their deployability to the separate "power zones" has actually been
demonstrated (e.g., through the "Reforger" exercises for the European
"power zone," airlift reinforcement exercises in which U.S. ground units are
flown to Europe), U.S. forces held back in the CONUS (continental U.S.)
produce a very low "output" in terms of power manifest to allies and
clients. Deployability demonstrations such as the "Reforger" exercises
seem to be interpreted in a double sense — as tests of mobility (including
political access), and as tests of political intentions on the part of the U.S.
government. For example, in answering both sets of questions, West German respondents gave a high weighting to the three armored and
mechanized divisions deployed in the CONUS but earmarked to reinforce
the Seventh Army in Europe, whose heavy equipment is pre-positioned; by
contrast, these respondents assigned a very low weighting to the National
Guard divisions, which they obviously regarded as not deployable in the
context of their implicit "short-war" time frame.

The significance of these findings may be disputed on the grounds that all
the respondents were politico-military specialists. Other kinds of respondents
— say, businessmen or conventional diplomats — may be inclined to attribute a far greater significance to the overall politico-economic strength of
the United States. And such respondents may be less likely to interpret non-
military strength in terms of war-fighting mobilization potentials, being more
cognizant of the leverage that non-military instrumentalities confer upon the
United States in the transactions of peace-time diplomacy. But even if these
specialist respondents were wrong, their answers remain of decisive
significance, because it is these same specialists who educate their respective
publics and the decision-making elites on the balance of power and the
magnitude of American military strength.

The Model Defined

Mobility constraints, including political limitations on transit and access, offset by such basing and pre-positioning facilities as are relevant, and modified by applicable force contributions by allies on the spot, together define the separation of the globe into discrete "power zones." These cannot of course correspond to any objective geographic areas, because each set of "power zones" is peculiar to a given party. For example, the Caribbean "power zone" is a function of *Soviet* mobility and access limitations while, as far as the United States is concerned, it is not a separate "power zone" at all but rather part of the continental periphery. By contrast, Korea is in a distinct Northeast Asian "power zone" as far as the United States is concerned, while being part of the Far East peripheral area as far as the Soviet Union is concerned. (It is clear, on the other hand, that the Soviet Union is so large a country that it has at least two distinct "power zones" within its *own* boundaries, and the resulting problem for its military planning is both unique and very serious.)

It is obvious that the value of the different "power zones" varies widely from the viewpoint of any given party; hence the effective worth of the "output" of manifest power generated by military forces with respect to each varies also. Other things being equal, the deployment of, say, a U.S. army division in Western Europe should generate a higher "output" for U.S. foreign policy than if the same division were deployed in, say, Korea — to the same degree that Western Europe is more valuable to the United States than is Korea, or rather its entire Northeast Asian "power zone." But there are two further factors that must be taken into account, either of which might easily reverse the result. First, the *salience* of military power as such in each of the different "power zones"; for example, it is clear that for all the chronic insecurity of Western Europe, Korea is much more insecure still, so that a given amount of American military power deployed in Korea will have a greater *relative* significance than the same force deployed in Europe. Second, there is the absolute commitment-making role of forces deployed in place, and especially ground forces, which adds greatly to the significance of the *first* of several formations that might be present in any one area. In terms of our example, if the division in question happens to be the *only* division in Korea, while being the nth division for Western Europe, then its *marginal significance* will be much higher in Korea.

The "power-zone" side of the model is therefore a function of: (a) the intrinsic worth of the geographic area in question; (b) the salience of military power within it; and (c) the marginal value of the forces deployed.

The force-deployment side of the model, on the other hand, is defined by the differential weighting that opinion-making observers on the scene assign to military forces. Three factors appear to dominate their calculations. First, the *operational relevance* of the forces in question; thus, for example, Japanese observers obviously attribute a far greater importance to U.S. naval forces than do the West Germans, and Norwegians are much more likely to highly value U.S. marine corps deployments (for Finnmark operations) than are Israelis, who believe them to be lacking in the heavy equipment needed for armored warfare in the Middle East. Second, the place of the forces in question in the hierarchy of deployability; as pointed out above, notions of deployability are heavily influenced by the pattern of past operational deployments or deployment exercises. Third, the readiness of the forces; this appears to be a distinctly less important factor. Moreover, it seems that perceptions of readiness reflect more the overall image of the United States and its armed forces than any more specific data available to respondents. (None of the respondents were aware of the fact that unit-by-unit readiness data for U.S. army CONUS-based forces has been published in unclassified form.) Quantification being impossible, it would be futile to set out in algebraic form a maximizing equation for manifest power "outputs." The characteristics of the model are obvious enough, and directly suggest some policy implications.

Notes

1. Elsewhere the present writer has classified the political functions of military force as varieties of "armed suasion"; see *The Political Uses of Sea Power* (Baltimore: The Johns Hopkins Press, 1975), chapter I.

2. By Wolf, Leites, Goldhamer and others; see, e.g., the author's article in *Survival* 19 (No. 1, January/February 1977): 2-8.

3. See, e.g., Herbert Goldhamer, "The U.S.-Soviet Strategic Balance as Seen from London and Paris," *Survival* 19 (No. 5, September/October 1977): 202-207; Goldhamer scrutinized *The Economist* and *Le Monde*.

4. The most important unclassified source being the *Military Balance* published annually by the London-based International Institute for Strategic Studies.

5. For an interesting collection of writings on the classic theory, see Moorhead Wright, *Theory and Practice of the Balance of Power, 1486-1914* (London: J.M. Dent and Sons, 1975).

6. For example, even with nuclear propulsion, it would still take a full week to concentrate Soviet submarines in the Caribbean "power zone" from bases in the Northern Fleet area; or, e.g., to move a U.S. marine division from the East Coast of the United States to the Persian Gulf by sea transport a minimum of 28 days is needed. As for air mobility, this is not a practical proposition for armor-mechanized units of divisional size unless their heavier items of equipment are pre-positioned.

On Diplomatic Surprise

Michael Handel

In the theory of international relations, and especially in strategic studies, much attention has been devoted to the development of a theory of surprise attack. Surprise is a relatively sophisticated and rich area of research, with its own jargon, theories, and classic case studies. However, while we know a good deal about the problems involved in surprise attack, surprise as a means of diplomacy and diplomatic maneuvering is relatively unresearched. Diplomatic history is rich enough to supply us with a large number of striking examples of diplomatic surprise of which Sadat's visit to Jerusalem in 1977 is only one of the most recent. Other examples of diplomatic surprise that come to mind are the 1922 Rapallo agreement between Germany and the USSR, the Ribbentrop-Molotov agreement of August 1939, Krushchev's diplomacy during the so-called U-2 incident of May 1960, and Nixon and Kissinger's Chinese "ping pong" diplomacy of 1971-72.

Why, then, haven't the scholars of international politics devoted any systematic attention to the study of surprise as a means of diplomacy, to problems of warning and hedging against such surprise, as they have with military surprise? What are the similarities and differences between military and diplomatic surprise? Is there a connection between the two modes of surprise? Which parts of the theory already available on military surprise are also applicable to diplomatic surprise and which are not? What are the causes of the failure to predict diplomatic surprise? What will be the value of a theory of diplomatic surprise if it can be developed?

While history can supply us with a fairly large number of examples of surprise in diplomacy, it has never been the fundamental tool for the diplomat as it has been for the soldier. While it is a necessary and inevitable part of war and military planning, surprise appears less frequently as a means of diplomacy, and when it does it is not necessarily integral to diplomatic conduct. It is true that since the beginnings of recorded diplomatic history, and certainly since Machiavelli, diplomacy has always been viewed as a world of deception, treachery and cunning, and therefore by implication as a world where surprise should always be accepted as part of the normal conduct of affairs. Diplomacy, however, involves much more continuity, tradition and conservatism — even inertia — than it does deception and treachery. After all, the major function of diplomacy is to further the interests of states by peaceful means, through improving mutual interests, ensuring stability and preventing crises and unexpected surprises from interrupting the normal fabric of the relations between states. In this respect, while surprise is accepted as normal and essential for the soldier, it is abnormal and pathological for the diplomat. This may have somewhat weakened the interest of the student of diplomatic history and international relations in surprise as a means of diplomatic conduct. Furthermore, while in war the consequences of a surprise attack are always dramatic, immediate and often disastrous, this is not always true of diplomatic surprise. While such surprise is, to be sure, always dramatic, the results are frequently neither catastrophic nor even immediate. The impact of a diplomatic surprise can often be *positive* in nature and its impact can be long-range. Thus, while for the strategist the dangers and problems of surprise are of critical importance, this has not necessarily always been the case for the student of diplomacy.

These, and perhaps additional considerations as well, can at least partly explain why surprise has not been much of a subject for research in the theory of international relations and diplomacy. Yet these explanations are not enough in the final analysis. I will therefore try to begin developing some initial insights into the question of surprise as a means of diplomacy.

What are some of the similarities and differences between military and diplomatic surprise? In the first place, military surprise is always one-sided, one party surprising the other. Surprise is therefore always a unilateral act; collaboration between the antagonists is non-existent or negligible. Diplomatic surprise, on the other hand, although it can be a unilateral act, is almost always the result of collaborative efforts between two (or more) antagonists who surprise the rest of the world (i.e., third parties). While in military surprise one of the two sides directly involved is always the object of the surprise attack, in surprise diplomacy the objects of surprise are usually third parties (including very close allies) affected indirectly and not always immediately. The Rapallo agreement, for example, was the result of the unexpected collaboration between two earlier antagonists, Germany and the USSR, the "victims" of the surprise being mainly Great Britain and France. The Ribbentrop-Molotov agreement was made after extensive and intense secret negotiation between Germany and the USSR, who again surprised third parties, especially

Great Britain, France and Poland, while Germany surprised its closest allies, Italy and Japan. In 1971, with the re-establishment of direct contacts between the United States and the People's Republic of China as a result of "ping pong" diplomacy, it was also third parties — and Russia in particular — that were surprised. Similarly, the main "victims" of Sadat's peace diplomacy and his visit to Jerusalem were not Israel and Egypt (though of course most observers in these countries were surprised), but rather the superpowers and the Arab states. The figure below illustrates this distinction between affected parties in military as opposed to diplomatic surprise.

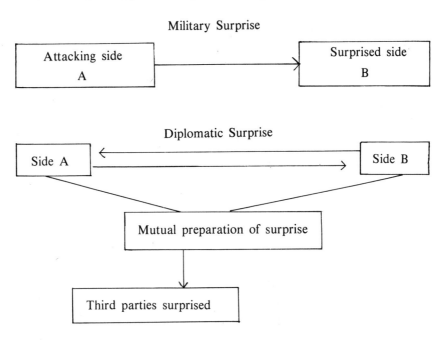

Military Surprise

| Attacking side A | → | Surprised side B |

Diplomatic Surprise

Side A ← → Side B

Mutual preparation of surprise

Third parties surprised

In military surprise attack, the intention of the initiating side is almost always to achieve immediate results so as to attain immediate, short-range military objectives: to throw the adversary off-balance, to dictate the direction and pace of developments, and to win as decisive a military victory as possible. Despite the immediate dramatic impact, diplomatic surprise usually leads to delayed rather than instantaneous results. Thus the Rapallo agreement led to the long-range economic, and later military, contacts between Germany and the USSR, gradually improved the diplomatic standing of both countries, and in the long run legitimized their acceptance and presence in world affairs. Similarly, both the U.S-China "ping pong" diplomacy and Sadat's surprise visit to Jerusalem were only the beginnings of processes that could lead to rapprochement, the improvement of bilateral relations and, eventually, to peace or to normal relations. The Ribbentrop-Molotov agreement signed in August 1939 is somewhat different from the above-mentioned cases, as it was Germany's intention to acquire almost direct benefits by clearing the way for an immediate attack on Poland. But even in this case the military attack came a week later (considering the previous German-Russian agreement, however, it should not have surprised Poland as it did) and did include as well many long-range arrangements between Germany and the USSR.

Military surprise differs from diplomatic surprise also in its much greater variety of possibilities. A military surprise attack can occur within a larger number of levels and modes than can diplomatic surprise. The former can be the result of a combination of the following elements: the timing of attack; the chosen area or areas of attack; the strategy, tactics and methods employed; the use of new military doctrines; the deployment for the first time of new and unexpected weapons technologies; and so on. For this reason it is much more difficult to predict, warn or hedge against a surprise attack than it is to forecast a diplomatic surprise. Given the concept of national interest or *raison d'état,* a state has only a relatively limited number of clear choices to make; the military planner, on the other hand, has a much larger combination of possible methods and means available to him. In international politics the number of exceptional or very important issues — vital interests — is small. In addition, the fact that most vital interests are handled routinely and are under control leaves only a very limited number of issues that need to be drastically changed. Therefore the number of possible *major* diplomatic surprises is limited.

Early in 1921 both Germany and Russia had only two major choices available to them. They could either improve their diplomatic and economic relations with the Western democracies or, alternatively, they could turn towards each other and improve their bilateral relations, despite all earlier animosities and conflicting interests, and thus break the isolation enforced on them by the Western democracies. They both preferred the first option, although they did not relinquish the right to later take up the second one. And having met with the obstinate and narrow-minded attitudes of the Western democracies, they had no choice but sooner or later to do just that. Given the limited options available to both Germany and the USSR, and considering their own policies, the Western powers should not have been surprised by the Rapallo agreement.

Once Hitler decided to dismember Poland by either peaceful means or force in 1939 — a decision which could be expected, in light of his earlier policies — he had to either obtain British or French agreement or Russian consent. As the West denied him either open or tacit agreement for such an act, he could turn only to Russia. The Russians, for their part, desired security against possible German aggression. This they could obtain either through a reliable defensive agreement with Great Britain or France, or by coming to terms with Germany. Again, both states first tried to reach an agreement with the reluctant French and British governments and, having failed to secure such an agreement, at a certain stage began to parallel their discussions in the West with direct negotiations with each other. Moreover, both the USSR and Germany had gradually developed a common interest — preventing the other from reaching a separate agreement with Great Britain and France — and thus their interests converged in more ways than one. For these and other reasons, France and Great Britain should have been prepared for the Ribbentrop-Molotov agreement. Yet that agreement came as a bombshell and the two Western powers were in fact surprised. The British tried to counter the Russian-German surprise with a bombshell of their own: ratification of the Anglo-Polish treaty on August 25, which surprised the Germans even more but, alas, came too late to prevent war.

Relations between the United States and the People's Republic of China virtually ceased to exist after 1950. War between the two, despite U.S. involvement in Vietnam, was highly unlikely; if any diplomatic surprise was possible, it could only be in the direction of improved Chinese-American relations. There were enough signals and feelers sent from both sides to indicate such a move but, again, everybody was surprised.

Sadat's surprise visit to Israel is analogous to the United States-Chinese rapprochement. In this case, all sides, *including* the Israelis, were surprised. For the second time, Sadat wrecked the "conception" of Israeli policy-makers and intelligence. This time, however, he wrecked not a military but a diplomatic conception. Yet given the relatively limited number of diplomatic options, and even Israel's own contribution to Sadat's move, the Israelis should have been less surprised than they were. Moreover, any other unexpected diplomatic move in a negative direction would *not* have surprised the Israelis, who have learned to always expect the worst possible initiative from the Arab states. Therefore the only diplomatic surprise possible from the Arab side would be a positive one.

A diplomatic surprise is somewhat easier to anticipate, and hence cancel itself, than is a military surprise attack, a situation determined by the fact that diplomatic surprise is almost always the end result of a long ongoing process which, because of certain developments, has unexpectedly been accelerated. In this respect, the acceleration is the cause of the diplomatic surprise. It is the recognition on the part of statesmen that a certain policy is desirable in the long run despite short-run difficulties. They therefore decide to shorten a process that will in any case take place sooner or later. Probably no one in the United States or China, for example, had any doubt that sooner or later the two states would resume their bilateral ties. If this is the case, why wait until the 1980s if this could be done at a reasonable cost in the 1970s?

Another reason diplomatic surprise should be easier to predict is that the number of alternatives for major diplomatic action is limited and, at a certain point, under the pressure of events (as shown above), they are still further narrowed down. Thus if Sadat (a) suddenly realized that there was a limit to the pressures the United States could bring to bear on Israel and hence he maintains no realistic military option against Israel, and/or (b) feared that the Egyptian economy would collapse completely unless a peace settlement was reached, his options are narrowed to two: either accelerating the peace settlement by direct negotiations with Israel, or going to war. Choosing the first option has certainly not precluded the second one. Nevertheless, the choice of the first option was the outcome of the narrowing down of other options to exclude those diplomatic and other non-military options that lead to a dead end. It is what Machiavelli has called *necessitas* — necessity — that dictates an almost inevitable choice.

There is only one factor that can make diplomatic surprise more difficult to detect: the ease of maintaining secrecy. At one stage or another, a military surprise attack must include relatively large numbers of participants and the movement of a large number of formations of material and the concentration of troops. A diplomatic surprise, on the other hand, can be prepared by a very limited number of top diplomats or negotiated directly between the leaders of states and their closest aides. It does not involve any physical movements of men and material and thus has in that respect an advantage over the planning of a military surprise.

There is another important difference between military and diplomatic surprise. A military surprise attack can offer only advantages; diplomatic surprise is almost always a compromise. A surprise military attack can help to throw the enemy off balance, dictate the shape of the war on the attacker's terms, and make victory easier to achieve. Surprise is an integral and natural part of any military planning. Diplomatic surprise, on the other hand, is a political decision; it always involves a trade-off. When Rathenau decided to sign the treaty with Russia at Rapallo he knew it would undermine Germany's relations with the Western democracies. By his decision to ally himself with Russia, Hitler to a certain extent also alienated the Italians and the Japanese. The Russians, by signing an agreement with Nazi Germany, considerably weakened their moral and political standing with the communist parties of Europe. The United States had to sacrifice its relations with Taiwan and reduce its credibility towards other allies in order to improve its relations with the People's Republic of China. Sadat alienated many Arab states, severed Egypt's diplomatic relations with others, and certainly lost much of his prestige in large parts of the Arab world.

In addition to the price involved in the relations with other states, there is always a price to be paid on the domestic scene. The reversal of a policy to which a state, and many groups and parties within the state, have been committed for many years provokes sharp reactions from those who object to the new foreign policy. The leaders deciding to choose the new direction must therefore be prepared to fight their opponents from within and must be sure that they have enough support to facilitate the change in policy they desire.

All these decisions involve a trade-off and sometimes bear a heavy price. The difficulties in calculating the costs and benefits of such decisions often make it still more difficult to be reached, and explain in part why surprise in diplomacy is not so common a phenomenon as it is in military strategy.

There is yet another difference between military and diplomatic surprise. In military surprise attention must be paid to two major dimensions in predicting the enemy's behavior: his intentions and his *capabilities*. Only correct evaluation of both in relation to each other can form the basis for any forecast of his expected behavior. In diplomacy we can focus on intentions only and must discount or ignore capabilities (if they exist at all in the same sense as in military strategy). In other words, here again the task of the diplomat as compared with that of the military intelligence analyst is somewhat simplified. This is also because the diplomat has the advantage of being able to discover his opponent's intentions to a large extent through a continuous dialogue with him. This option is, of course, never directly available to the military intelligence analyst. He cannot probe the intentions of the enemy by direct negotiations or by any other direct contact.

The differences cited above between military and diplomatic surprise are briefly summarized below:

Military vs. Diplomatic Surprise

Military Surprise	Diplomatic Surprise
1. Very great variety, hence forecasting, warning and prediction very difficult	1. More limited variety; forecasting, warning and prediction relatively easy
2. Always unilateral: initiating side surprises attacked side	2. Almost always involves collaborative effort between two (or more) sides who surprise third parties
3. Impact felt in immediate, short run	3. Impact felt in short and long run
4. Offers only advantages from military point of view	4. Always involves trade-off
5. Attention must be paid to enemy's intentions and capabilities	5. Attention paid only to enemy's intentions which can, to a large extent, be explored by direct and immediate negotiations
6. Eliminating emission of signals difficult as troops and material must be concentrated and final preparations for attack made — relatively large number of people involved	6. Easier to control emission of signals as very few top-level decision-makers participate and no movement of materiel involved

The Pattern of Diplomatic Surprise

Almost all diplomatic surprises follow a common pattern, which can be divided into three basic stages (see above). During the first stage one or both sides re-evaluate their basic interests and reach the conclusion that a reorientation or change in their foreign policy is necessary. During the second stage they begin a dialogue between them to establish whether they can reach an agreement. The third stage follows if such an understanding has been reached; it is then made public and other parties are surprised.

Stage I. One or both sides begin to realize, independently of each other, that earlier policies must be revised or drastically reversed. This can be the result of the bankruptcy of policies that have gradually become archaic or no longer serve their original purpose (e.g., the U.S.-China policy of the 1970s). Often this change in orientation is the result of a change in leadership or the formation of a new government that is not so powerfully identified with or committed to earlier policies. A new government (or leadership) can thus also change

The Three-Stage Process of Surprise Diplomacy

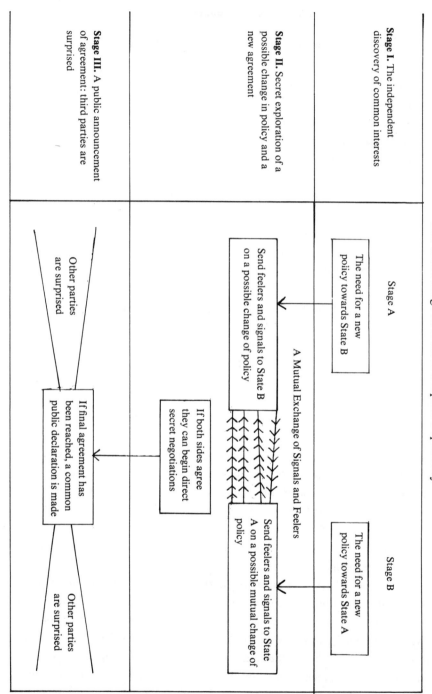

Stage I. The independent discovery of common interests

Stage II. Secret exploration of a possible change in policy and a new agreement

Stage III. A public announcement of agreement: third parties are surprised

Stage A

Stage B

The need for a new policy towards State B

The need for a new policy towards State A

A Mutual Exchange of Signals and Feelers

Send feelers and signals to State B on a possible change of policy

Send feelers and signals to State A on a possible mutual change of policy

If both sides agree they can begin direct secret negotiations

If final agreement has been reached, a common public declaration is made

Other parties are surprised

Other parties are surprised

the order of national goals and priorities (for example, the new Nixon-Kissinger administration and the change in attitude towards China; Sadat's and Begin's lesser commitments to Nasser's and the Israeli Labor government's policies, respectively). On other occasions existing governments set themselves new goals that require a drastic shift in their foreign policy (for example, Hitler's decision to crush Poland which dictated a new orientation in his policy towards Russia; Russia's search for security and its disappointment with the Western democracies; a possible decision on Sadat's part to pursue a new policy of "Egypt first" and to concentrate his efforts on Egypt's economy). The first stage often follows a long gestation period and involves an agonizing re-evaluation of policy and search for a new alternative.

Secrecy can easily be maintained during the first stage, as the number of decision-makers involved in the formation of the highest level of foreign policy is minimal. It is, of course, of great importance that a similar revision in the evaluation of national interest simultaneously occur on both sides. This does not mean, however, that a perfectly synchronized and symmetric evaluation in terms of pace and timing must exist between the two parties. One of the sides may be further ahead in its re-evaluation and may, perhaps, be in greater need of more rapid change. For example, while both Germany and the Soviet Union began to recognize the need for a change in policy at about the same time, Hitler was under much greater pressure as he had set himself September 1 as the latest date for war against Poland. The Russians were much less rushed, but could not refuse Hitler's offers and his corresponding pressure for speed. Similarly, while both Egypt and Israel were interested in direct negotiations leading to peace, it was Sadat who was ahead in his decision and who insisted on a faster pace to reach an agreement.

A symmetry of interests and their re-formation is not necessary, but a new realization of the existence of a common interest, and thus the congruence of such interests, is of course essential. This leads to the second stage.

Stage II. Once each of the sides has separately recognized the need for change, the major problem that remains is to discover whether the other side has reached similar conclusions and is ready to reach mutual agreement. The motives and intentions of the other side must be established. At this stage diplomacy must be kept secret, as neither side to the possible diplomatic revolution is certain of his adversary's intentions. Secrecy is essential so that each side will be able, if necessary, to withdraw without a loss of face or an undermining of his relations with his other allies (who would object to such a move), should the move fail.

At this stage both sides employ "informal diplomatic methods." These include mediators or go-betweens (like the good offices of Rumania employed by Israel and Egypt) and a variety of feelers and signals. Most of these exchanges between the parties are done in secret — especially if direct negotiations take place — but some signals are publicly transmitted. The latter may encompass a reduction in the level of propaganda directed against each other, the mutual publication of some positive statements, or a relaxation of tourist restrictions or trade regulations (as the U.S. did in relation to China in 1970).

The exchange of feelers and signals can be spread over an extended period of time as each side evaluates the signals and responses of the other side. An intricate zig-zag process of action and reaction takes place between the sides until they are certain of the other's intentions. Once both sides have satisfactorily reassured each other, the process can be accelerated. For example, German relations with the Soviet Union began before Rapallo, as early as 1920. Germany and the Soviet Union started to exchange signals at least six months before the Ribbentrop-Molotov agreement. The United States began sending signals to the People's Republic of China during the Nixon election campaign, and continued this gradual exchange of signals for three years.

After the basic decisions concerning the possible reversal of foreign policy have been made at the highest level during the first stage, the early exchange of signals can be undertaken by low-level officials, not always immediately on a political level. Early German-Soviet contacts were made by low-level economic representatives of both states; the Chinese chose to signal the United States by inviting a U.S. ping pong team. As the exchange of signals is gradually intensified and the sides become more certain of each other's intentions, they also raise the level of contacts and move on to a discussion of political issues which have only been mentioned obliquely before.

Together with the second stage of exchanging signals and making probes to establish mutual intentions, the process of re-evaluating new directions and basic interests continues. Earlier policies are not simply terminated suddenly: an internal struggle of contradicting forces, pushing and hauling in different directions, takes place. Often, up to the very last moment, neither side is certain of the course of actions to be taken, as additional avenues are explored. The possibility of a last-minute change of heart always hovers in the background. Stages one and two must therefore not be seen as consecutive, but as simultaneous. To be sure, the evaluating of basic interests comes *first;* but it is not terminated with the beginning of stage two.

The second stage is also the stage when secrecy becomes more difficult to maintain. The exchange of feelers and signals between the two sides leads to the inevitable emission of signals (as well as noise) that cannot be hidden. These signals can alert experienced political and intelligence observers. Surprise can fail at this point if third parties discover the contacts between the two sides. Both sides therefore try to throw third parties off by covering their discussions with a veil of secrecy, by deception, and by distorting the available signals emitted by producing contradictory noises.

Stage III. Once an understanding has been reached, the third and last stage takes place. The new agreement and course of action are now made public. All that remains is to iron out the final lines of agreement and implement the new policies chosen. Most often, third parties are totally surprised despite the earlier availability of a large number of signals that should, but did not, indicate what was about to happen, either because such signals are ignored or because they are misunderstood. In this respect, despite the simpler warning problems involved in forecasting a diplomatic surprise, its results are similar to those of military surprise. It strikes out of the blue like a bombshell or explosion.

A Note on Diplomatic Surprise and Different Types of International Systems

One definition of diplomatic surprise is an "unexpected change of allegiance in the international system which has an effect on the division of power in the international system and hence on the structure of the system." A major diplomatic surprise would therefore be one executed by one or more of the great or superpowers, with the effect on the division of power in the international system being considerable. Its global impact can alter the structure of the system by adding or eliminating a major pole in the system.

Diplomatic surprise on a small scale, presumably initiated by second-rate states or by a great power together with weak or weaker states, would thus differ from a major surprise by bearing only a regional and not a global impact, by being subject to a change of the resultant events, and by marginal shifts in the division of power.

Diplomatic surprise can be expected in any type, structure or nature of the international system. The difference between various types of systems as far as diplomatic surprise is concerned is in the *degree* to which states expect diplomatic surprise to occur in different types of systems. In other words, surprise can be more or less surprising in one type of system rather than another.

Thus, for example, in the classical balance-of-power system, diplomatic surprise should be more expected than in a tight bipolar system, in a multipolar system more than in a bipolar system, in a homogeneous system more than in a heterogeneous system, and in a moderate system more than in a revolutionary system. On the other hand, the impact of diplomatic surprise will stand in *inverse* relation to its probability and to the degree it was expected, as will be shown below. Therefore in systems in which surprise is, or seems to be, less probable, the impact on the system's structure and character will be much stronger.

Surprise in diplomacy is most often a move that leads to the formation of a new and unexpected alliance or the withdrawal of support from an old ally. This also explains the connection between the structure and nature of the international system and the probability or degree to which a diplomatic surprise can be expected. The larger the number of poles in a system, the larger the number of theoretical combinations of new alliances (according to the standard formula for possible pairs $N(N-1)/2$). Thus the number of possible new, and hence surprising, alliances will be greater in a balance-of-power or multipolar system than in a tight or loose bipolar system. For that reason, decision-makers and diplomats can be expected to face a surprise more often in multipolar types of systems. This must be combined with an explanation concerning the probability of surprise and the nature or character of the international systems. The inhibitions of forming *new* alliances in a homogeneous system — in other words a system in which all or most states have a similar ideology or act according to similar rules of conduct — are much lower than in a heterogeneous system split by competing ideologies, by tensions and wars, and in which communication between states is difficult. The character or nature of the system can thus also limit or encourage the possibilities of making a surprising move. The stronger the ideological antagonism within a system over a period of time, the more difficult it will be to expect new alliances or a surprise move to form an alliance between states that have been competing for some time. However, once two ideologically competing states open the way for agreement, the effect of surprise will be enhanced and much more dramatic than in a system in which the possibility of a surprise move is always present. Therefore when Nazi Germany and the Soviet Union (1939 — an ideological, revolutionary and heterogeneous, but also multipolar system) and the United States and the People's Republic of China (1971 — ideological, heterogeneous, loose bipolar system) decided to ignore ideological differences and form alliances, the impact of diplomatic surprise was considerably amplified. Of the two major traits of the international system — structure (or number of poles) and nature (heterogeneity or homogeneity) — the latter seems to create opportunities for more dramatic surprises while the former lends itself to a larger number of surprises.

This can be seen for example from the description of the balance-of-power system by Raylam: Actors in the balance-of-power system are only loyal to their own interests and to the maintenance of the equilibrium in the system in general — but not to other specific allies. Therefore they will tend to switch alliances (i.e., make surprise moves) often in order to enhance their own power or maintain the equilibrium of the system (i.e., a balanced division of power) by shifting their alliances to counter alliances or states which seek to assume a position of predominance. In order to facilitate rapid changes, in which no time is allowed the other side to make a counter-move or obstruct the shift in alliance sought by the opposing states, surprise is one of the best means to secure a smooth and rapid transition from one alliance to another. Surprise can therefore be seen as part of the accepted rules of the game in a balance-of-power system.

Bridging the Image-Reality Gap:
An Empirical Perspective *

Jonathan Wilkenfeld, Gerald W. Hopple, Paul J. Rossa

Perception and misperception of reality have been the subjects of important recent work in the fields of international politics and foreign policy. The predominant approach attempts to systematically account for the various factors contributing to misperceptions or distortions of reality, and the effects of these factors on the behavior of states and their leaders.[1] Among the most widely discussed factors are those pertaining to the psychological characteristics of leaders and the extent to which these factors give rise to particular and identifiable perceptual patterns. The underlying assumption is that as we increase our understanding of the psychological make-up of key national decision-makers, we will be in a better position to understand how they will interpret various actions taken by other states in the international arena.

While acknowledging the importance of the perspective on perception and misperception as outlined above, it should be pointed out that there is a second perspective from which the notion of perception can be usefully analyzed. In this case, we can speak of the correct perception of overt events that do not, in turn, accurately reflect the intentions of the initiating state. Thus, for example, in periods of intense conflict between states, decision-makers of one party must interpret reality as that which is reflected in the overt signals of their adversaries. Obviously, what is missing from this image or perception is the process that brought about the decision that resulted in the overt act. In such situations, usually characterized by limited communications between adversaries, the possibilities for misperception are abundant.

It should be noted that this approach to the perception-reality issue de-emphasizes the psychological make-up of the perceiving decision-maker and the possible distortions it introduces into the perceptual process. Under the present formulation, misperception of reality can occur even when perfectly rational decision-makers are involved. Therefore we can define this type of misperception, based on a rational actor model of the perceiver, as the *literal*

34

reading of events of complex origins. These are distortions that result from a lack of comprehension of the dynamics behind overt actions taken by one's adversaries.

An initial question that can be raised concerns the types of situations most likely to give rise to this special case of misperception. Obviously, in any situation in which two parties confront each other, the potential for distorted images of reality exists. A critical element in this process is any limitation on the ability of the parties to communicate directly with each other. The inability of one party to ask the other, "What did you mean by that?" will create a potential for misperception. Generally, in conflict situations, the level of direct communications between adversaries decreases as the level of conflict increases. This being the case, we have the potential for an increase in the level of uncertainty concerning intentions, and therefore an increase in the possibility of a divergence between perception and reality.

At the interpersonal level, the sort of situation described above is potentially damaging to the relationship between parties, since once a process of misperception has been initiated, it tends to escalate. Unless the parties involved can discern that such an escalatory process has begun, and take remedial action, the ultimate result may be the destruction of the entire relationship. At the international level, the problems of misperception arise from similar causes, but the dangers are more far-reaching and can ultimately involve the states in overt conflict or war. Because of the high level of risk involved, pairs of states that we can cite have been able to recognize the dangers inherent in a continuation of the process of escalatory mutual misperception and have decided on bold initiatives in order to rectify the situation.

Two examples drawn from very different experiences serve to highlight this process. The initiative that President Anwar Sadat of Egypt undertook in November 1977 can be seen against a backdrop of the type of process we have been discussing. In fact, much of the Egyptian rhetoric surrounding the event and its immediate aftermath was couched specifically in terms of breaking through years of hostility and misperception in a bold move designed to begin a real dialogue. One of the major tangible outcomes thus far has been the establishment of a communications network between Egypt and Israel, which can be used in cases where misperceptions of intentions can be particularly dangerous. In fact, there is some evidence that this communications process was employed by Israel prior to its incursion into southern Lebanon in March 1978.

A second case, which we need not belabor at this point, concerns the evolution of the cold war into something that we have termed "détente" as regards the relations between the United States and the Soviet Union. The outstanding characteristic of the twenty-odd years of cold war was the inability of the parties to correctly perceive each other's intentions in the context of a lack of appreciation for the underlying causes of overt actions. In both of the examples cited above, states were caught up in an escalatory process, with the potential dangers perhaps clearly seen for the first time by leaders capable of strong actions. That is, while they could do nothing about the misperceptions of each other's overt acts, they could understand that they were in fact misperceiving and that a dialogue had to be initiated to break the pattern.

Barring the sorts of diplomatic breakthroughs we have mentioned above, as potential aids in coping with the negative outcomes of such a process, what can we as social scientists offer policy-makers of states caught in such situations in order to contribute to a reduction in the level of misperception? Let us for the moment exclude from consideration those intelligence-gathering tools designed to aid this process. Rather, let us concentrate on those techniques that can be applied to an analysis of overt actions of states towards each other in an effort to enhance their ability to properly perceive each other's intentions.

In this regard, the identification and systematic analysis of trends over time is perhaps the greatest single contribution that rigorous social science can make. By this we mean the identification of past trends in the overt behavior of states, the conversion of such trends into indicators, and the systematic monitoring of such indicators in order to detect sharp divergences from the norm. These divergences can be matched with observations of other changes within the state under examination in an attempt to explain these changes. In other words, the change in the overt behavior level need no longer be interpreted at face value, but rather in conjunction with other (observable) societal and interstate phenomena, thus enabling us to more easily interpret overt behavior.

What is required here is the development of a series of causal models, subjected to a certain amount of empirical testing, that will establish, within the probability limits of standard statistical procedures, the parameters of behavior for states. With the aid of these models, we will then be in a position to assess the proper meaning of overt actions whose sharp fluctuations might otherwise be uninterpretable and dangerously misleading.

Before discussing several of these models in some detail, let us examine one such preliminary model as an example of how this process might work. In earlier work,[2] the notion was explored that leaders of states experiencing internal difficulties will, under certain conditions, attempt to undertake externally aggressive behavior in order to divert attention and reunite. What should be the response of the state on the receiving end of such overt behavior? Should the increase in aggressiveness be interpreted as a true manifestation of the intentions and desires of the leadership of the adversary? Or should these unusual acts be interpreted with the aid of models that help to explain them on the basis of internal requirements? While this is an empirical question — and obviously a large number of factors go into this calculus — a mutual sensitivity to the dynamics of the conditions surrounding the overt actions undertaken by one's adversary, and a knowledge of the range of options open to that country at any given point in time, should be quite useful in the process of minimizing misperception.

Models as Aids for Proper Perception

In the preceding section we have argued that an alternative view of misperception, based on the literal reading of events of complex origins, is a reasonable alternative to the standard view of perception based on the psychological predispositions of the perceiver. Because it is not sufficient to simply alert decision-makers to its existence, we must now turn to an examination of possible strategies for coping with this problem. We must be prepared to offer systematic strategies for detecting the problem and coping with it successfully. Several existing models can be useful in this regard, and we will review them briefly before proceeding to the preliminary empirical model offered here.

A considerable amount of empirical work has been done across a variety of disciplines on the phenomena of diffusion and contagion. With regard to the process of diffusion of innovations, four distinct sets of variables have been considered: (1) the innovation; (2) channels of transmission; (3) the spread of diffusion over time; and (4) the members of a system among whom the innovations spread. Almost no work has been done on the extent to which these types of processes characterize the foreign behavior pattern that states exhibit. Yet a careful reading of this literature indicates a great deal of potential for the transfer of portions of this theoretical perspective to the problem of misperception as investigated here.

If conflict and crisis behavior are conceptualized as "innovations," the principles of diffusion research can be applied in the area of misperception. Such independent variables as the characteristics of the various innovations, the various sources and channels of information and influence, the social structure of the adopter population, and the characteristics of potential adopters should be investigated. Prior inquiry shows that the rate of diffusion is generally S-shaped; the process begins slowly and then increases with a gradually accelerating rate. Furthermore, the cumulative diffusion rate sometimes approaches or approximates a normal curve. To the extent that these generalizations also characterize the diffusion of innovations in the realm of conflict and crisis, these processes will be much more amenable to explanation and prediction.

With regard to contagion, the question for the social scientist is whether the patterns of increases and decreases in certain types of conflict and crisis behaviors follow specific identifiable and describable rules. One model with potential value involves the concepts of contagion and epidemics. There has been a considerable amount of work by mathematicians on epidemics, fads, rumors, and other types of mass behavior in an effort to identify consistent patterns that characterize these different phenomena. Such notions as the nature of the transmission, differences in susceptibility, temporal elements, the development of immunity, and the process of termination have been examined. From these characteristics, mathematical models have been developed to fit the various stages of contagion.[3]

While mathematical models of contagion have been developed most elaborately in the biological and medical sciences, there has been at least one notable effort to apply these notions to international events. Specifically, Richardson developed a mood theory of war, drawing upon the types of notions developed above to put together a quantitative picture of war moods in Great Britain and Germany immediately before, during, and immediately after World War One.[4] It is our expectation that these notions can be successfully applied to conflict and crisis, particularly in tracking the origin, development, spread, and decline of certain types of actions.

Another set of potentially useful models for coping with the phenomenon of misperception is related to the notions of status inconsistency and aggression. This corpus of theory, following the pioneering work of Galtung,[5] postulates that aggression is most likely to originate in social positions that are in states of rank disequilibrium. Depending upon the unit of analysis under consideration, this aggression will manifest itself in the form of crime, revolution, and war.

The notion of rank disequilibrium can be integrated into a general framework for the analysis of conflict in the form of relational considerations. Thus the structural attributes of states can also be viewed as relational attributes, with each state occupying a certain rank on various status dimensions. Furthermore, states will have status rankings on both the global and regional levels. Perceived status inconsistency can then be viewed as a contributing factor to the level of foreign behavior in general, and foreign conflict behavior in particular, that the state exhibits.

A third area in which models may be constructed concerns the widespread notion that conflict begets conflict. In the present situation, it would be advisable to refine the action-reaction model that has appeared with such regularity in the foreign policy and conflict behavior literature.[6] While the conflict-received/conflict-sent nexus is robust, this finding is neither astonishing nor helpful to theorists or policy analysts. The extent to which the process is automatic is the key issue. Is a crude and mechanistic stimulus-response model satisfactory? Does the strength of the action-reaction linkage vary by type of state, type of issue, type of conflict, etc.?

The approach we wish to briefly outline here develops a fourth perspective based on the distinction between those factors that can be viewed as the basic underlying preconditions of conflict behavior and those determinants that actually precipitate such conflict. This distinction, originally developed by Eckstein and applied specifically to the phenomenon of internal war,[7] is modified for use at the interstate level of analysis. According to this scheme, precipitants are events that actually contribute to the initiation of foreign conflict behavior. The preconditions are those circumstances which provide the necessary context in which the precipitants operate. Sensitive models of the foreign conflict realm should clearly identify and distinguish between these two factors.

This distinction between preconditions and precipitants has been largely overlooked in the empirical studies of foreign conflict behavior. As Eckstein points out, the greatest contribution of this distinction is to shift attention from those aspects of the conflict process that defy systematic analysis as a result of their uniqueness — precipitants — to those amenable to systematic inquiry. For our purposes, a clear understanding of the preconditions as they exist for one's adversary, and an understanding of the circumstances in which one or another precondition emerges as dominant, will greatly increase our ability to cope with misperception of the type under discussion here.

With this basic rubric in mind, let us then turn to a brief description of an analytic scheme designed to systematically incorporate sets of preconditions of foreign behavior and foreign conflict. This will be followed by a brief discussion of some preliminary findings in terms of their potential usefulness in minimizing misperceptions.

The research projects from which the current effort evolves had as their goal the development of a framework for the comparative analysis of foreign behavior in general, and foreign conflict in particular.[8] In this connection, an elaborate set of indicators has been developed, designed to serve as tools for the systematic monitoring of state behavior, in an effort to develop a capability to anticipate conflict and crisis. To the extent that we can develop a reliable set of indicators, coupled with an ability to specify the relative importance of these indicators as circumstances change and as we shift our focus from state to state, we will move closer to our goal of reducing that portion of misperception that results from a lack of understanding of the motivating forces behind overt acts. Thus the indicators examined here, as well as the state classificatory scheme, are designed to assist us in understanding complex conflict interactions.

It should be noted at this point, that we will treat the notion of action-reaction, or stimulus-response, in a somewhat unusual manner. As we have noted, prior research has stressed the centrality of an action-reaction process in the study of conflict interactions. The notion that conflict begets conflict, and that this process underlies the basic interactions between states, is of far-reaching consequence. We contend, however, that this underlying process, while explaining large portions of the statistical variance, explains little of the dynamic of foreign policy formulation. Rather, it can be argued that the action-reaction element constitutes the context within which one can observe the operation of other determinants of foreign behavior, rather than being a legitimate determinant in its own right. Thus we will attempt to specify a model of determinants of foreign conflict that excludes action-reaction, but that will occasionally refer to effects of its incorporation at certain stages of the analysis.

The model we will outline here is relatively straightforward; yet its underlying logic, as well as the methodology developed for its implementation, are potentially valuable in the development of more accurate monitoring and forecasting tools. Clearly, there are a myriad of factors that intelligence analysts would like to systematically track in order to provide accurate information on the motivations behind the actions of states and leaders. Our contention is that a relatively small number of key indicators can serve this purpose. The prime advantage of working with a small number of indicators is that the monitoring function becomes more manageable. In addition, the present context is a comparative one, hence the emphasis on the development of indicators of a cross-national nature. Work with a small set will allow us to concentrate on those most appropriate and amenable to cross-national data collection. Obviously, while this scheme can also be developed in a fashion tailor-made for the particular state being monitored, that task, and the case-study orientation it entails, is beyond the scope of the present study.

The model developed here is composed of three basic elements: indicators of the determinants of foreign behavior; dimensions of foreign behavior; and a state classificatory scheme. The determinants of foreign behavior are grouped into three broad categories or components: societal/political; interstate; and global. At the conclusion of the paper, we will also briefly report on the incorporation of a fourth set of determinants, pertaining to the value systems of the decision-makers of the states whose behavior is being investigated.

Concerning the societal/political component, a determination was made to specify variables in three distinct domains: population characteristics; economic performance measures; and indicators of domestic conflict behavior. Attributes of a state's population may be expected to be related to its external behavior, and *rate of population growth* has emerged in prior research as a factor of some significance.[9] In the domain of *economic performance*, certain types of foreign actions are dictated by fluctuating internal economic conditions. These may manifest themselves in the choice of trading partners, in the need to adopt more aggressive foreign policy stances, and so on.[10] In this study, general economic performance is assessed indirectly by the merchandise balance of payments situation. Finally, in the realm of domestic conflict, a series of studies has attempted to demonstrate empirically that states experiencing such problems may be more likely to engage in conflict behavior at the interstate level than are more stable states.[11] Two basic indicators are incorporated here: *societal unrest* (riots, strikes, and demonstrations), and *governmental instability* (coups, revolutions, purges, changes in cabinet, executive, and constitution). In summary, it is contended that this rather small number of indicators serves to summarize the basic situation at the societal level.

Turning to the interstate component, our concern here is with indicators that tap various aspects of interaction between states. As we indicated earlier, we will concentrate primarily on a formulation that excludes from consideration the behavior-received/behavior-sent realm, and will concentrate instead on indicators related to the economic sphere of interstate behavior. These indicators take into account the following units of information: export and import flows; production and consumption within states; and commodity specific relationships. The contention here is that interstate economic exchange captures the most central aspects of interaction in the economic sphere. When we deal with states as entities, relationships are formed by the absolute and relative importance of various types of exchange. Resource production, consumption and flow define the exchange relationship among states. Exports and imports serve to describe interstate economic relationships, supplemented by information regarding the consumption and production of commodities within a state.

Eight specific interstate economic indicators were incorporated into the present analysis:

(1) *International economic involvement (total value of merchandise trade):*
$$\text{total exports} + \text{total imports}$$

(2) *Food dependency index:*
$$\frac{\text{Food imports} - \text{food exports}}{\text{food imports} + \text{food exports}}$$

(3) *Export concentration index:*
$$\sqrt{\frac{(Ti)^2 - 1/10}{1 - 1/10}}$$

where Ti is the percentage share of export income percentages in commodity class i, where 10 categories exist.

(4) *Import concentration index:*
$$\sqrt{\frac{(Si)^2 - 1/10}{1 - 1/10}}$$

where Si is the percentage share of import expenditures in commodity class i, where 10 categories exist.

(5) *Energy dependency index* (energy consumption dependency index):
$$\frac{\frac{\text{energy imports}}{\text{energy consumption} + \text{energy exports}}}{\text{energy production}}$$

(6) *Energy interdependence index:*
$$\frac{\text{energy imports} + \text{energy exports}}{\text{energy consumption}}$$

(7) *Energy seller index* (energy market supplier ability index):

$$\frac{\text{energy exports}}{\text{energy production} + \text{imports}}$$

(8) *Neo-colonial dependency index:*

$$\frac{(\text{industrial imports} + \text{unrefined exports}) - (\text{unrefined exports} + \text{industrial imports})}{\text{total imports} + \text{total exports}}$$

The global component contains non-static attributes of the international system that the state confronts and according to which its actions must be undertaken. The non-static stricture eliminates from consideration a host of indicators that have traditionally been considered as attributes of the global system, such as power stratification, alliance aggregation, systemic turbulence, status rank, subsystemic phenomena, and global scarcity. Two classes of indicators are delineated here: international governmental organization memberships, and the extent of conflict within bordering states. The extent to which a state is involved in the international system can be assessed by attention to the number of international governmental organizations (IGOs) to which it belongs. Two indicators were developed: *total IGO membership per year;* and *total new IGO memberships during the year.* The second set of global indicators evolves from the contention that states that border on other states which are, in turn, involved in conflict behavior, have a greater probability of becoming involved in these conflicts themselves than do states with more peaceful neighbors.[12] The specific indicators are the following:

1. Direct land borders: conflict
2. Direct land borders: force
3. Colonial land borders: conflict
4. Colonial land borders: force
5. Direct sea borders: conflict
6. Direct sea borders: force
7. Colonial sea borders: conflict
8. Colonial sea borders: force

The dependent variables in the present model concern the foreign behavior of states. Foreign behavior is conceptualized in terms of its action element, with an event being viewed as a distinct portion of reality.[13] In the most elaborate formulation, events can be decomposed according to the following questions: "*Who* does *what* to *whom, where, when,* and in what immediate *context?*" For our purposes, we utilize the World Event Interaction Survey (WEIS) categorization and data collection. Factor analysis of the twenty-two WEIS categories of cooperation and conflict yielded three distinct behavioral dimensions: *constructive diplomatic behavior* (yield, comment, consult, approve, promise, grant, reward, agree, request, propose, reject, deny, warn, and impose negative sanctions); *non-military conflict* (accuse, protest, demand, threaten, demonstrate, expel, and seize); and *force* (force acts). It is within the context of these types of foreign behavior that our analyses will be conducted.

We also postulate that static structural characteristics of states intervene between the sources of determinants of foreign behavior and foreign behavior itself. For analytic purposes, the state classifactory scheme can be viewed as a filtering screen whereby the stable structural characteristics of states provide the context in which the determinants of foreign behavior operate. Twenty-three structural characteristics of states were identified, and a series of factor analyses resulted in the assigning of scores to each state according to its summary ranking on four general structural dimensions: economic structure; governmental structure; capabilities; and instability. Q-factor analysis then identified five major groupings of states which for descriptive convenience were labelled as follows: Western, Closed, Large Developing, Unstable, and Poor.

The analysis here pertains to fifty-six states. Included in this sample are virtually all major actors in the interstate realm. The criterion for inclusion required that the state initiate forty or more foreign events during the 1966-70 time span. This criterion guarantees the inclusion of major actors in terms of volume and activity. All geographic regions are represented, and the states constitute a reasonably heterogeneous "sample" of the international system. Table 1 lists the states for which data were collected for the period 1966-70.

In summary, then, the model of foreign behavior utilized here consists of societal/political, interstate, and global determinants of three types of behavior: constructive diplomatic; non-military; and force. Furthermore, we will assess the intervention of four structural characteristics of states — economic, governmental, capability, and instability — and the distinct groupings of states these structural characteristics form. We now turn to a description of the analytic procedures and a brief overview of the major findings.[14]

Analytic Procedures

The purposes of the analysis were to identify the component or components that contain the most potent indicators for explaining foreign behavior, as well as to pinpoint the central indicators in each component. That is, the contention

Table 1

GROUPING OF STATES BASED ON STRUCTURAL CHARACTERISTICS, 1966–1970*

West

Belgium	.83**	United Kingdom	.73
Sweden	.80	Israel	.72
Denmark	.79	Japan	.70
West Germany	.77	France	.68
Netherlands	.77	Chile	.64
Canada	.76	USA	.61
Australia	.75	South Africa	.52
Italy	.74		

Closed

Poland	.84	USSR	.66
Rumania	.81	Hungary	.62
Czechoslovakia	.71	East Germany	.60
Bulgalua	.69	Portugal	.55
Spain	.67	Yugoslavia	.51

Large Developing

India	.83	Brazil	.67
Pakistan	.75	China	.65
Turkey	.72	Philippines	.62
Indonesia	.69	South Korea	.57

Unstable

Syria	.76	Egypt	.60
Iraq	.76	Iran	.59
Algeria	.75	Cuba	.59
Zaire	.75	South Vietnam	.53

Poor

Cyprus	.77	Laos	.60
Lebanon	.69	Malaysia	.59
Cambodia	.65	Yemen	.58
Jordan	.63	Ethiopia	.55
Albania	.61		

* States for which data were colleced but which could not be classified according to this scheme are: Thailand, Ghana, Kenya, Nigeria, Saudi Arabia, and Greece.

** For Belgium these numbers represent factor loadings on the Q-factor analysis, and can be interpreted as indicating the extent to which a state is closely identified with the factor.

is that the identification of these central indicators will bring us closer to our goal of minimizing misperception based on incorrect assessments of our opponent's motives. These goals are combined with an analysis of the effects of the mediation of state structural characteristics on these relative potency assessments.

We have utilized for this purpose some recent methodological developments from causal modeling and econometrics. The latent variable — a stand-in for a block of variables — is the central concept in this approach. We allow each component of the model to represent such a latent variable, with the indicators within each component serving as directly observed or manifest variables. Thus the latent variable is specified in terms of the parameters of the model and the directly observed variables.[15]

In the current analysis, four latent variables are defined, representing the societal/political, interstate, and global independent variable components, and foreign behavior, the dependent variable cluster. Each weighted variable is defined as a weighted interaction of its manifest indicators, where weights are determined as estimated parameters of the model. The structural specification of the model relates blocks of variables rather than single variables. That is, the latent variables, specified as linear combinations of manifest variables, are linearly interrelated.

Since relationships involve both unknown parameters and unknown variables, the problem of estimation is non-linear. This non-linearity problem is solved through an iterated series of estimations, each confronting a portion of the model (which is linear in isolation) with ordinary least squares regression. "Each such regression gives proxy estimates for a subset of the unknown parameters and latent variables. . . . and these proxy estimates are used in the next step of the procedure to calculate new proxy estimates."[16] The cyclical procedure, called PLS (Partial Least Squares), stabilizes until consecutive estimates do not significantly differ. Figure 1 provides a graphic representation of the PLS model as adapted to the present research problem.[17]

Overview of Findings

The PLS procedure generates a wealth of information pertaining to all aspects of the process under investigation. For present purposes, we will highlight those portions of the analysis that focus on four central questions: (a) Which indicators are the strongest contributors to each of the three latent independen-

Figure 1

PLS Model of Foreign Behavior

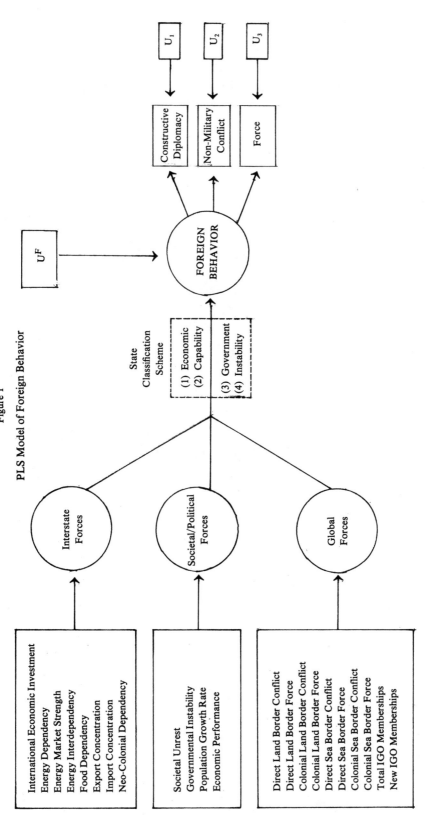

dent variables? (b) How are the effects of the components mediated by the structural characteristics of states? (c) What types of foreign behavior are best explained by the current model? And (d) What is the relative potency of each of the latent variables for each of the fifty-six states under analysis? Consideration of these four question will be followed by a discussion of the results as they pertain to the overriding concerns of this paper — the development of tools for a reduction of misperception in interactions among states.

Composition of Latent Independent Variables

It should be pointed out that we are not engaged here in standard clustering procedures. Rather, in the present case we identify those variables that contribute most strongly to the composition of a latent variable that in turn most adequately explains the latent dependent variable, foreign behavior. Normal index construction proceeds independent of the power of the index to explain a dependent variable. The difference, then, is between clustering, on the one hand, and a best fitting operation, on the other.

Our findings indicate that among the societal/political variables, societal unrest and economic performance yield the strongest betas, indicating their centrality to the societal/political latent variable. For the interstate latent variable, international involvement, energy dependency, and energy market strength stand out as critical in their impact. Finally, the global latent variable is composed primarily of the four manifest variables representing conflict (rather than force) in direct and colonial land and sea border countries.

Mediation of Structural Characteristics

An assessment of the mediatory effects of the four structural dimensions was undertaken: the results are quite revealing. The global and interstate latent variables have their strongest impact on foreign behavior when a control for capability is imposed. The global component also shows the mediating effect of economic structure, while the interstate component shows the effect (somewhat limited) of a control for level of instability. The societal/political component, which, as we shall see below, generally shows little impact on foreign behavior, is most potent in its uncontrolled state, although some limited impact is also noted with the mediation of governmental structure and level of instability.

Overall, then, we note that in the cases of the interstate and global components, and to a lesser extent in the case of the societal/political component, the mediating effects of state structural types are important. Furthermore, it is important to point out that these effects differ sharply from one component to the next, thus adding emphasis to the importance of properly identifying states in terms of their underlying structural characteristics.

Types of Foreign Behavior Explained by the Model

The set of three latent variables representing the three components, as mediated by state types, explains 69 percent of the variation in foreign behavior. This rather impressive figure is even more striking when we recall that the present analysis has purposely excluded the action-reaction element on the grounds that its overwhelming impact serves to mask the more subtle, although no less important, effects of the remaining determinants of foreign behavior.[18] Up to now, we have discussed the model as terminating with the latent dependent variable, foreign behavior. Now, however, let us explore the links between this latent variable and the three manifest foreign behavior variables.

The present model does extremely well in explaining the variance in constructive diplomatic behavior (72 percent of the variance), and moderately well in explaining non-military conflict behavior (47 percent of the variance). The force dimension, however, which is composed of the most extreme forms of conflict behavior, is virtually unrelated to any of the indicators explored in the present model. This sharp contrast among the three types of foreign behavior is further highlighted by an examination of the results of the analysis that incorporated the action-reaction element (i.e., foreign behavior received) in the interstate component.[19] This addition resulted in almost no change (from 72 percent to 74 percent of the variance explained) for the constructive diplomatic type of foreign behavior. Here, then, is clear evidence that the more routine, constructive, and cooperative types of behavior are dominated by situational factors rather than by those evolving from patterns of interstate interactions.

Quite different are the conclusions with respect to the two purely conflict-behavior-related dimensions. Regarding force, we observe a striking increase (from 1 to 50 percent of variation explained) in our ability to explain this type of phenomenon once behavior received is incorporated into the interstate component. It is apparently the case that, for this type of intense interstate conflict behavior, the dynamic of the conflict situation itself takes precedence over other potential determinants of conflict. Other research has found that type of state has very little bearing on this process.[20] Clearly, then, at very high levels of conflict behavior, little maneuvering room is left to the decision-makers out-side the dynamics of the situation itself.

The third dimension, non-military conflict, also showed a clear improve-ment in the model's ability to explain its variation once the action-reaction ele-ment had been incorporated (from 47 to 61 percent). In this case, however, in contrast to that of force, we are already starting from a base in which the other determinants have explained nearly half the variance. Clearly, the deter-mination of the level of non-military conflict exhibited by states is the most complex of the three behavioral processes examined here in that we observe the simultaneous operation of a large number of determinants.

The implications of these findings are clear. Force actions are deeply rooted in a stimulus-response dynamic; once conflict between states reaches this level of intensity, it is unlikely that factors other than those directly related to the dynamic and rhythm of the conflict will exert serious impact. On the other hand, constructive diplomatic (mostly cooperative behavior) and non-military conflict (less serious conflict indicators) will be much more susceptible to the impact of the whole range of potential influences on state behavior. The dif-ferentiation among types of foreign behavior and the differing impacts of various types of determinants are potentially significant to our conceptions of foreign behavior generally. Since the behavior of states in the international arena — even when dominated by conflict — is never unidimensional, it is vital that as both scholars and policy analysts we recognize that not all behavior is subject to the same dynamic. To so treat it is to oversimplify and to open oneself up to serious and justifiable criticism (as a scholar) and poten-tial disaster (as a policy-maker).

Relative Potency of Components in Explaining Foreign Behavior

Relative potency scores are computed based on the betas of the components as multiplied by the control dimensions. These scores show a pattern consis-tent with earlier findings. In the majority of cases for which the model is ap-propriate, the interstate latent variable is the most potent. A small number of states show exceptional strength for the societal component, while the global component is occasionally significant but never to the exclusion of one of the other two latent variables. Rather than engage in a long (although important) presentation of the relative potency scores for the individual states, we will at-tempt to highlight some of the major findings.[21] For this purpose, Table 2 pre-sents a list of states whose scores are particularly high (or particularly low) on each of the three latent variables.

Table 2

STATES WITH STRONG RELATIVE POTENCY SOURCES*

SOCIETAL/POLITICAL		INTERSTATE		GLOBAL	
Kenya	−.61	USA	1.29	USA	.48
Syria	−.56	USSR	1.10	USSR	.46
Zaire	−.47	China	.93	China	.32
South Vietnam	−.41	France	.80	Albania	−.30
France	−.34	India	.70	Jordan	−.30
Egypt	−.32	West Germany	.62	Cambodia	−.32
Japan	−.32	Brazil	.59	Yemen	−.37
Laos	−.31	Japan	.59	Lebanon	−.40
Chile	−.30	Syria	.56	Cyprus	−.54
		Canada	.55		
		U.K.	.53		
		Jordan	−.53		
		Albania	−.54		
		Lebanon	−.63		
		Yemen	−.69		
		Cyprus	−.98		

*For the societal/political and global components, a cutpoint of ±.30 was used. For the interstate component, a cutpoint of ±.50 was used.

Concerning the global component, it should be recalled that the critical manifest variables involve conflict actions taking place in bordering states. Six of the nine states that show strong impact of this factor fall in the "Poor" category (see Table 1), whose outstanding characteristics are their very low scores on capability and economic structure. While these states react negatively to conflict in bordering states, China, the U.S., and the USSR, the top three states on the capability dimension, react strongly and positively to such conflict. Thus the global component is most potent for states ranking unusually high or unusually low in terms of their capabilities. Those with strong capabilities, not coincidently the three superpowers, will react to nearby conflict by increasing their activities, perhaps even to the extent of intervention, in the hope of influencing the outcome. By contrast, states with few resources will withdraw from the arena when faced with conflict in the local environment. States in the middle range of capability and economic structure will be less constrained in policy-making by spillover from the problems of their neighbors.

The interstate component shows a much larger group of states with high relative potency scores. Six of the sixteen are from the "Western" group, five are from the "Poor" group, and three from the "Large Developing" group.

Once again, the capability dimension appear to be critical. In reference to the major manifest variables of the interstate component, we find that strong states act in accordance with their relative position in the international economic hierarchy. For example, a large volume of trade and energy interdependence would indicate a strong position and frequent participation in international politics. States with few resources will match their foreign behavioral output volume to the dominant pattern of economic interchange; activities increase when energy dependency or insufficient trade prevails, while energy self-sufficiency and a high volume of trade have the effect of reducing the need for external involvement.

Finally, we turn to the societal/political component. Here we find a relatively heterogeneous group of states with high scores, confirming our earlier finding that type of state has little impact on the operation of the societal/political component in its relation to the foreign behavior of states. It is of interest to note that there is a lack of strong positive relative potency. Neither societal unrest nor poor economic performance predict an increase in foreign behavior or conflict, but instead may lead to a decrease in such activity.

Fourteen states show a particularly poor fit between model and data, i.e., none of the three latent variables show any particular potency. Seven of these states — East Germany, Hungary, Yugoslavia, Bulgaria, Romania, Spain, and Portugal — came from the "Closed" group. It would appear that the particular configuration of structural characteristics that typifies the "Closed" group creates a situation in which the types of determinants examined here are not relevant. The "Closed" group could be roughly described as follows: strong on economic structure; quite closed on the governmental dimension; relatively strong on capabilities; and high on stability. Thus, the two dimensions in which the "Closed" group is highest — governmental structure and instability — are precisely those that contribute least as mediating variables in our model.

Before concluding, let us briefly turn to an additional set of considerations, that of the psychological make-up of the decision-makers with which the state on the receiving end of actions must attempt to cope. As we have noted, while the psychological make-up of the decision-making elite of the perceiving state is not of concern to us in the present analysis, the extent to which psychological predispositions cause the leaders of the adversary to initiate certain types of actions with certain frequencies should be of major concern in the present context. That is, there is once again a problem in misperception as we employ the term in this study.

The psychological realm constitutes a fascinating area of inquiry for the crisis analyst. Shapiro and Gilbert's comprehensive literature review[22] suggests that individual (psychological) and small-group (social psychologial and sociologial) research is clearly relevant to the task of conflict and crisis management. Given the impact of high-level elites in the crisis milieu,[23] political psychology can be expected to contribute to the analysis of sources of and decision-making processes associated with crisis and conflict phenomena.

The psychological data set analyzed here adopts content analysis as a research technique and concentrates on the value subsystem of a decision-maker's belief system as the substantive focus of inquiry.[24] These data are collected on the foreign policy elite of the state (i.e., the head of state and the foreign minister) based on their speeches during the period under investigation. The specific variables are listed below:

Decision-maker Values

1. A comfortable life
2. A world of peace
3. Equality
4. Freedom
5. Happiness
6. Governmental security
7. Honor
8. Justice
9. National security
10. Public security
11. Respect
12. Social recognition
13. Wisdom
14. Progress
15. Unity
16. Ideology
17. Cooperation
18. Support of government

The eighteen values are derived from Rokeach's list of universal values and from exploratory research; the last five foreign-policy-specific values were added as a result of preliminary content analyses. The source for speech material was the *Daily Report* of the U.S. Foreign Broadcast Information Service (FBIS).[25]

Only preliminary analyses were undertaken with this data set. The most pertinent findings for our purposes concern the impact of decision-maker values on external behavior. In a multiple regression analysis in which the eighteen values were employed as predictors of foreign behavior, the values accounted for almost 40 percent of the variance in the case of constructive diplomatic behavior and almost 25 percent of the variance in the case of non-military conflict. Once again, the force dimension was the least well-explained, with the eighteen variables accounting for a statistically insignificant 19 percent of the variance.

While the above findings are only preliminary in nature, they do indicate a substantial impact of psychological factors in the determination of various types of foreign behavior. Furthermore, as was the case with the earlier analysis, it is clear that a differentiation among various types of foreign behavior is quite important in that it highlights the specific operation of psychological considerations on foreign behavior.

Conclusion

We should now return briefly to the issues with which we began the current research. That is, our concern was with the concept of misperception as it arises from the assessment of events of complex origins. Thus the indicators we have discussed here were developed in order to provide the decision-maker with greater systematic information concerning the types of factors that serve as important inputs into the process of policy formation and execution for various types of states under varying conditions and circumstances. While the system of indicators presented here is merely a prototype, it nevertheless provides us with an insight into how a system such as this could function, based on a wide array of internal and external characteristics of states and the context in which interstate interactions are undertaken.

The ultimate goal of this type of research is to sensitize the parties to a conflict situation to the contextual realities as they exist for their adversaries. As we have noted, conflict situations are typified by a reduction in the direct communications between parties concerning the meaning behind their overt actions, whether verbal or non-verbal. In such situations, there is a natural tendency to accept events at face value, as an accurate reflection of the intentions of the sending party. The danger in this situation lies in the misperceptions that can result and their translation into policy outputs. To the extent that we can gain a greater understanding of our adversaries' context, we will be able to reach more informed decisions concerning our responses to such actions.

Notes

* This research was supported in part by the Advanced Research Projects Agency of the U.S. Department of Defense and was monitored by ONR under Contract No. N00014-76-C-0153.
    1. For an excellent review of the extensive literature on this subject, see R. Jervis, *Perception and Misperception in International Politics* (Princeton: Princeton University Press, 1976).
    2. J. Wilkenfeld, "Domestic and Foreign Conflict Behavior of Nations," *Journal of Peace*

Research 1 (1968): 65-69; idem, "Models for the Analysis of Foreign Conflict Behavior of States," in B.M. Russett, ed., *Peace, War, and Numbers* (Beverly Hills: Sage Publications, 1972), pp. 275-298.

3. F.A. Beer, "The Epidemiology of Peace and War," *International Studies Quarterly* 23 (March 1979): 45-86.

4. L.F. Richardson, *Arms and Insecurity* (Pittsburgh: Boxwood Press, 1960).

5. J. Galtung, "A Structural Theory of Aggression," *Journal of Peace Research* 2 (1964): 95-119.

6. See, e.g., W.R. Phillips, "The Conflict Environment of Nations: A Study of Conflict Inputs to Nations in 1963," in J. Wilkenfeld, ed., *Conflict Behavior and Linkage Politics* (New York: McKay, 1973), pp. 124-147; W.R. Phillips, "The Dynamics of Behavioral Action and Reaction in International Conflict," *Peace Research Society Papers* 17 (1971): 31-46; and J. Wilkenfeld, "A Time-Series Perspective on Conflict in the Middle East," in P.J. McGowan, ed., *Sage International Yearbook of Foreign Policy Studies,* Vol. 3 (Beverly Hills: Sage Publications, 1975), pp. 177-212.

7. H. Eckstein, "On the Etiology of Internal Wars," in I.K. Feierabend, R.L. Feierabend, and T.R. Gurr, eds., *Anger, Violence, and Politics* (Englewood Cliffs: Prentice-Hall, 1972), pp. 9-30.

8. We refer here to the Interstate Behavior Analysis Project and the Cross-National Crisis Analysis Project. For detailed discussions of these projects and earlier analyses, see S. J. Andriole, J. Wilkenfeld, and G.W. Hopple, "A Framework for the Comparative Analysis of Foreign Policy Behavior," *International Studies Quarterly* 19 (June 1975): 160-198; G.W. Hopple, J. Wilkenfeld, P.J. Rossa, and R.N. McCauley, "Societal and Interstate Determinants of Foreign Conflict," *Jerusalem Journal of International Relations* (Fall 1977): 30-66; J. Wilkenfeld, G.W. Hopple, S.J. Andriole, and R.N. McCauley, "Profiling States for Foreign Policy Analysis," *Comparative Political Studies* 11 (No. 1, April 1978): 4-35; and J. Wilkenfeld, G.W. Hopple, and P.J. Rossa, "Indicators of Conflict and Cooperation in the International System, 1966-1970," in J.D. Singer and M.O. Wallace, eds., *To Augur Well: Indicators of Conflict at the Interstate Level* (Beverly Hills: Sage Publications, 1979).

9. See N. Choucri, *Population Dynamics and International Violence* (Lexington, Massachusetts: D.C. Heath, 1974) and N. Choucri and R.C. North, *Nations in Conflict: National Growth and International Violence* (San Francisco: W.H. Freeman, 1975).

10. See I.K. Feierabend and R.L. Feierabend, "Level of Development and International Behavior," in R. Butwell, ed., *Foreign Policy and the Developing Nations* (Lexington, Kentucky: University of Kentucky Press, 1969), pp. 135-188; and P.J. Katzenstein, "International Relations and Domestic Structures: Foreign Economic Policies of Advanced Industrial States," *International Organization* 30 (Winter 1976): 1-45.

11. See Wilkenfeld, "Domestic and Foreign Conflict Behavior"; D.A. Zinnes and J. Wilkenfeld, "An Analysis of Foreign Conflict Behavior of Nations," in W.F. Hanrieder, ed., *Comparative Foreign Policy: Theoretical Essays* (New York: McKay, 1971), pp. 167-213; L. Hazlewood, "Diversion Mechanisms and Encapsulation Processes: The Domestic Conflict — Foreign Conflict Hypothesis Revisited," in McGowan, *Sage International Yearbook,* Vol. 3, pp. 214-244; and D.A. Zinnes, *Contemporary Research in International Relations* (New York: Free Press, 1976).

12. M. Midlarsky, "Power, Uncertainty, and the Onset of International Violence," *Journal of Conflict Resolution* (September 1974): 395-431.

13. W.H. Riker, "Events and Situations," *Journal of Philosophy* 54 (January 1957): 57-70.

14. A more extensive discussion of these findings can be found in Wilkenfeld, Hopple, and Rossa, "Indicators of Conflict and Cooperation."

15. Detailed discussions of the PLS procedure (formally known as NIPALS — Non-Linear Partial Least Squares) can be found in H. Wold, "Methods II: Path Models with Latent Variables as Proxies for Blocks of Manifest Variables," in idem, ed., *Modeling in Complex Situations with Soft Information,* presented at the Third World Congress of Econometrics, Toronto, Canada, 1975; idem, "Causal Flows with Latent Variables: Parting of the Ways in Light of NIPALS Modeling," *European Economic Review* (June 1974): 67-86; and I. Adelman et al., "Applications of Methods I-II to Adelman-Morris' Data," in Wold, *Modeling in Complex Situations.*

16. Wold, "Methods II," p. 71.

17. For additional details on the adaptation of the PLS procedure to the IBA framework, see R.N. McCauley, "Analytic Strategies in the Comparative Study of Interstate Behavior," Interstate Behavior Analysis Research Report No. 19, University of Maryland, 1976; P.J. Rossa, G.W. Hopple, and J. Wilkenfeld, "Crisis Analysis: Indicators and Models," *International Interactions,* 1979; and Wilkenfeld, Hopple, and Rossa, "Indicators of Conflict and Cooperation."

18. In fact, incorporation of the action-reaction element results in the explanation of 94 percent of the variance in foreign behavior. In addition, its incorporation has the effect of drastically reducing the statistical impact of the other indicators within the interstate component, as well as reducing the overall impact of the societal and global components. Our feeling is that the model as presented in the body of this paper more accurately reflects the balance of potency among the determinants of foreign behavior.

19. Rossa, Hopple, and Wilkenfeld, "Crisis Analysis."

20. Hopple, Wilkenfeld, Rossa, and McCauley, "Societal and Interstate Determinants."

21. A more detailed presentation of these findings is available in Wilkenfeld, Hopple, and Rossa, "Indicators of Conflict and Cooperation."

22. H.B. Shapiro and M.A. Gilbert, "Crisis Management: Psychological and Sociological Factors in Decision-Making," Human Science Research, Inc., McLean, Virginia, Final Technical Report, 1975.

23. M.G. Hermann, "When Leader Personality Will Affect Foreign Policy: Some Propositions," in J.N. Rosenau, ed., *In Search of Global Patterns* (New York: Free Press, 1976), pp. 326-333; O.R. Holsti, "Foreign Policy Formation Viewed Cognitively," in R. Axelrod, ed., *Structure of Decision* (Princeton: Princeton University Press, 1976); and M. Brecher, "Toward a Theory of International Crisis Behavior: A Preliminary Report," *International Studies Quarterly* 21 (March 1977): 39-74.

24. Details are provided in G.W. Hopple, "Elite Values and Foreign Policy Analysis: Preliminary Findings," in L. Falkowski, ed., *Psychological Models in International Politics* (Boulder: Westview, 1979); and M. Rokeach, *The Nature of Human Values* (New York: Free Press, 1973).

25. In order to determine the annual state samples for the 1966-70 period, coders generated lists of heads of state and foreign ministers for all fifty-six states and then recorded all *Daily Report* speeches (interviews, broadcasts etc.) by the decision-makers. For each year, states for which there were three or more "cases" (i.e., speeches) were included. A total of thirty-nine states satisfies this criterion one or more times during the 1966-70 time span. Because a different set of states satisfied this criterion in each year, this data set could not be incorporated into the PLS analysis performed earlier. For an analysis that incorporates the four components simultaneously, see G.W. Hopple, P.J. Rossa, and J. Wilkenfeld, "Threat and Misperception: Assessing the Overt Behavior of States in Conflict." in P.J. McGowan and C.W. Kegley, eds., *Sage International Yearbook of Foreign Policy Studies,* Vol. 5 (Beverly Hills: Sage Publications, 1979).

History as Reality Shaped by Images

Yehoshua Arieli

Two assumptions seem to underlie the title given this volume, "Images and Reality in International Politics": that there exists a reality or structure of facts and events in international politics that, at least in theory, is recognizable and comparable with those images of the validity of this reality held by the political participants; and that the relation between "image" and "reality" is of critical importance for the actors, as it will to a certain degree determine the outcome of their actions.

If we define politics as measures and actions taken to achieve aims related to society, the state and the public, then we assume that the success or failure of such measures depends on, among other factors, the capacity to discern the elements by which political action becomes organized, on the capacity to correctly assess the suitability of the means to the ends and to correctly estimate the chances of achieving the ends in a given situation. In the context of politics, reality is counterposited to political action as the framework of necessary conditions, as the field of forces to be encountered, and as the criteria for the evaluation of the feasibility of political action.

"Image" and "reality" are polar terms inside a conceptual continuum, complementary opposites in meaning. They connote subjectivity as against objectivity, the representation of something that exists independently of the representer.

Reality is a regulatory concept — *ein grenzbegriff* — connoting actuality, being, having existence. It is that which underlies appearance, the sphere of action, force and events. As such it is the object of knowledge and cognition, the criterion of truth, the opposite of illusion. Reality as being possesses structure and attributes. It is either comprehensive or part of a comprehensive totality in harmony with a general structure.

The ideal type of the concept of reality is nature as that which exists independently of the mind and is the object of knowledge. Knowledge of nature is gained by systematic observation and conceptualization, by the application of mathematical models and the postulation of general laws that adequately explain the individual case. Such knowledge can then be used for prediction that to a certain degree confirms the truth of our assumptions and the adequacy of our image of nature.

Images, on the other hand, are products of the mind. They are integrative: out of a multitude of cognitive, perceptual and emotional elements drawn from experience, memory, tradition and language, fashioning an integrated whole — a view. They are a stabilized and ordered world of things that are for the mind what the vision of the world in space is for the eye, and are to a certain degree fashioned after the likeness of the spatial vision. The functions of images related to human life are not limited to representations of the outside world. They create frameworks of personal and social cohesion; and through them personal and group identities are established. They relate to individual and public purposes, serve as ideal representations of behavior, and embody beliefs about the nature of the visible and the invisible world. They serve to integrate the personality of the individual by integrating the elements of past experiences, present desires, needs and anxieties with expectations about the future, and by relating the individual to the group and the social environment. In short, they create structures of meanings and mental entities that are necessary for orientation and action in the present and, even more so, for future-oriented behavior.

The contradistinction between image and reality relative to nature is therefore only one type of relation between the two concepts in the sphere of politics or the wider sphere of social action, behavior and social life.

All expressions and dimensions of human life are permeated and shaped by representations (*Vorstellungen*), ideas, conceptions, beliefs, purposes, and images that transform the basic and recurrent biological and psychological needs and behavior patterns into a world dominated by meanings and mental constructs, images and symbols. They are constituent parts of human reality. We can neither conceive nor understand the individual and society unless we relate to mental constructs and images inherent in their make-up. The units comprising social reality are conscious agents, a myriad of wills, minds, mentalities and behavior patterns held together by semiconscious and conscious relations that contain structures of meanings and images of a meta-natural world. The way to understand this world is by understanding its language and forms of communication; by analyzing the intentions, motives, conceptions and purposes embodied in actions, institutions and patterns of behavior, as well as the nature and the logic of the relations between individuals and groups; by taking account of material, social and mental resources organized for the satisfaction of needs and the employment of power.

While images and representations of nature cannot influence or change nature unless an action taken is based on a correct understanding of its structure, images about nature or the human world *can* change human reality, irrespective of their truth value, as soon as they are translated into actions and patterns of behavior and gain power over the minds of men.

This permanent transfer of individual or group images into the objective sphere of human reality through action and patterns of behavior is a fundamental characteristic of all social life and history. The basic assumption about human life is that it is shaped by consciousness and that it experiences reality by translating it into the medium of mentality. Language, behavior patterns, customs, institutions, all forms of social organization, of production and economic relations belong to this sphere. Through this medium the specific forms of individual and social life are made possible and are maintained. This socio-mental world is grafted onto the biological structure and needs of the species and onto the conditioning forces of its natural environment. Through the latter, a framework of stable structures and constant variables is given in the form of basic needs, capacities, behavior patterns and environmental determinant factors. The prototypes of this interaction between the mental sphere and that of nature as related to man in the wider sense are presented by the transformation of nature through work; by the transformation of sexual and reproductive drives into patterns of kinship and child-rearing, and of the instincts of self-preservation and herding into patterns of primary social relations and organization. Yet even in these most stable and biologically rooted forms of human life, the impact of changing concepts, beliefs and images is decisive for the actual form and structure they possess at a given time and place.

The relation between reality and image taken in its widest sense in the human world is then radically different from that vis-a-vis nature. It is one of permanent transfer from the mental sphere into that of actuality and factuality by formative human action and behavior. Man lives at one and the same time in the natural and in the socio-mental environment that he has created. He is largely the maker of the world he lives in, although at any given time the world confronts man as a determining reality. This apparent paradox of the human situation underlies human philosophy from Vico to Hegel and Marx. It underscores the fact that man is simultaneously the product and producer of history; that the mind, ideas and images become objectivized as the historical world through actions and attitudes, and as social, cultural, religious-ideational, economic, and technological structures maintain and determine human life.

This two-fold aspect of human reality — man as producer and product of his social existence — can only be understood in terms of history; and the paradox inherent in this statement can be resolved only if we conceive the structure of human reality as historical.

Unlike nature, the reality of human existence is unfinished and open-ended. Being permanently determined by action, by the active maintenance of social relations and by the unceasing impact of events, the historical world is one of change and development, of continuities and discontinuities; a world in which contingencies, new forces and factors, accidental events and continuous relations are intricately interwoven into one texture.

Nature is structured by the axis of space-time. The world of history is structured by the axis of time, by duration, sequence, succession, and concurrence. This is of course true for all life. Yet while biological life develops according to an imprinted structure and is cyclical in its course, human life, taking its course in the socio-mental sphere, possesses an open-ended, linear time axis embodied in history.

Reality in the strict sense, as a given structure of things, as determined existence, belongs in the human experience only to the past, or rather to the sphere of the past-present. Human past, whether individual or social, is human life completed; that which has taken place is irreversible and has conditioned the present. The sphere of the past-present is therefore the situational framework of existence that the individual and society have inherited, and presents the given data of human experience that determine the situation in which man finds himself. This inherence of the past in the present is transmitted in the form of cultural inheritance, language, habits, behavior patterns, norms, values, beliefs, and images, as well as the institutional framework of social life, of the existing structure of social relations and the distribution of power, status and resources, and as the inherited world of artifacts and material environment produced by man.

History, as the story of human life and events, as the record of and reflection upon human existence, is therefore concerned only with the past as formed reality.

The present, on the other hand, is the focus of action and experience; the sphere of determination that reaches out toward the future as the focus of the possible and not yet determined existence. As the succession of events and as the dimension in which human life unfolds, history then proceeds from the present to the future — from the actual to the possible. The sphere of the present-future is that of evolving reality actualized by action, experiences and events occurring in the present. Two spheres thus intersect in the present: that of the past-present, the sphere of a given reality and situational framework of life, and that of the present-future, the sphere of action and evolving reality — the sphere of freedom and anticipation working within the framework of a given reality.

A basic concern of human life, whether individual or social, in facing the future is to foreclose its unknown elements by present action, implying that the present be organized so that future events will be determined by it. All private and public action includes future-directed elements and is based on anticipations, perceptions, predictions — in short, on images of a future. Estimates of future needs, developments and resources are basic components of public action. So is policy-making. The will to organize the future in predictable terms lies at the root of all law- and institution-making.

In facing the future, man is guided by conjectural images of likely events, as well as by images of desirable events. Like all images, they are integrated mental constructs composed of elements of knowledge, experience, stereotypes of realities and emotional factors. They are rational to the degree that they are based on the analysis of the present situation and estimates of the probable configuration of forces, resources and events at a future date. Yet the span of foresight is by its very nature limited and its measure of reliability uncertain. Both depend on the range of objects sought, on the range of factors involved, and on the degree of mastery over these factors.

Change and continuity are thus the outcome of actions and events occurring in the present in the framework of a reality created and transmitted by the past, and the modifications of this framework are produced by the sum total of events, activities and mental attitudes that impinge upon the individual and society in the present.

Keeping in mind the fundamental importance of time awareness for man, which is closely welded to the consciousness of change and to the insecurity concerning the future and the outcome of the clash of innumerable factors, the supreme importance of mental constructs for the cohesion and the ordering of human life becomes evident.

Being from the phenomenological point of view timeless, these constructs serve as frameworks to subject the flow of phenomena to meaning structures; to unify the multiplicity of events into patterns of order; to create a community of beliefs, loyalties, norms and values; and to forge instruments for dominating reality by knowledge, techniques and power.

For the historian, the problem of the relation between image and reality bears several aspects. It may be defined as the question of the nature and structure of knowledge about human existence, about human life in the past. It may relate to the question of the role of mental constructs, images, in history or, again, be related to the problem of the capacity of man to shape history — the relation between man the maker and man the product of history.

All historical knowledge is constructed, selected and bound to the present as a point of perspective, as a limiting horizon of knowledge and understanding, and as a sphere of belonging. This is because, by its very definition, the past is gone and exists only to the degree that it inheres in the present as tradition, traces and sources and as transmitted and inherited structures of social life in the widest sense. The image we gain of the past is inevitably based on our own experiences, perspectives, interests, our mental horizon and sense of belonging and relevance. We reconstruct the past from these elements by integrating them into images that bear the semblance of human life in the past. The process of re-creating the past through image formation remains basically the same whether we refer to the images of the past that form part of the cultural tradition of a group, a society or a people, or whether we refer to images that the trained historian creates by critical analysis of historical evidence and data.

In both cases the image formed of the past goes beyond knowledge, which of necessity is limited and composed of a multitude of separate data. It represents an integrated view of human life particularized by known or assumed knowledge that relates to it. The method by which this image is formed proceeds by way of analogy. We project our concepts and images of the structure of present life and of human existence into the past, while our knowledge of data of past life determines the content of this constructed past and modifies the structural elements of its image. Historical empathy and imagination, as well as generalizing conceptions, serve as instruments through which such images are evoked, and the separate data serve to stand for multiple and continuous phenomena. Yet this, after all, is the way by which the mind interprets the elements of experience into a coherent view of human life and nature.

Moreover, all knowledge of the past is imbued with and guided by the concept and image of history as a fundamental, almost *a priori,* idea that inheres in man's consciousness and grows out of his time awareness. The idea of history implies that the life of individuals or groups is basically a story, a narration of what happened and became meaningful for man, individual and collective, and for the the course of human life. It implies that history is the account of events and factors that shaped the life of man and societies and that are therefore memorable, worth remembering. All men at all times carry within themselves this concept of history and act accordingly. History as an idea is the imposition of *Gestalt* on the life of man and the flow of events in time. This urge to impose meaning structures on the flow of time and events becomes a formative element of human action that attempts to bind the past, the present and the future of the individual and the group into a unity of identity and destiny.

The image of the past and its meaning for the present differ in different cultures and societies and change with their internal transformations. Traditional societies, in which the rate of social and cultural change is slow and imperceptible, which are regulated by customs and whose institutions are legitimized and sanctified by the past, will conceive the past as a source of order and as standard for behavior, norms and beliefs.

The past, the present and the future are conceived as a continuum revealing the chain of being, the timeless order of existence or the superhuman origins of its foundations by mythical or heroic figures. To the degree that they are dominated by religious-monotheistic concepts, the images of the past will be translated into terms of revelation and a religious normative order of life. History may then be conceived as the revelation of divine will and purpose in time, and the future is conceived as *telos,* the consummation or the denouement of human existence in time.

Societies in which the rate of change is more rapid, in which the present is different from the past and the future becomes uncertain, develop different attitudes towards the past and towards history in general. They will be permeated by the awareness of distance, by elements of reflection and value judgment, and by conscious endeavors of reconstruction. These are the periods to which Johan Huizinger's definition of history applies: the intellectual form through which a culture renders account to itself of its own past.

History as an idea serves in such periods to maintain or create social identification by creating a community of past memories and experiences and belongings, and a common destiny in the present and the future as a people or a state. This consciousness of historic community, of peoplehood and common destiny, may take the form of the sacred history of the Jewish people as exemplified in the Bible, created by a covenant between God and the people, or the more mundane version of community of descent, history and fate as expressed by Edmund Burke in his famous passage: "[The State] is a partnership in all science; a partnership in all arts, a partnership in every virtue, and in all perfection. As the ends of such a partnership cannot be obtained in many generations, it becomes a partnership not only between those who are living, [but also] those who are dead, and those who are to be born."

Yet beyond this elementary idea of history with its quest to know whence we come, whither we are going and who we are, there exists the intellectual desire to discover the structure and nature of human life as existence developing in time: to discover the factors that shaped the past. This approach posits history as a structure of human reality against nature. It thinks in terms of causation, processes, development; in terms of social, cultural and ideational structures, as well as in terms of events that shape human reality in their interaction.

History as a comprehensive concept of human reality attempts to explain the course of events and developments of human societies by analyzing the factors, forces and situations considered relevant. It uses the methods of interpretation, exegesis and dialectics necessary for understanding human phenomena, alongside theories and models concerning human behavior taken from the realm of the social and natural sciences.

This is not the place to enter into the discussion whether the type of explanation and description prevalent in the natural sciences is also applicable to the humanities and social sciences, or whether the latter must use different modes and methods; whether history deals with the unique and with irrepeatable facts or should adopt the more analytical and generalizing approaches of the social sciences; whether the one is ideographic, based on the category of "understanding" as against the nomothetic postulates of the sciences. Yet it seems reasonable to assume that the very fact that history and human reality are permeated by and take their course in the socio-mental sphere demands that the modes of understanding and explanation should be at least partly different from those of the natural sciences. The vocabulary needed for dealing with history and the social sciences is completely different. It deals with norms, values, aims, reasons, motivations; with the whole range of human attitudes, feelings and behavior patterns; with knowledge, experience and systems of beliefs; with social organization, communication and institutions; with tradition and cultural inheritance; and with the frameworks of social, economic, political, cultural, and intellectual-religious order that unite individuals as society and differentiate them from each other in space and time. This world is far more fragile and unstable than that dealt with in the natural sciences. It is a world of transition, change, breakdowns and multiple perspectives; of failure of nerves and misconceptions; of power struggles and clashes of interests and forces. Yet above all it is the world of images, private and public, stable and changing, emergent and disintegrating, that motivate and shape private and public life.

Historical inquiry aims to discover, understand and describe these images that give cohesion and content to individual and social life and relate them to specified historical, social and personal contexts, evaluate their roles and efficacy, and explain them in the framework of their historical environment. Images may also be called "outlook," views, general and particular conceptions of private and social life and order, of values and norms, of the "what is" and "should be," of the real, possible and desirable.

Being mental constructs, they tend to fuse, create clusters and hierarchies like the monads of Leibnitz's universe. In this they reflect, express and interpret the complexity and multidimensional character of social life; the interrelationship between individuals, groups and society at a given time. They are expressive as well as interpretative, functional as well as normative, directed toward the outside world or to the emotional, spiritual sphere of individual and social life, and these dominant characteristics define their relation to reality. Expressive and interpretative images are embodied in creative art, in play, styles of life, philosophies and religious forms and expressions. They guide men in search of meaning, self-realization and self-expression. They are inner-directed and their relation towards reality as a given world is that of ends towards means, a situational framework, a stage on which the performance takes place.

Functional images are reality-oriented. They aim at action, at the mastery or the ordering of life, at the correct orientation; as such they aim at the adequate understanding of experience and of the factors determining the given world. When we speak of a culture or a civilization we refer at least partly to that pattern of interrelationships between these images prevalent in a society or group that differentiate them from others, and we assume that there exists a specific hierarchical structure that characterizes this interrelationship.

Such are our concepts of the classical culture of Greeks, of medieval European culture, of the civilization of the Renaissance, of Puritanism, or the Catholic culture of the Counter-reformation. The same applies to all the categories used to describe historical reality and to the whole inventory of social, political, cultural, religious, economic and legal entities. There exists the image of the Christian medieval world order, which contains the image of the

Church as institution of grace, *as civitas dei* — a distinct hierarchical order of priesthood related in specified ways to the other orders of the Christian commonwealth. The image of kingship, different in the world of Judaea from that of the European medieval world, is intrinsically related to the wider image of a world order and the narrower image of place and time, of specific traditions and a social and legal order.

It may be argued that the term "image" misleads, and that the terms "concepts," "ideas," "conceptions," etc., should be used in order to describe those mental constructs inherent in the phenomena of the human world. Yet, as explained before, "image" is used in order to signify the composite and synthetic character of these constructs, their analogous structure to that of the external world, their elasticity and tendency to coalesce with other mental constructs, and their innate tendency to be externalized from the realm of consciousness into patterns of behavior, action and life styles.

The relations between image and reality in the historical realm are those of a two-way transfer and are of mutual impact. Mental constructs tend to influence existing configurations of the personal and social world, and the latter condition and shape the socio-mental sphere. This relationship can be described and analyzed only historically, as a process shaped by diachronic and synchronic sequences developing dialectically through the mutual impact of distinct and disparate factors.

The quest of history and the social sciences is after permanent structures, after the elimination of the accidental, to analyze the relations and factors active in these structures in the form of quasi-functional, formal-logical or causal laws, generalizations and ideal types that can serve as explanations of social, political and economic behavior and as models for prediction.

While by its own definition history cannot forgo the narrative descriptive element, the social sciences proceed by the elimination of the time structures and the uniqueness of the historical phenomenon in order to gain models of explanation that would then be applied to the individual case. This quest can never be fully achieved. All historical knowledge remains hypothetical and provisional. The past can never be wholly retrieved, as all historical knowledge is selective, choosing from an infinite number of events and data only a limited number — those considered to be of "historical importance." Moreover, historical reflection deals with irrepeatable events and constellations that cannot be satisfactorily explained by generalized theories. It is conditioned by our own position and point of view which, stemming from the perspective of the present, is itself part of the course of history.

The hypothetical and provisional character of our historical knowledge is infinitely heightened when applied to the present as the sphere of action and reality moving toward the future. True, this present is structured by the frameworks of social life and organizations: the state, laws, by the economic and technological nexus, by cultural inheritance, and by the unceasing effort to create and maintain social cohesion. Yet the present is also the sphere of action and interactions, events and processes that can be only partially known. It presents innumerable actors and factors who know each other only partially if at all, who hardly know yet what they will do, and whose knowledge and understanding of their own needs and deeds, present and future, is as vague as their needs and intentions are pliable and changeable.

In order to be effective, individual, social and political action can therefore rely only partially on knowledge. The success or failure of action, the historical potency of ideas, purposes and images that underlie social actions do not and cannot depend on their truth value in relation to historical reality. Men act in order to safeguard needs, satisfy desires, achieve ends considered worthwhile, and solve problems arising from a given situation. The potency of mental constructs vis-a-vis action lies in their capacity to supply motivations, to guide action, create consensus, present solutions, and evoke support and strength by their appeal to the mind and the heart.

The limits that reality sets to their efficacy is their *compatibility* with reality, not their truth value. This is a cardinal point that indicates the pliant, open and indeterminate nature of history as reality. The compatibility of reality with mental constructs and images directing action means the possibility to organize elements of reality so that they will be consonant with the construct, and at the same time capable of persisting — or rather coexisting — with reality and forming a part of it. Incompatibility means that mental constructs cannot be translated into terms of existence, cannot persist.

The concept of compatibility as a limiting term of the relation between reality and the efficacy of images as determinant factors in history is based on the assumption of the pliability of reality, its dynamic character as the framework of the interplay between a vast number of forces. The infinite variety of social relations and institutions, of beliefs and styles of life, of patterns of behavior and of cultures, of types of events, personalities and configurations of human activities are, in the last resort, based on the pliability of human and material nature and the wide range of possibilities given within the limits of compatibility. This is also the basis of freedom, of the uniqueness of historical phenomena, and of the emergence of the "new" in reality.

As noted before, mastering reality as a present leading toward a future means possessing the ability and capacity to organize its elements in accordance with the requirements of the aims set by purposive action. This implies, among other things, the capacity of gaining power to impose one's will on reality, on nature or human environments. From this point of view all mental constructs possess reality when they possess power or are capable of mobilizing power — by influencing the minds of men, by the capacity to embody them in material forms as artifacts or instruments, by possessing residual physical power of coercion as state or political authority, or by gaining sufficient brute force to destroy or change physical or human existence.

Power connotes the capacity to act, to overcome resistance, to create change, to possess force. As such it possesses reality and, used for purposive action, can change reality.

The will to power as the way to shape the present and the future in accordance with one's desires and needs is one of the basic factors in history and cardinal to the understanding of the relation between image and reality. The greater the measure of power one possesses, the greater seems the capacity to dominate the present and foreclose the future, and the less seems the need to correctly evaluate the compatibility of one's purpose with the factors that compose reality or to judge the justifications of the uses of power in relation to the purposes to be realized. *This is the temptation of power.* It both corrupts and misleads. It corrupts because power as force of coercion has its own structure and dynamics that tend not only to become independent from the purposes for which it was to be used, but also to dominate the user by the need to maintain it and by the incapacity to relinquish it once it has been applied and created a chain reaction of resistance, fear, hate and violent revenge. It misleads because it creates the illusion of being sufficient and therefore tends to disregard the limits set by the rule of compatibility and the elementary truth taught by historical experience: that man's capacity to predict the outcome and consequences of action, especially of coercive action, is narrowly limited.

The closer the aims of action are to a given historical structure, the more they answer distinctly defined and widely felt needs, the less they need coercive power, and the better is their chance to be realized and incorporated into the general structure of social life and history. The more radical the aims are, the less they express real needs, the more they require coercive power, and the more counter-productive will be the consequences of their action.

Although history is to a great degree shaped by mental constructs and images, the formative and lasting influences of images and ideals on humanity were not achieved by the uses of coercive power and violence. I speak of great ideas that have shaped the outlook of nations, societies and individuals; of concepts, attitudes and values that inform the manners of societies and the intercourse of men; of the great religions, systems of thought and cultures, visions of the good life, the idea of science and social ideals. Their power lay in the influence they gained over the minds of men, in their capacity to enlighten the mind or satisfy the quest of the heart; to solve complex problems of the social order; to unify societies in a common belief; to provide man with the instruments to better his life and make it more abundant.

Yet even these ideational forces could not escape the law of change, adjustment and transformation once they had been translated into the terms of reality by action and institutionalization and had been embodied in patterns of social relations, political authority and personal behavior. Reality, whether social, political, economic or material, is subject to the inherent logic of facts and relations existing and arising out of the composite character of the elements that compose this reality. It is subject to the interplay of concurrently existing forces and to the changes caused by this interplay that create new patterns of relations and constellations of forces and factors.

Once embodied in terms of historical existence, mental constructs can only set the initial terms of their course; they cannot escape the unforeseen consequences and counter-productive side-effects common to all historical existence. History is prophecy looking backward. Only in the past can we discern the course of events and see at one and the same time the beginning and the end. Only in the past can we discern the interplay of forces in their full complexity, the distance between intentions and outcome, the ironic fate of great visions once translated into praxis, and the absolutely unforeseen consequences that follow purposive action.

The tension between image and reality is permanent. Out of this tension the existence of human life is dialectically developed. It is the motor power of human reality, the warp and woof out of which the texture of history is woven.

Images and Reality in International Politics: Security Perceptions in the Foreign Policy of the Netherlands

J. H. Leurdijk

Introduction

The main title of this article, "Images and Reality in International Politics," suggests a contrast that does not really exist. Images, defined as *perceptions* of reality, are a two-fold *part* of reality: They are shaped by reality, and they help shape it. One may even say that images cannot be contrasted with reality, because one image of reality can only be contrasted with another image of reality.

This leaves the subtitle, "Security Perceptions in the Foreign Policy of the Netherlands." In the context of this article, images will be understood to mean perceptions of reality held by the decision-makers. Reality will be understood to refer to the "objective" factors that, in each time period, determine the broad outlines of a country's foreign policy. In this sense, the actual foreign policy of a country mediates between the "images" of the position of their country in the world that its decision-makers hold, and the "reality" of that position. Accordingly, this paper will be divided into two parts, an analysis of the security perceptions of the foreign-policy-makers of the Netherlands, and a brief description of some main aspects of actual Dutch security policy.

The Netherlands as a Small Country

The "reality" within which the foreign policy of the Netherlands operates consists of three constant factors that, at any time, shape the outlines or orientation of the foreign policy of a country: (a) its geographic position; (b) the structure of the overarching international system; and (c) the "size" of the country.[1]

In the historical development of the international system, global wars are
watersheds that lead to its complete restructuring and to a new division of
responsibilities between the major powers. The Netherlands was newly constituted as an independent country in 1815, and the Second World War served
as the principal watershed that caused it to change from a policy of neutrality
to one of alliance. Security policy ultimately serves to maintain the independence of a country: before 1940, Dutch independence was safeguarded by the
balance of power between the European major powers, and hence Dutch
security policy was one of neutrality. After 1945, the same factors compelled
the Netherlands to develop an alliance policy that linked its independence to
an extra-European major power, the United States.

Before 1940, the Netherlands' geographic position at the mouth of a number of important European rivers dictated that none of the European major
powers could allow another one a dominant influence in the Netherlands. Yet
the independent existence of the Netherlands was seen as a condition for,
rather than as the result of, the European balance of power. The passivity of
the foreign policy of the Netherlands — an aloofness towards international
politics rather than a more active neutrality — also led to the sublimation of
its position as a small country, dependent for its security on the balance of
power of other countries. The Netherlands regarded itself as a main defender of
international law and an enlightening example in a world dominated by the
rude principles of power politics. But at the same time, its geographic position
led to an outward maritime orientation and placed it in an economic position
in which foreign trade and colonial possessions constituted the two pillars of
its material wealth which international law was supposed to maintain. Dutch
internationalism and legalism were therefore not altogether altruistic.

The outbreak of the Second World War and the German occupation of the
Netherlands testified to the failure of the European balance of power, at the
price of the disappearance of the Netherlands as an independent country. The
European balance of power had broken down definitively, and the war
resulted in a global bipolar balance in which the same three constant factors
more or less compelled the Netherlands to a policy of alliance with the United
States as the main guarantor of its security. It took some three years to make
this change, for in the first immediate postwar years the Netherlands hoped for
a reaffirmation of the alliance between the United States and the Soviet Union,
based on an agreement on the German question. When in 1948 the
Netherlands had to acknowledge the fact that the cold war was a reality, unchallenged by internal opposition or even debate, the fundamental reorienta-

tion of its foreign policy towards alliance with NATO was made, already in the belief that only the United States could safeguard European security. Since then, this basic orientation of foreign policy has never constituted a divisive issue in internal Dutch politics, although parties and factions do quarrel about the modalities of alliance policy. In fact, there is a broad consensus among the foreign policy elite and the public in general on the main principles of foreign policy.

In this situation of membership in an alliance, the acknowledgement of its position as a small power led the Netherlands to a policy guided by a continuous effort to prevent the possibly concomitant implication of irrelevancy. The basic conception of the national role of the Netherlands has been described as that of "a faithful ally." As a faithful ally, the Netherlands has fulfilled a specific, recognizable role, a recurring behavioral pattern characterized by unconditional (or almost so) support for the leader of the alliance, a marked identification with the aims and interests of the alliance as a whole, the desire to serve as an example to the other allies, efforts to reinforce the military integration and the political cooperation of the alliance, and conscientious fulfillment of any promises or guarantees the Netherlands has made.[2]

In general, it cannot be said that the perception of the "objective factors" mentioned above reduced the image of the foreign policy of the Netherlands to an exercise in futility for its foreign policy elite. A majority of this foreign policy elite (61%, according to a 1976 inquiry into the opinions and attitudes of the Dutch foreign policy elite on international politics) does agree with the "objective fact" that the Netherlands is a small country in the arena of international politics. A surprisingly high percentage (78%, in fact) of this elite maintains that the Netherlands could influence international politics, and over half (54%) believe it could do this less by exercising power than by setting a good example.[3]

Thus, both before 1940 and after 1945 the foreign policy of the Netherlands was based less on expedient principles than on deep-felt principles, and although the actual orientation of its policy may change, the deeper inspiration remains the same. Before 1940, the practice of international law served as a substitute for foreign policy; after 1945, the Netherlands abandoned an independent foreign policy altogether. This broad consensus on the basic principles of its foreign policy tends to turn into a disadvantage when it can be interpreted as a "lack of originality or creative thinking with regard to foreign policy."[4] In fact, Dutch foreign policy, at least until the beginning of the 1970s, has been described as reactive rather than initiative.

Security Perceptions

Security is a core value of any nation, and the foreign policy of a nation is aimed basically at maintaining the independent existence of the country. From this perspective, it appears quite natural that a nation put itself in the center of the world. As viewed from the Netherlands, therefore, the world can be divided into four spheres:

1. *The global-international system:* There is strong feeling in the Netherlands on the need to maintain the quality of life on earth (a great deal of attention was given to the Club of Rome) and on the potential dangers inherent in the uncontrolled spread of nuclear energy. In past decades, this inspired Dutch governments to an active policy against the spread of nuclear weapons. It has been consistently maintained that in the long run the international system can survive only if it is based on an international legal order.

2. *The Third World:* Development assistance has been one of the tenets of the foreign policy of the Netherlands. In a wider context, it is recognized that the international economic order is in need of revision; and in implementing its policy the Netherlands certainly proved receptive to the needs and views of the developing countries.

3. *East-West relations:* The security perceptions of the Netherlands are closely linked to the development of East-West relations, which have always held priority in Dutch foreign policy. The central factor in the security policy of the Netherlands has been "the American nuclear guarantee."

4. *The European Community:* Although the Netherlands has always advocated a supranational form of European political integration aimed at creating a new political entity, it has also consistently maintained that the security of this new entity could only be safeguarded in the context of the Atlantic community working in close cooperation with the United States. In fact, it can be argued that the basic consensus on Dutch security policy was to a large extent a condition for the near-unanimity in the Netherlands as to the goal of European integration. Had there been no such consensus, disagreement on the security implications of European integration might have resulted in disagreement on political integration as a goal.

In the 1976 inquiry mentioned above, it became evident that the results of the disappearance of the American nuclear guarantee were largely perceived as highly negative (an increase in armaments, greater discord in Europe, and greater Soviet influence), while only a small percentage of the respondents expected such effects to serve as positive stimuli encouraging rapprochement

73

with the Soviet Union and integration in Western Europe (69% and 9%, respectively). There were strong differences of opinion as to the alternatives to an alliance with the United States. And although Dutch governments were in general opposed to European nuclear arrangements to replace or augment the American security guarantee, the least one may say is that the foreign policy elite's rejection of the idea of a European nuclear force is highly ambiguous.

The basic security condition of the Netherlands is determined by the interrelatedness of three dyads that together constitute what is termed a situation of "extended deterrence"; a situation in which one nuclear power extends its (nuclear) protection over its junior alliance partner by threatening the other superpower with (nuclear) retaliation in the event of an attack on its allies. There are three dyads that together constitute this triangular system of extended deterrence: (a) The fundamental perception of a "Russian threat" to Western Europe; (b) the American security guarantee to Western Europe against this threat; and (c) the substantiation of this guarantee by the threat of American nuclear retaliation on the Soviet Union.

This interrelatedness can be depicted thus:

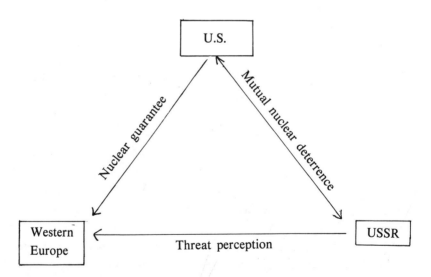

Accordingly, from the Dutch viewpoint the security of the Netherlands resides in what has come to be known as the American nuclear guarantee. This factor is so central that an analysis of the security policy of the Netherlands can easily begin with Dutch perceptions of this nuclear guarantee. Obviously, the American nuclear guarantee is only one aspect of the triangular relationship and therefore subject to changes as the perceptions of the other relations change. In fact, however, changes in the perceptions of these relations did not detract from the centrality of the American nuclear guarantee in the foreign policy of the Netherlands.

Despite the gradual movement toward détente in international relations, the "Russian threat" continues to be felt as real, and the changes in the way in which it manifests itself are viewed as tactical adaptations on the part of the Soviets to changing circumstances, the ultimate aim remaining unaltered. Over the years, however, there has been a change in the perception of the threat: fear of mass attack gave way to fear of local aggression, which again gave way to expectations of political pressure that could result from a weakening of Atlantic ties. In the present circumstances, however, the Dutch government does not discount or deny the sincerity of Russian efforts to achieve détente, but views those efforts primarily as military ones. In recent years, Dutch governments have taken an active part in the efforts toward détente, giving emphasis to respect for and implementation of the human rights articles of the Helsinki Declaration, and to the need to translate this détente into agreements on military disengagement.

It might be said that the official perceptions of the Russian threat are the embodiment of the general image the Dutch hold of the Soviet Union. While this image has become more favorable over the years, the view of a Soviet lust for power tends in particular to persist. It may be added that the bilateral relations between the Soviet Union and the Netherlands have never been particularly good. The supposedly aggressive intentions of the Soviet Union at first constituted sufficient justification for Western defense efforts, but for the past few years the guiding emphasis has been on the implications of the (steadily increasing) military power of the Soviet Union.

For the various Netherlands governments, there has never been any uncertainty as to the effectiveness of the threat of American nuclear retaliation, and it was recognized at an early stage in the nuclear arms race that the Soviet Union would not use nuclear weapons to achieve its ends. This did not, however, exclude the possibility of the aggressive use of other means by the Soviet Union, notably conventional weapons. The view obtains that, as a result of its favorable position in terms of conventional arms, the Soviet Union would not be the first to resort to nuclear weapons. Accordingly, in Dutch defense policy priority has been given to NATO's conventional armaments rather than to nuclear superiority. The Netherlands harbored no doubts as to the willingness of the United States to abide by its nuclear guarantee; but the

Dutch were apprehensive that the aggressive tendencies and powers ascribed to the Soviet Union might induce the latter to exploit its conventional superiority. Since the use of nuclear weapons is not an attractive option in any situation, an adequate conventional force would be a necessary supplement to nuclear deterrence. In fact, Dutch governments have always advocated pushing the role of nuclear weapons as far as possible into the background, and this was proclaimed the cornerstone of the "active peace policy" advocated by the progressive cabinet in 1973. The changing strategic relationship between the United States and the Soviet Union did not have any influence on Dutch perceptions of the reliability of the American nuclear guarantee.

In the view of Netherlands governments, maintaining the effectiveness of the nuclear deterrent required that certain organizational requirements be met, notably: that there be (a) central decision-making on the use of nuclear weapons, the sole power of decision resting with the American president; (b) a United States monopoly on the possession of nuclear weapons; and (c) military integration in NATO, especially in the field of conventional arms.

The American Nuclear Guarantee

The third aspect of the triangular relationship called "indirect deterrence" is the American nuclear guarantee, *the* central factor in the security situation of the Netherlands. Since its introduction in the debate on foreign affairs in the Netherlands in the early 1960s, the term "American nuclear guarantee" has been used very often, the suggestion of its self-evident nature prevailing over a sober analysis of its meaning. Accordingly, two aspects may be considered: (a) what kind of nuclear guarantee is it that the United States has given (to Western Europe); and (b) in light of the fact that explicit policy statements on a number of important and often basic problems have been made, based on this notion of the American nuclear guarantee, what has been the operational significance of the guarantee in the formulation of the foreign policy of the Netherlands.

The perceptions of the American nuclear guarantee have been remarkably consistent despite changes in the two other elements of the indirect deterrence situation. In the 1976 inquiry into opinions and attitudes of the foreign policy elite of the Netherlands, 63% of the respondents believed in the reliability of the guarantee, while 17% had lost their earlier confidence in the guarantee over the years.

The American nuclear guarantee is perceived as a definite commitment on the part of the United States to use (ultimately strategic) nuclear weapons for the defense of Western Europe. The certainty implied in the term "guarantee," however, has never been translated into anything but a reference to "the American promises." There is neither an international obligation nor a definite nuclear strategy that contains explicit references to the use of strategic nuclear weapons (although the "Schlesinger doctrine" apparently does provide for the use of strategic weapons in the European theater). This is a central factor, because the use of American tactical nuclear weapons in Europe would only result in the nuclear devastation of Central Europe. Although this prospect does not particularly appeal to the Netherlands, a part of Central Europe in this respect, the Dutch have never doubted the readiness of the United States to use strategic nuclear weapons that might result in the nuclear devastation of the United States.

Promises made only verbally are of little value in international politics; in the context of the American nuclear guarantee, however, they could be perceived to be real. First of all, there is a strong belief in the indivisibility of the Atlantic security system and in the intrinsic importance of Western Europe for America's own security. Moreover, the United States has provided Western Europe with "securities" constituting material proof that the promises will be honored: the presence of about 300,000 American troops and some 7,000 tactical nuclear weapons in Europe. In the past, however, Dutch governments have put much greater stress on the psychological function of the presence of American ground forces and tactical nuclear weapons (deterrence of Russian aggression), and on their indispensable contribution to the defense of Western Europe, than on their "security" function. Statements of Dutch governments do not give the impression that the former two aspects of the American presence in Western Europe furnish material evidence that an otherwise not entirely reliable guarantee will be upheld.

It is relevant to distinguish between the reliability of the American nuclear guarantee and its credibility. Reliability refers to the confidence of the allies in the American nuclear protection; credibility refers to the credence of the potential opponent against whom the guarantee is given. We have already noted that Dutch governments have never debated the reliability of the American protection, although other allies have, notably France. Neither did the Dutch question the credibility of American retaliation. But the 1972 SALT agreements, which included the ABM treaty establishing strategic parity and reinforcing the idea of mutual vulnerability, prompted new discussion of nuclear strategy, now initiated by the United States itself. And this discussion has also met with a certain response in the Netherlands, where the meaning and credibility of the American nuclear guarantee have been explicitly mooted.

The risk that the United States would run if called upon to abide by its guarantee has never been an important consideration for Dutch governments, but since the 1972 SALT agreements, this point has been raised by others, who saw a very definite link between credibility and reliability. In this context, the Dutch government in 1975 reinterpreted the credibility of the American nuclear guarantee. At the time Foreign Minister Van der Stoel (a socialist) recognized a logical contradiction between the expectation that the Soviet Union would be deterred by the specter of a nuclear war from taking rash steps against Western Europe on the one hand, and the expectation that the United States, despite that same specter, would not be prevented from abiding by its guarantee to Western Europe, on the other hand. But he did not consider this logic relevant to the relationship of mutual deterrence. The point was not to prove that the United States would with all certainty risk such nuclear confrontation on account of a conflict in Western Europe. That could never be proved. "The crux of the matter has nothing to do with logic, but with the inherent uncertainty of the situation, with the impossibility of being sure that the other side will not, after all, turn to nuclear weapons in the hour of danger."

Just as in the case of tactical nuclear weapons — in which constant reference is made to the imperative of keeping the opponent in the dark about the moment when, the circumstances in which, and the extent to which these weapons will be used, because this produces the maximum deterrent effect — the uncertainty factor also appears to apply to strategic nuclear weapons. The views of the various Dutch governments can be summed up in the statement that nuclear weapons possess the unique quality of having a moderating and stabilizing effect on the international situation, an influence that extends to a much wider scale of actions than the use of these weapons themselves.

Conclusion

In recent years, too, these pertinent perceptions with regard to the American nuclear guarantee have been translated into policy, with considerable operational significance. Definite policy statements have been formulated with regard to a whole range of security problems, with explicit reference to this crucial factor.

1. *Conventional armaments:* Over the years the Netherlands has argued in favor of improving conventional defenses rather than making various nuclear arrangements within NATO (e.g., Atlantic nuclear forces or a European nuclear force). It has left no doubt that it regarded the provision of these conventional forces a special task for the European NATO partners. Dutch initiatives have been taken mainly in this sphere, and can be accounted for by the fact that, although it harbored no doubts as to America's willingness to abide by its nuclear promises, the Netherlands was apprehensive that the aggressive tendencies and powers ascribed to the Soviet Union might induce the latter to exploit its conventional superiority, thus possibly forcing NATO to resort to nuclear weapons at an early stage. Reducing the role of nuclear weapons requires, *a priori,* that a conventional balance of forces be established in Europe, and that this should be the first aim of the MBFR talks;

2. *Nuclear Armaments:* The view of the United States as the sole power responsible for the nuclear protection in Western defense led to a definite policy with regard to nuclear problems in NATO. The emphasis has been on the obligation of sharing nuclear responsibilities by accepting the nuclear duties agreed upon in NATO, rather than on claims to a decisive say in nuclear matters. Dutch governments have consistently argued in favor of consultation and the right to be informed, but no more than that. In practice, this was evidenced by the priority given to the achievement of a universally acceptable treaty on the nonproliferation of nuclear weapons as against the formulation of nuclear regulations in NATO (which issue stood in the way of an early agreement on nonproliferation between 1964 and 1968); the willingness to confer direct powers of inspection on the IAEA as the universal atomic organization within the Euratom area; and finally, no insistence on a European nuclear force in the nonproliferation treaty.

Although between 1973 and 1977 the progressive cabinet made the reduction of the role of nuclear weapons a cornerstone of its "active peace policy," it is clear from the exposition of the Dutch view with regard to the essential role of nuclear weapons in Western defense that the attempts to reduce the role of nuclear weapons can be of only marginal significance. This government has favored the inclusion of the tactical nuclear weapons in Europe in the course of the MBFR talks in Vienna, but it envisages a reduction in the number of these weapons, not a change in strategy. And even though this same government made efforts to reduce the nuclear responsibilities of its armed forces, it did not reject the principle of sharing, as an ally, in the nuclear responsibilities of the alliance. Alongside certain pragmatic arguments, it maintained the fundamental argument that such sharing demonstrates the willingness to bear joint responsibility for implementing the nuclear aspects of an accepted strategy. Nuclear proliferation has again come to the fore as a major issue of foreign policy (c.f. the delivery of nuclear materials to South Africa and Brazil), and although less than optimal, the policy in this field is motivated by a deep concern for the future of international relations.

But as long as nuclear weapons have such an essential function in the international relations of the Northern hemisphere, preventing the spread of nuclear weapons to other areas does not have much real chance of success.

Notes

1. See in general, J.H. Leurdijk, ed., *The Foreign Policy of the Netherlands* (Alphen aan den Rijn: Sijthoff & Noordhoff, 1978).

2. A. van Staden, "The Role of the Netherlands in the Atlantic Alliance," in J.H. Leurdijk, *The Foreign Policy of the Netherlands,* p. 152.

3. P.R. Baehr et al., *Elite en buitenlandse politiek in Nederland* (Elite and Foreign Policy in the Netherlands) (The Hague: Staatsuitgeverij, 1978).

4. H. Daalder, "The Netherlands and the World: 1940-1945," in J.H. Leurdijk, *The Foreign Policy of the Netherlands,* p. 80.

Change and the Chinese*

Davis B. Bobrow, John A. Kringen, Steve Chan

In recent years, it has been commonplace to note that the international environment is changing in some specified direction. The now almost ritual references to the "increasing interdependency of nations" are representative. Data are often advanced to "prove" that such changes have occurred, and policy implications are drawn from these changes. Rarely, however, are the perceptions of important actors in the international system taken into account in assessing change or in deriving those policy implications.

The possibility that perceptions of change on the part of significant actors may alter the policy consequences of the "objectively" occurring change is almost never considered. Yet a moment's reflection suggests the naiveté of analyses of this sort. Take the hypothetical case of changes in the military balance between two nations. Policy guidance on how each party should act in a crisis would vary considerably depending upon whether this "objective" change was recognized by both parties, by only one of the parties, or by neither. And if we are concerned with perceptions, we must explore them on the basis of the words and actions of those whose perceptions we want to understand. As de Callieres observed long ago, "Most men in public affairs pay more attention to what they themselves say than to what is said to them."[1] An emphasis on perceptions follows not from a belief that the problems between states are primarily ones of communication, but rather from the view that regimes pursue relations of deterrence, defense or pragmatic adjustment in terms of the world as they see it.

Understanding perceptions of change is, of course, just one aspect — albeit an important one — of understanding foreign policy more generally. Because historical generalizations relating classes of situations to overt actions often provide an inadequate basis for understanding the specific foreign policy choices that different regimes make, knowledge of the perceptual basis of those decisions is needed. The crucial question has been whether or not such knowledge could be developed in a systematic, reliable fashion.

Over the past several years, we have tried to develop a research strategy capable of producing sound knowledge about the logics that regimes use to reach foreign policy decisions. As a test case we have examined the foreign policy of the People's Republic of China, on the grounds that it is both a sufficiently important and a sufficiently difficult problem to warrant particular concern. Our approach involves numerous methods — including traditional qualitative analysis of documents, systematic historical case studies, and semantic analysis of perceptions — to arrive inductively at the precedents, rules and precepts that shape foreign policy choices. From this analysis of Chinese decision logics, we have gone on to draw hypotheses about how the Chinese will treat various situations and regimes and to submit at least some of these to systematic statistical tests.[2] Our results have been sufficiently encouraging to suggest that this approach may be useful for the analysis of other regimes as well.

The aim of this article is not to summarize or review all the work that we have undertaken — an impossible task given space limitations. Rather, we intend to discuss the key assumptions that underlie our approach and present some findings about one domain of Chinese beliefs. Because of their critical importance in a rapidly changing international environment, and because of their significance to an understanding of the dynamics of Chinese foreign policy, we report here on Chinese beliefs about change.

Our Assumptions

In the manner of attribution theorists,[3] the present writers assume that foreign policy elites, like most human beings, try to predict social behavior (and avoid surprise). In their efforts to do so, they search for causality and order, ignoring randomness interpretations. Further, foreign policy participants, like most social scientists, realize that particular isolated acts may signal many alternate combinations of actor intention and capability. Accordingly, foreign policy decision-makers tend to rely on previous attributions of intent and capability, disregarding occasional behavior that contradicts those attributions unless the behavior in question is extremely deviant from the pattern of expectations.

If one accepts these assumptions, two conclusions follow. First, the interpretations that foreign policy elites make regarding the international environment, the behavior of foreign regimes and movements, and the past and probable future behavior of other institutions and individuals in their own national foreign policy process are patterned and, thus, are in principle predictable. Second, if we are to realize these predictive possibilities in actual analysis, we must capture the already established structures of causal interpretation and expectation held by decision-makers. Foreign policy decision-making involves processing new situations and courses of action through these structures. Therefore, in order to understand decision processes we need to identify the historically established categories and decision rules that will be brought to bear, the sorts of behavior that will or will not seem extremely deviant, the central points for revision in existing structures, and the consequences of such revision. Since there is little reason to expect that foreign policy decision-makers with grossly different experiences have developed the same set of interpretations and expectations, it is reasonable to begin with the notion that the pertinent structures differ across foreign policy decision systems.

Note that we do not contend that *all* the beliefs we present are unique to the Chinese. We know from research on other national decision cultures[4] that other national elites share some particular elements of Chinese beliefs. We are fundamentally concerned with the relative distinctiveness of Chinese policy analytics as a whole system, rather than with the uniqueness of its particular components. Also, we are alert to the possibility that the Chinese may differ from those who hold some similar beliefs in terms of the conditions under which they invoke these beliefs, and the interpretations and emphases that they attach to the shared beliefs.

Because we believe that foreign policy decision processes involve beliefs about one's own policy system as well as about an external environment, the cybernetic conception of communication and control is particularly attractive. Decision processes involve a number of attempts to cope with an environment, in our case an international environment, through cycles of information assessment, decision choice, and policy implementation.[5] A simple representation of this system can be seen in the figure below.

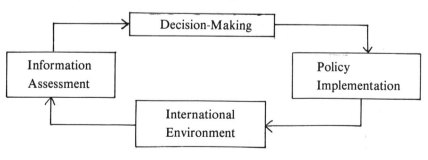

Our task, then, is to deal with beliefs pertinent to all four elements in this representation. Foreign policy actions are the joint product of these several sets of cognitions, not of any single one. In line with our view that decision-makers are not devoid of a sense of history, the structures we seek should contain beliefs about sound and unsound decision practices, drawn from what are thought by the groups under study to be cases of notable success and failure. And the structures of interpretation and expectation we discover should include some process rules as well as beliefs about the characteristics of domestic and foreign individuals, groups, and institutions.

In searching for the Chinese structures of policy interpretation and expectation, we seek to learn the answers to two general questions. First, what is for the Chinese a sound description, explanation or prediction of how other nations act in foreign affairs? Second, what is for them a compelling prescription to induce other nations to act in particular ways?

As these questions imply, we work with the national culture as our unit of analysis. Our contention is that we will gain some knowledge by working at the national-culture level, knowledge we would otherwise lack. Structures of interpretation and expectation that operate at this level determine in important ways how the phenomena emphasized by those who work with broader units (e.g., the international system) will be treated for policy-making and international bargaining purposes. They also set boundaries and issue agendas in terms of which the more limited units of analysis (e.g., those featured in bureaucratic politics perspectives) will have to operate. The structures at the national-culture level set an acceptable range for policy dialogue and mandate that certain issues be dealt with. They provide conventions to which individuals and organizations are under great pressure to conform if they wish to be treated as "serious" and "responsible." Whether or not these conventions yield falsifiable predictions about foreign policy behavior is an empirical question. We believe that they do, and that they vary across national decision systems, with important substantive implications for foreign policy outcomes. The issue, then, is not that foreign policy participants in any given nation are homogeneous in a strict sense; of course, they are not. The issue is whether they are sufficiently like each other as compared to participants in other national decision systems for the similarities to matter.

We deal then with general tendencies in the thinking of Chinese leaders, but do not take the position that all members of the Peking elite hold identical beliefs. We also avoid analysis of individual Chinese decision-makers or factions because, with the notable exception of a handful of leading cadres, only the most fragile and fragmentary understanding of the beliefs and roles of particular participants in Chinese foreign policy decision-making is possible. We consciously sacrifice some amount of analytic precision in favor of findings more likely to be applicable to decision situations in general and to have continued importance despite changes in office-holders. Basic beliefs and logics inculcated by the national decision culture seem especially likely to outlast the political and natural lives of specific leaders, to characterize officials in different institutions and organizations, and to have pertinence for diagnosing and treating a wide variety of issues and problems.

The above approach to the analysis of belief systems and foreign policy choice should not be interpreted to imply that an understanding of the belief systems of regimes will provide either a simple or a complete explanation of all their foreign policy decisions. Besides obvious data limitations, it is important to recognize that beliefs may vary considerably in the degree to which they entail unambiguous policy consequences. In order to allow for adaptation to new circumstances, policy beliefs must have some "open" elements — that is, elements that allow policy-makers some flexibility in deciding whether or not to bring the more fixed, unambiguous decision rules to bear.

This point is worth stressing because attempts to explain foreign policy choices in terms of attributions about policy-makers' beliefs frequently have assumed some simple correspondence between single belief elements and policy behavior. Studies investigating the role of "ideology" in determining the foreign policy behavior of China illustrate this point. The tendency has clearly been to assume that, if a simple correspondence did not exist, then "ideology" had no impact. Rather than assessing some simple correspondence, our analysis of Chinese policy beliefs has consciously attempted to be alert to elements of "openness" in Chinese beliefs. Such "openness" may take the form of either ambiguity in specific belief elements or inconsistency between different elements. This effort is useful in several respects. First, analytically, it allows us to distinguish areas where our understanding of Chinese policy beliefs is strong from those where it is weak. Second, identification of ambiguous elements in Chinese beliefs allows us to identify likely areas of elite conflict. Finally, since these areas are likely to be sources of conflict, they provide useful policy information about key leverage points for modifying Chinese policy.

While details of our methods have been presented elsewhere,[6] it is helpful to summarize here our general strategy of inference. We opt for an ensemble of methods, rather than relying on any one, because we believe that the tools at hand to inform us about inaccessible decision processes are, in essence, "weak." Evidence about the validity and reliability of these methods in informing us about foreign policy decision processes is sparse. Consequently, we stress the need to assess areas of convergence and divergence in findings produced by alternate research techniques.[7] Further, we emphasize the development and testing of propositions regarding decision processes that imply that a regime will behave in some ways and not others in situations of foreign affairs interest. In short, our strategy of inquiry seeks to test substantive propositions about structures of interpretation and expectation, and to assess alternate methods and data sources.

The foundation of the strategy — and the source of the findings we report here — is a qualitative content analysis, conducted in an operational code fashion, of a wide variety of Chinese documents. Content analysis of this sort has a long history in research on the foreign policy beliefs of inaccessible decision-makers.[8] Although an imperfect tool, it has been underutilized in comparative foreign policy research.[9]

Our findings are based on analyses dealing with two historical periods, the mid-1960s[10] and the mid-1970s.[11] We are relatively confident about the stability of Chinese "core beliefs" because these analyses suggest very similar findings. To guard against source biases in our research materials we have examined standard doctrinal treatises, cultural materials (e.g., revolutionary plays), and some political-military documents with restricted access inside China. Similarity in the policy analytics articulated in these various sources increases our confidence in the validity and strength of the inferred belief elements.

Chinese Beliefs About Change

We present the beliefs and decision logics central to Chinese analysis of change in a series of rule-like statements. These "axioms" purport not only to describe, explain and predict change, but also to prescribe sound ways to manage it. In analyzing Chinese views about change, it is important to bear in mind that the Chinese world view stresses both the inevitability and the desirability of conflict.

1. The world is constantly changing; the history of material, personal or social development is a continuous series of contradictions and resolutions of contradictions.

(a) Social development passes through distinct historical stages, with each successive stage taking place on a higher dialectical plateau.

(b) The transition between these stages is a wave-like or screw-like, rather than a straight-line, progression. Temporary reversals of historical processes are inevitable, but in the long term these processes cannot be blocked or deflected.

2. So long as they correctly grasp and act in accordance with the laws of social development, communist actors will be successful agents of change. While current international conditions and their development in the immediate future may be unfavorable to the communist cause, the long-term trend is always favorable.

3. In order to become successful agents of change, communist actors must achieve a basic understanding of the nature and bases of change.

(a) Factors internal to things are the causes of their change while factors external to things are the facilitators of their change.

(b) There is usually a considerable time lag between the development of conditions for change and any visible results of change.

(c) Small incremental changes in the capabilities of actors may, in the long term, lead to a significant structural change in their relationship.

(d) However, quantitative changes in actor capabilities (i.e., marginal revisions in the gap between the superior and the inferior parties) are inherently unstable and transient and can be easily compensated for or reversed by the opposing party.

(e) Qualitative changes in actor capabilities (i.e., the attainment of parity between actor capabilities or the reversal of positions between the superior and the inferior party) indicate that a structural transformation in actor relationships has taken place.

(f) The transition from quantitative change to qualitative change is likely to be turbulent because the parties involved will be more prone to take risks to either promote or prevent the new stage.

(g) Confrontation is especially likely under conditions of parity, and the ensuing struggle will eventually lead to the subjugation of one of the parties.

(h) Structural change in actor relationships accomplished through qualitative change is more enduring than the fluctuations resulting from quantitative adjustments.

(i) However, this change is not always conclusive and may be challenged by the newly inferior party, thus renewing the cycle of contention.

Axiom 1 rules out the possibility that the status quo can continue indefinitely. In turn, belief in the permanence of change calls for capabilities to monitor and forecast environmental change, to constantly update knowledge, and to adjust policy. Change stems from contradictions — that is, from confrontation and struggle between opposing forces. To quote Mao, "Contradictions take place constantly and are resolved constantly; this is the dialectical law of material development."[12] Mao explained that "the generality and absoluteness of contradictions have two meanings. First, it means that contradictions exist in the development of all things. Second, it means that the development process is a series of contradictions from beginning to end."[13] Notions of "contradiction" and "change" are closely related in the Chinese world views: contradictions generate change, and change produces new contradictions. The Chinese assert that both are present in all things and at all times.

Axiom 1(a) treats the development process as unfolding in distinct "stages" marked by some basic transformation in actor relationships. Stages are distinguished by changes in the nature of the main contradiction among the actors or by massive changes in their capabilities or behavior. Shifts in actor capabilities, especially qualitative leaps (Axioms 3e-3h), indicate the imminent resolution of contradictions. A change in strategy is called for to deal with the new situation.

Parenthetically, we expect that disagreements among the Chinese leaders are more likely during the transition periods between stages because of differences in the assessment of the nature and degree of changes and of their policy implications. Also, new policy objectives and strategies are likely to bear differential impact on the power and interests of groups in the Chinese leadership. Historically, periods of major policy review have been accompanied by leadership dissent. Those who continue to apply methods or views that are no longer appropriate for the new stage are indicted for "defeatism" and "failism," while those who attempt to apply methods or views that are not yet warranted by altered objective conditions are accused of "adventurism" and "leftist opportunism."

While Axiom 1(b) suggests that setbacks in the communist cause are inevitable, these setbacks are manageable with only temporary adverse effects. To quote Mao again, "The setbacks, failures, and deaths of socialism are temporary phenomena, and it will be able to recover quickly. Even in case of total failure, the setbacks are temporary and could be recovered."[14] So long as the communist cause represents the laws of objective social development, ultimate victory is assured (Axiom 2). "The socialist system will eventually replace the capitalist system; this is an objective law that cannot be altered by people's wishes."[15]

Axiom 3 makes effective control of change contingent on proper causal analysis. Specifically, it should be borne in mind that internal factors are the primary cause of change (3a). In Mao's words, "dialectical materialism recognizes external causes as conditions for change and internal causes as bases for change; external causes would have effect only if they operate through internal causes."[16] This axiom underlies the Chinese tendency to explain the behavior of foreign governments primarily in terms of domestic pressures. It also implies the judgment that domestic political and social conditions, especially the political consciousness of the people, determine the success or failure of a nation's efforts to develop its capabilities. Correct political thought provides the key to manipulate material conditions; therefore, changing the political thought of people makes possible all other kinds of changes. Concomitantly, "self-reliance" becomes a hall-mark of Chinese domestic and foreign policies.

Of course, change requires a considerable period of gestation and development (3b). Successful transformation of external attributes, such as economic and technological capabilities, will lag behind successful transformation of internal attributes (e.g., political consciousness). Socio-economic changes are expected to require long, hard struggle. During this struggle visible accomplishments are incomplete and tentative (3i).

This is not to dismiss small and often latent changes over a protracted period of time as unimportant (3c). Incremental quantitative changes provide the basis for qualitative changes. As Mao explained,

> Change in all things takes two forms: the form of [apparent] opposing stagnation and the form of manifest change. . . . When things are in the first form, there is only quantitative change and no qualitative change and, therefore, they give the appearance of stagnation. When things are in the second form, the quantitative change in the first form has reached a certain high point, causing the breakup of the unified existence [of their elements] and creating qualitative change. . . .Things are constantly changing from the first form to the second form. The struggles between contradictions take place in both of these two forms, but the resolutions of contradictions are reached through the second form."[17]

This reasoning suggests that quantitative changes, which leave intact the basic power relationship between the opposing forces, are particularly fragile and reversible (3d). Qualitative breakthroughs are far more stable and ongoing because of the decisively changed distribution of power associated with them (3e, 3g, 3h).

These premises lead to the expectation of intensified conflict between actors when their capabilities undergo qualitative change (3f). The Chinese will attend closely to developments in other countries that suggest basic changes in their capabilities. They are not likely to make significant policy realignments when only quantitative changes in actor capabilities occur. They will reexamine major policies if they perceive that qualitative changes favoring them or their opponents are taking or have taken place. The Chinese will expect their opponents to launch foreign "adventures" if the qualitative change is adverse to China; they themselves will act more boldly when they perceive such a change in China's favor.

The major elements of Chinese beliefs about change identified above clarify some of the more distinctive features of recent Chinese policy that have seemed anomalous to external observers. Chinese beliefs about change, for example, provide the crucial theoretical underpinning for the well-known flexible posture that the People's Republic has adopted in recent years. While the decision logic of Chinese leaders, like that of most national elites, focuses heavily on historical precedents, their views about change facilitate adaptation to a fundamentally changing international environment. At the same time, however, Chinese beliefs about the inevitability of change, and the fragility of any particular change, operate to prevent them from changing policy stances incrementally in response to the frequent events of everyday foreign affairs. Parenthetically, it is worth commenting that both of these postures seem markedly different from those operating within the U.S. policy community, where the tendency is to focus more on the preservation of the status quo and on daily events that seem to threaten it.

Similarly, the beliefs about change identified previously also explain the actively confident long-run posture that the Chinese have displayed in recent years, despite the fact that they perceive one of the superpowers to be actively hostile to them (the USSR) and the other as a somewhat uncertain coalition partner (the U.S.). The Chinese belief that long-term development is inevitably in their favor allows them to rationalize changes opposed to their interests. The appearance of Soviet revisionism, for example, is dismissed as only a temporary adverse current in the large flow of favorable development.[18] And, as indicated in Chou En-lai's 1973 report to the Tenth Party Congress, even international chaos can be interpreted as favorable to Chinese communist interests.[19]

Most specifically, the impact of Chinese beliefs about change can be seen in their treatment of U.S.-Soviet relations. The campaign of a few years ago, to warn the world of the likelihood of world war, is obviously based on Chinese views about the increased probability of conflict in a situation that has been shifting from U.S. superiority to one of parity, or at best essential equivalence. Their increasingly activist anti-Soviet stance follows clearly from the basic principles we have summarized. First, the prospect of a qualitative change favoring the Soviet Union poses a major threat to China — a threat sufficiently severe to warrant unprecedented efforts to prevent the change. The danger is especially great when the Soviet military build-up is placed in the context of U.S. domestic disarray and the long gestation period required for plans to improve China's economic and technological capacity to bear fruit. Second, in Chinese eyes, the relative parity in capability between the United States and the Soviet Union means not only that they are more likely to contend, but also that the People's Republic can play a significant role in influencing the course of events. In a competition that threatens to change the structure of the international system in an unfavorable direction, modest Chinese capability, and those of other third parties, can affect the balance against the somewhat more powerful Soviet Union. A passive, bystander approach is unwarranted, given both the dangers of the decline in U.S. superiority and the opportunities of checking the Soviet progress toward supremacy. This combination of perceptions motivates relatively recent intense Chinese steps to build anti-Soviet coalitions in Western Europe, to buttress American leaders who favor greater military expenditures and a hard line towards the USSR, to work together with "strange bedfellows" to oppose Soviet political and military moves in Africa, to court the more independent East European nations, and to modify long-standing technology acquisition policies by exploring the purchase of off-the-shelf military hardware and weapons systems.

Lest these correspondences be interpreted as an argument that we have achieved a complete understanding of Chinese treatment of change, it should be noted that the beliefs about change that have been identified provide rather open decision guidelines for the Chinese. The Chinese can only make decisions about change if the assessments required for the application of these belief principles can be made in a timely and compelling fashion. For example, the decision to intervene in a strategic parity situation can be made only after the relative capabilities of the competing parties, as well as the nature of recently realized and approaching changes, have been assessed. Determining precisely how the Chinese make such assessments is difficult. In our own research we have attempted to determine what the Chinese expect to be "qualitative changes" through statistical analysis of their responses to different events, but without much success. Perhaps this is due to the fact that consensus among Chinese leaders about these assessments is more likely to be on a *post hoc* than an anticipatory basis. If so, assessments before the fact seem likely to be the focus of substantial policy debate within the Chinese elite. Major changes in policy are stressful for most national elites, and the Chinese are no exception. Given the especially high stakes they associate with the prospect of qualitative change, and their expectation that others do so as well, conflict over this assessment is especially likely to be severe. Undue delay in moving to block the possible "qualitative change" in favor of the Soviet Union places China in a situation of severe and possibly avoidable danger. Yet actions that strongly commit the Chinese to the side of the U.S. and other anti-Soviet parties only increases the hostile consequences the Chinese will face from Soviet power if the change has already occurred, and make it less likely that China will have the grace period needed to substantially improve her power position relative to the USSR.

Conclusion

While the illustrative analysis presented represents only a minor portion of our work on Chinese foreign policy, the results presented here are suggestive in several respects. Most importantly, the rather distinctive features of Chinese views about change suggest that analyses of the consequences of changes in the international system should incorporate some assessment of the perceptions of change by the relevant groups, since those perceptions may vary significantly across national elites. This point can be extended more generally to an argument for the importance of examining perceptions in foreign policy analysis. On the limiting side, the findings reported here are also important in suggesting that we should not expect the analysis of perceptual dimensions to yield simple, deterministic models of decision choice.

Notes

* The research reported in this article was supported by the Defense Advanced Research Projects Agency of the U.S. Department of Defense and was monitored by the Office of Naval Research under Contract N00014-75-C-0846. The views and conclusions presented are those of the authors and should not be interpreted as representing the official policies, expressed or implied, of the Defense Advanced Research Projects Agency or the U.S. Government. This article is drawn from a large report published by the Free Press of New York in mid-1979 under the title *Understanding Foreign Policy Decisions: The Chinese Case.*

1. Quoted in R. Fisher (with W. Ury), *International Mediation: A Working Guide* (New York: The International Peace Academy, 1977), p. 1.

2. See D.B. Bobrow, S. Chan, and J.A. Kringen, *Understanding Foreign Policy Decisions: The Chinese Case* (New York: The Free Press, 1979).

3. A.H. Hastorf, D.J. Schneider, and J. Polefka, *Person Perception* (Reading, Massachusetts: Addison-Wesley, 1970), pp. 61-90.

4. For example, M. Brecher, *The Foreign Policy System of Israel* (London: Oxford University Press, 1972); and N. Leites, *A Study of Bolshevism* (Glencoe, Illinois: The Free Press, 1953).

5. See J. Steinbruner, *The Cybernetic Theory of Decision* (Princeton: Princeton University Press, 1974); S.J. Thorson, "National Political Adaptation," in J.N. Rosenau, ed., *Comparing Foreign Policy: Theories, Findings, and Methods* (New York: John Wiley, 1974), pp. 71-114; F. Bailey and R.T. Holt, "Towards a Science of Complex Systems" (mimeo), Minneapolis: University of Minnesota, 1971; H.A. Simon, *The Sciences of the Artificial* (Cambridge, Massachusetts: The MIT Press, 1969); K.W. Deutsch, *The Nerves of Government: Models of Political Communication and Control* (New York: The Free Press, 1966).

6. Bobrow et al., *Understanding Foreign Policy Decisions.*

7. D.T. Campbell and D.W. Fiske, "Convergent and Discriminate Validation by the Multi-trait-multi-method Matrix," *Psychological Bulletin* 56 (1959): 81-105. The study of foreign affairs belief systems at a distance is particularly vulnerable when based heavily on public statements authorized by the regime. The major problem is that of the correspondence between the beliefs and perceptions manifest in public statements and those really internalized by the elite. We have resorted to semantic analysis using two groups of native Chinese speakers, one raised in Hong Kong and the other composed of recent Mainland refugees, to establish the extent to which persons socialized in the People's Republic seem to use cognitions different from those of a linguistically similar community. We find that these two groups differ in ways that have important implications for how they analyze political affairs, and that there is some evidence of mass internalization of the beliefs explicit in People's Republic official statements. Such evidence does not conclusively resolve the issue. It does, however, support the view that the elite takes the beliefs in question seriously and not as mere propaganda; thus it is more likely to hold them, albeit augmented with more specific views and greater information than is available to the broader Chinese population.

8. For example, A.L. George, *Propaganda Analysis* (Evanston, Row-Peterson, 1959).

9. A.L. Horelick, A.R. Johnson, and J.D. Steinbruner, *The Study of Soviet Foreign Policy: Decision-Theory-Related Approaches* (Beverly Hills: Sage, 1975).

10. D.B. Bobrow, "Chinese Communist Response to Alternative U.S. Continental Defense Postures," in idem, ed., *Weapons System Decisions: Political and Psychological Perspectives on Continental Defense* (New York: Praeger, 1969), pp. 151-213.

11. S. Chan, J.A. Kringen, and D.B. Bobrow, "Chinese Views on Crisis Diagnosis and Management: Insights from Documentary Analysis," in "Crisis Warning and Management Report " (mimeo), College Park: University of Maryland, 1976.

12. Quoted in Worker-Peasant-Soldier Team of the Central Party School for Studying Philosophy, *Thoroughly Study Marxist Theory of Knowledge* (Peking: People's Publishing House, 1971), p. 8.

13. Quoted in Tientsin Writing Group, *Talks on Dialectical Materialism* (Peking: People's Publishing House, 1975), p. 42.

14. Quoted in Worker-Peasant-Soldier Team, *Marxist Theory of Knowledge,* p. 84.

15. Quoted in Study Team, *Study to Realize "The Critique of the Gotha Programme"* (Shanghai: People's Publishing House, 1974), p. 48.

16. Quoted in Worker-Peasant-Soldier Team, *Marxist Theory of Knowledge,* p. 9.

17. Quoted in Tientsin Writing Group, *Dialectical Materialism,* pp. 87, 90.

18. C. Chang, "Imperialism is the Eve of the Social Revolution of the Proletariat," *Peking Review* 39 (September 28, 1973): 6-10.

19. Chou en-Lai, "Report to the Tenth National Congress of the Communist Party of China," *Peking Review* 35-36 (September 7, 1973): 6-10.

The Interaction of Policy and Religion:
The Vatican and the State of Israel

J.W. Schneider, s.j.

The somewhat distant relations between Israel and the Vatican are no more surprising than the feuds that exist between closely similar churches: it is precisely the differences that tend to shape the core of the relationship and to overshadow the points of convergence. It is of course true that religious motives play their role in many of the political relationships between Israel and its neighbors. But there is one point that singles out the rather unique relationship between Israel and the Vatican: both are, though each in its own way, interested in the country of Israel, and primarily so in terms of the religious nature of the titles to the country. For the one it is the promised land, a fundamental and integral part of its national identity; for the other it is the country of its founder, Joshua of Nazareth. To put it briefly, for one it is the land of the Old Testament, for the other, the land of the New Testament. Modern Israel is a product of Zionism with the political goal of providing a haven for Jews, but Zionism can scarcely be understood without reference to the Bible. The Vatican, hardly a worldly power in our days, harks back to its most essential origins by stressing its interest in the holiness of the land, though it could, like Israel, live without it, if necessary.

For both, thus, this is the Holy Land; and for both the meaning of "Holy Land" is summarized in the Holy City of Jerusalem. Though Israel was prepared to become a state without the inclusion of Jerusalem, it is hardly possible now to contemplate its parting with it, after being in possession of this city that has come to symbolize for the Jews, through the ages, the vital center and the sharpest symbol of its longing for Palestine. The Vatican is likewise interested in Jerusalem as the most essential summing up of its interest in Palestine, which for well over fifteen hundred years, has centered on Jerusalem. For Israel, Jerusalem, and particularly the old city with its temple site, has moved to the fullest extent to the center of its political interest since

1967. I think it is fair to state that the entire relationship between the two countries is primarily shaped by the conflicting perceptions of Jerusalem in the light of the changing political realities.

The interest of both parties in Jerusalem has to a large extent shaped their relationship from its inception to the present day. The more or less concrete translation of the Vatican's motives and perceptions vis-à-vis the Holy Land into a system of diplomacy can be said to have begun with the Balfour Declaration and, more particularly, its role during the peace conferences that followed World War One when its political impact had to be defined in some more precise detail.

The Interest of the Vatican

The Vatican's ultimate interest in Jerusalem is relatively easy to state: the holy places and shrines, mainly in old Jerusalem and Bethlehem, have since early times been places of intense veneration for Catholics and precious goals for pilgrimage — and not only precious among others, but by far the most outstanding. So much for the material reason. But Jerusalem, thus defined, has also become an important object of Vatican diplomacy because the access of Christians to these places has often been in jeopardy. To use a somewhat profane expression, the Vatican has always considered the holy places to be its "back-garden," a view that has by no means died out. In this connection it may be observed that the first distant journey undertaken by a pope in modern times was precisely to Jerusalem.

But this interest does not only stem from the intrinsic holiness of this place. The Vatican — or here I should say the Holy See, as the highest organ of the Catholic Church — used to consider itself the only true Church of Christ and, therefore, as a main interested party in Jerusalem in its own right. These are considerations that the Church can hardly relinquish in full, whatever political theories or religio-historical considerations may say. Or to put it differently, as a religion founded by Jesus of Nazareth, as the Church fully and necessarily believes itself to be, it cannot write off Jerusalem. One may, of course, say that the Vatican view stems from irredentist considerations and motives.

This material interest is compounded by the special concern it has for the right of the Latin element on the spot. The Vatican has been locked in occasionally bitter infighting with the Orthodox churches, who are not united with Rome, and also, though less so, with the Eastern rites, that do live in community with Rome. Vatican claims concern the property rights, in a more legal sense, to the Holy Places, the freedom of religion and religious expression for its institutions, but also the implantation and well-being of the (Latin) Christian community on the spot. Only so, the Vatican believes, can its interests in the Holy Places be safeguarded for Christians from everywhere. Protection against desecralization — not something of the past — and expropriation; room for reconstruction and scope for the activities of its institutions; the possibility of more or less neutral arbitration in cases of encroachment and "fraternal" disputes with other custodians of the holy places: they all underline the need for the protection of vested rights and they explain the concern of Vatican diplomacy for an internationally guaranteed, statutory arrangement in relation to Jerusalem.

Another point that should be mentioned is the Vatican's attitude towards the "Jewish problem." Whatever the probably deeply differing perceptions Jews have of themselves and of their relation to Palestine, the Vatican has almost rigorously adhered to its own conception of the Jewish problem. Though something will later be said about the rather radical change resulting from the Second Vatican Council, one factor remains constant: the Jewish problem is viewed from a religious angle. The paradoxical result of this approach is that the Vatican has considered Jewish relations with Palestine not as a religious problem but as a political one: the Jews cannot pretend to have title to the Holy Land, and especially Jerusalem, by laying claims to it on the force of biblical authority. The Vatican view is that its own long-standing contacts with the Holy Places and its physical presence there, notwithstanding Moslem rule, give it a better, more substantial and, above all, moral title for legitimate interest than Israel could ever raise.

This proposition was sharply set forth in 1950 in the *Osservatore Romano*. The newspaper reacted to a declaration made by the Commissioner for Palestine to the effect that the actual situation showed signs of returning to normal, and also to the declared willingness of Israel to accede to such normalization as evidenced in its proposal to internationalize the Holy Places only. The newspaper observed that Jerusalem and its environment had to be subjected, in their entirety, to an international regime, and that access to the other holy places, the historical rights of the Church and the functioning of its institutions had to be secured over the whole of Palestine. This statement was equally exasperating for Israelis and Arabs alike, but the *Osservatore Romano* countered by saying that the moral interests, precisely in Jerusalem, were such that they deserved the highest consideration from all parties.

While it is true to say, as we did, that the concern of the Holy See was mainly with the holy places, it would be wrong to belittle that interest by restricting it almost entirely to them. Vatican diplomacy, and especially so after World War One, viewed the problem in its wider setting. Given its religious concern for the city as such and the nature of that concern, the Vatican held that only within the bounds of a more or less autonomous position for Jerusalem could the Vatican's interest find the proper atmosphere in which to be preserved and to prosper, and only thus could the religious nature of the city, for all the three monotheistic religions, be maintained. The moment Jerusalem became the center of political infighting, and even war, its exalted nature would suffer irremediably. We may note in passing that this perception has probably been conditioned by the relatively stagnant character of the city and, after 1967, by the alarm caused when the Jewish annexation threatened to change the nature of Jerusalem by transforming it into a bustling but also sharply contested capital.

The Political Goals of the Vatican Diplomacy

However religious the interest of the Holy See may be, the means to secure its objectives have, of necessity, to be of a more diplomatic and therefore political nature. If there is one thing of which the Vatican diplomacy has become rather painfully aware—and not only in this instance—it is its lack of power and the inherent difficulty of translating its lofty moral aims into political pressure through appeals to conscience. Whenever the Vatican has sought to ally itself with this or that state or organization, it has all too often found that its own motives and objectives became firmly wedded to and made an ally to national interest or drowned in organizational pressures. Nevertheless, no other road remains open to the Vatican.

If the Roman objectives have been religious and straight-forward enough, if changes in those objectives have been compelled by considerations of a religious nature, the same cannot be said of the diplomatic goals by which the Vatican has tried to secure its fundamental objectives. The traditional diplomacy has been a strictly bilateral one and, in the case of Palestine, such a policy imposed itself because only the Ottoman Empire held sway over the entire territory of Palestine. However, the nationality of various institutions in Jerusalem — and the traditional pre-eminence of France as a sort of worldly custodian for religious interests of the Church — brought into play a variety of relations in which the Vatican had but little part. These various powers were anxious to protect the interests of their nationals, and it is probably the weakness of the Ottoman Empire that prevented it from vigorously objecting to the special statutes which these powers sought to secure for their national interests. To an extent, at least, the Church was the indirect beneficiary.

The end of World War One and the competing influences of France and Britain in the Middle East as the new holders of actual power opened the way to replace the existing structure, possibly on a less precarious footing, from the Vatican's point of view. The Vatican objected to the influx of Jews as a politically destabilizing factor. In the background, so one may read from the allocution of Pope Benedict XV, lingered the idea that the Jews had been justly punished with their ejection from the Holy Land in the first and second centuries, that they had forfeited any *political* right — apart from their access to their holy places, though little mention is made of this — and that the establishment of a Jewish national home might give rise to efforts to repay in kind the not always charitable Christian attitude. The Vatican was certainly moved by the pogroms in Eastern Europe, which also struck at Christians, but it was not prepared to see a solution in massive immigration. Proposals were even made to bring Christians from Malta to forestall and counter any increased Jewish presence in the Holy Land.

The Vatican's traditional adherence to bilateral diplomacy and the suspicion with which it viewed the League of Nations did not predispose the Vatican towards that organization. Yet little choice remained once the subject had become a major preoccupation of the League. The League remained the only way to forestall English efforts to install a commission for Jerusalem that might possibly be presided over by an agnostic, and the Vatican fought a long and tenacious battle for which the League gave it the opening. Once the subject faded from the agenda of the League and the proposed commission did not get off the ground, the Vatican also settled for a more quiet diplomacy. The British success in creating a quiet atmosphere in the area was helpful.

The sequels of World War Two brought another dimension sharply into focus: the political antagonism of the feuding factions. The respective religious elements in Jerusalem began harking back to their respective religious-political powers and that, of course, left the Vatican, a non-political power, out of consideration. A second feature also sprang into often stark prominence: the Vatican had to take into account the various Christian communities in the area which could be held hostage to pressure the Vatican. The Church should, of course, exist in the first place for its own faithful; but the interests of the

Church at large and its concern for particular groups of believers may be at variance.

These difficulties have changed the attitude of the Vatican and go far to explain its diplomacy after the last world war. The prominence of humanitarian motives, both the massacre of Jews and the displacement of Palestinians — a good many of them Christians — the danger of theocratic structures, the withdrawal from Palestine of what traditionally were considered more or less Christian nations, and the dumping of the Palestine problem in the lap of the U.N. brought the Vatican to concentrate on the religious nature of its interests and to prefer the more all-round approach of the U.N. over the uncertain results of fighting. The religious interest found its expression in the prominence now given to Jerusalem as a center of veneration to the three monotheistic religions, and became most prominent through the long efforts taken to draw up a declaration on the Jews. This latter episode particularly has drawn sharp criticism both from Jews and Arabs, and heavy pressure was brought to bear on the Vatican to desist from its efforts at the Second Vatican Council. Everyone suddenly knew where the proper and most religious concerns of the Church should lay and how they had to be expressed.

The U.N. has been, in its first series of efforts, the best hope for the Church. To a certain extent, this hope was realized by the propositions about the internationalization of Jerusalem, which the Vatican, though it did not entirely approve of them, viewed not as a makeshift proposal but as the considered consensus of the international community. This view may explain why the Vatican has so often afterwards referred to the idea of the internationalization of Jerusalem. The solution of a *corpus separatum* has been the explicit yardstick used by the Vatican to measure its judgment on the political changes that have taken place.

The Counter-perceptions

Notwithstanding its claim to superior interests, the Vatican is not the only party to the problem. While we have dwelled long enough on the religious concern of the Vatican, one should also pay attention to the motives of the other parties. Jerusalem has become something of a Berlin. Its symbolic character made it one of the most prized objectives to be secured by political sovereignty. Arab reactions against the internationalization of Jerusalem even included the suspicion that behind the Vatican's approval lay the distant goal of resurrecting the times of the crusades. The mirror image of these strivings towards sovereignty was the Vatican's fear that the emergence of *any* national sovereign would imply grave dangers for minorities and, by implication, for Catholics. It is tragic to state that developments have largely confirmed these fears.

One may also ask why the Christian minority in the Holy Land was at the receiving end of subtle — or gross — discrimination. How is it that the Vatican, whose political motives can hardly be suspected and whose political clout is so regrettably poor in its own eyes, has made so little headway with its endeavors? This question is all the more intriguing because, ever since 1948, the previous system of foreign powers protecting their nationals and their institutions has lapsed. No longer did protecting powers stand behind the Church. The answer most probably is that the interested countries today are, without exception, theocratic to a greater or lesser degree. Theocratic regimes, of whatever shade, by definition *always* have to profess that theirs is the best or only religion; the rest are there only on sufferance. But theocratic regimes remain irremediably underdeveloped in terms of their thinking on sovereignty. Security arguments may be bandied about, Trojan horses may be seen in the smallest exceptions, third powers may be deemed to shuffle their pawns: the truth is that theocratic regimes tend to be monolithic. Everything else is a *corpus alienum,* a body of unbelievers and, finally, infidels.

It is important to note that both Jordan and Israel have shown behavior that should allay the Vatican's fears, as they have freely permitted religious performances and pilgrimages and have taken ample measures to allow unhampered access to the holy sites. To my knowledge, there are no telling examples of Vatican complaints on this score. But, in a way, this argument against further Vatican insistence is beside the point. Of course the Church is interested in open and unhampered access and all the measures that allow things to proceed peacefully; it is the very core of Christian interest. The goal of Vatican diplomacy, however, is to secure a firm and unalterable basis for this religious generosity. The Vatican does not object to the goodwill shown, but it prefers to have something better than unilateral goodwill, which may change for reasons entirely unconnected with the religious concerns of the Church. As an international and independent personality, the Vatican seeks what every state seeks: to shore up goodwill by agreement, an agreement that binds a party not to change its behavior for purely national reasons. On this point, as already indicated, the Vatican sorely notes the absence of an internationally safeguarded regime. Indeed, the Vatican is interested in a living

Jerusalem, also from a Christian point of view, that is, it wishes the Holy
Places to function in a living Christian environment. And that Christian population is shrinking. Jerusalem has been the cradle of the Church and the
Vatican Council has again picked up the New-Testamentary veneration for
this mother community. There is sufficient continuity to link up with that
primitive church. Both from the point of view of historical presence, and hence
political title, and from a moral — theological, perhaps — point of view the
Vatican is deeply interested in the continuity of this community. A series of
Holy Places functioning, or rather not functioning, like museums is the ultimate
specter dreaded by the Vatican. A nationalistic, and certainly a theocratic,
state need not lead to such a situation; but it usually will. One need but recall
that only a few years ago in Israel a statute was passed forbidding the making
of conversions for money. All talk of flexible interpretation has the beauty and
sincerity of powerless goodwill, because no theocratic state, even of a more
"secular" complexion, is fully able to satisfy its rigid orthodox elements
through liberalization. The history of the inquisition remains, I am afraid, a
most modern reminder of this observation.

A Collision Course?

It is easy to indicate the long-standing trends and perceptions that underlie
Vatican diplomacy towards Israel. Some of these are inherent in Vatican
diplomacy as such, others stem from the fact that, in this case, the matter in
hand concerns a Palestinian state and the Holy Land, and finally, some elements have to do with the fact that Israel is a Jewish state. While most of
Vatican policy, as far as imposed by the two first strands of motives, would
have remained basically the same regardless of the sort of state existing in
Palestine, on the third point the thinking in the Church has evolved considerably. Both the horrors inflicted upon the Jews during the Holocaust and
World War Two and the changes that have resulted from the Second Vatican
Council have transformed the Church's attitude towards the Jews. Much of
the old antagonism is gone and a far more positive appreciation of Jewish
religion has replaced it. But something similar can be said of the Church's attitude towards other religions, including Islam. The new trend finds its expression in the designation of the three religions most interested in Jerusalem as the
"three great monotheistic faiths" — a description far more positive than the
previous curt dismissal of Jews and Moslems as "infidels."

This change in Church thinking has had its impact on Vatican diplomacy. Jerusalem has become the symbol of a city that should provide the living encounter and fertile soil for the meeting of these three religions. The Vatican has not fully dropped its claims and wishes for its own property rights and the statutory basis underlying them. But the less exclusive attitude held by the Vatican is no longer so rigidly insistent on sharply divisive rights. One would thus have expected the Vatican to find an additional argument for a continuing, and perhaps even increased, insistence on internationalization and the establishment of a *corpus separatum,* be it more territorial or more functional. Surprisingly enough, however, the Vatican has, if anything, muted its insistence on this point.

One can surmise the reasons. One is purely political: the Vatican does not want to add at this time to the formidable obstacle that East Jerusalem already constitutes in peace talks and thus possibly threaten future developments. A second reason may very well be that the change in Vatican thinking makes the insistence, at this juncture, less opportune. If this is the case, the Vatican may be paying the price, as it were, for its increased religious approach to the entire problem. By showing its more ecumenical approach, the Vatican intends to defuse at least part of the problem. A further reason is that the present Vatican reticence is a necessary precaution so as not to damage a slow evolutionary process; the Vatican is keeping a "low profile." Moreover, the Vatican's attitude towards Jerusalem has been, and remains, attentive to the interests of the Arab Islamic countries, both for the sake of the dialogue with Islam and for the sake of the Christian communities living in Arab countries. This applies also to Israel: since 1967 Israel has gained authority over even more Arab Christians. And the solution to the problem of the Palestinians, among whom there are quite a few Christians, forces the Vatican not to remain too predominantly concerned with Jerusalem only.

If these reasons are more or less correct, I presume that the Vatican intends to create a more propitious atmosphere that would allow full normalization of its relations with Israel and thus would permit it to continue to secure the objectives it views as legitimate and profitable for the other interested parties as well.

Why, then, hasn't the Vatican recognized Israel? In a way, the Vatican considers that it has already made a major move by recognizing the Jews for what they are — a Jewish people — and by undertaking a dialogue with them on an equal basis. The political difficulty is compounded by the dual role the Jews play: a religious entity *and* the holders of sovereignty in the Holy Land.

The development of further relations depends on the course along which Israeli positions will develop. If, once its most basic and pressing security problems are solved, Israel became, religiously speaking, a more liberal state, the opportunities for all the faithful would probably improve. If Israel is not able to make up its mind about its theocratic nature, I am afraid that the religious minorities might pay the price the Vatican seems to dread.

East-West Détente: Perceptions and Policies*

Frans A.M. Alting von Geusau

East-West détente in Europe has been with us now for almost twenty years. During this period "détente" has unquestionably been the single most widely used term for characterizing the present stage of development in East-West relations. Of French origin, it defies proper translation into Russian, Polish, Dutch or German; it cannot be translated at all into English, today's first diplomatic language. Its proper meaning has never been adequately defined. The policies it is said to identify continue to diverge widely, yet the profound changes that have taken place in East-West relations have hardly tarnished its power. While the chances for further progress toward East-West cooperation are now in serious doubt, it has even been suggested that the term détente be employed in other areas, including relations between Egypt and Israel.

Détente, as these opening remarks suggest, thus combines the features of an image in international politics: it speaks to the imaginations of political actors and the public, it is ill-defined, it serves to justify a variety of one side's policies while condemning the policies of adversaries, it disguises realities one prefers not to talk about too openly or directly. It evokes feelings of holy indignation whenever the other side fails to prostrate itself in veneration to the image made in the absence of a common purpose.

It should be noted here that images, whenever they emerge, reflect both policy aims and perceived reality. It therefore appears useful to deal first with the history of détente.

History of the Détente Image

Authorship of the triad: *détente-entente-coopération* is generally ascribed to President Charles de Gaulle of France in the early sixties. Although the reality of East-West relations permits us to deal only with détente, the triad must be mentioned for one specific reason: détente in that connection was presented as the first stage in a process of gradually improving East-West relations. Détente thus not only envisaged a state of mind or climate different from that prevailing in the era of the cold war, it also promised progress toward more cordial relations (*entente cordiale*) and toward overcoming East-West divisions through cooperation. Thus from its inception détente evoked associations of moving forward. Even if the direction of the movement is unclear, one cannot in this century afford to be against progress.

De Gaulle's triad succinctly reflected an effort to promote a specific, short-term gaullist desire and a general, long-term gaullist dream: the restoration of French autonomy — at that time autonomy *from* the United States — and of French world influence in international politics, and the creation of a Europe of states from the Atlantic to the Urals in which France could play the role of holder of the balance between the two superpowers. In that dream — still dreamed today by Giscard d'Estaing — France (Europe) would shift its favors from one to the other of the two superpowers, depending on the balance of power existing between them.

Détente also reflected the way in which de Gaulle perceived reality: a world unduly dominated by two superpowers that were in conflict and unable to manage their relationships in the direction of accommodation (a reality perhaps epitomized by the abortive 1960 summit). That world also failed to recognize that France, and perhaps Europe, had recovered enough strength to be accepted as a force in its own right.

The handling of the Cuban missile crisis in October 1962 significantly changed the reality as perceived by de Gaulle. It inaugurated an era of Soviet-American negotiations and arms-control efforts. In the West, this new era was quickly labeled détente, and was presented as a climate favoring Soviet-American negotiations on arms control and limited cooperation — almost the direct opposite of the initial gaullist image. France, of course, continued to pursue its own goals: a special relationship with the Soviet Union, a special adversary relationship with the U.S., autonomy in defense and withdrawal from the military organization of NATO, non-participation in arms-control negotiations, expansion of cultural relations with the East. The other Western countries viewed détente as a climate in which economic and cultural relations with the East could be prudently improved in the wake of Soviet-American negotiations. For the East European states, détente thus offered a restoration of contacts with the West.

The Soviet leadership at the time studiously avoided using the term détente. For the Soviets, a "relaxation of tensions" afforded an opportunity while simultaneously posing a danger: the opportunity to embark upon a long-term program of improving and expanding their military capability, and the danger of possibly seeing their control over Eastern Europe eroding through improved East-West contacts. The spring of 1968 in Prague illustrated the extent of that danger, and the Soviet-led invasion of Czechoslovakia underscored the narrow limits of détente as perceived by the West Europeans. At the same time, American and Western reactions to the invasion proved to the Soviets that they could have their cake and eat it too: the restoration, maintenance and strengthening of Soviet control over Eastern Europe had hardly been challenged and might even be recognized by the West; relations beneficial to Soviet economy and technology were unlikely to be hampered by the invasion.

As of 1969, multilateral talks with the aim of culminating in a conference on security and cooperation in Europe (CSCE) could begin. The French goals remained what they had been. The American administration showed little interest in CSCE. The concept of détente according to Kissinger was designed to prevent competition from sliding into military hostilities and to create conditions for the relationship to be gradually and prudently improved. Kissinger referred primarily to the bilateral Soviet-American relationship, which should be marked by mutual restraint in foreign policies through the medium of SALT and other arms-control agreements.

The government of the German Federal Republic viewed détente primarily as a climate in which relations with its Eastern neighbors — including the German Democratic Republic — might be gradually normalized. West Germany approached the multilateral CSCE negotiations as the follow-up to the bilateral treaties already reached with Moscow, Warsaw and Pankow and the new four-power agreement on the status of Berlin. The other Western governments hoped that CSCE would promote progress toward arms control and troop reductions in Europe. They also emphasized the need for agreement on less restricted human and humanitarian contacts across the East-West divide. The non-aligned and neutral European countries perceived détente as one step in an ongoing process eventually moving beyond détente itself, i.e., in the direction of a situation in which the European scene would no longer be dominated by the adversary relationship between two opposing systems or military alliances. To them CSCE meant definite progress in several respects. It multilateralized the process of détente, thus moving it from a bloc-to-bloc process to a broader international level. It contributed to what their representatives termed a "democratization" of European relations, enhancing the influence of the smaller participating states, and holding out the promise of improved security and strengthened independence, especially their own. During the talks they especially advocated the need to develop better relations among all states, irrespective of differences in their economic, political and social systems. They also tried to use the CSCE platform for discussing the military aspects of détente, the so-called confidence-building measures in particular.

In 1973, the Soviet Union adopted the term détente into its official ideological jargon. Henceforth, we are told, détente would indicate a new stage in relations between the two camps in which the changes in the "correlations of forces" have compelled the "capitalist" states to give wider recognition to the principle of peaceful coexistence. Détente would consequently be used to mark the era in which power relations shift in favor of the Soviet Union as a result of the crisis of the capitalist system (the oil crisis), the increasingly anti-Western attitudes of many developing countries, and the continued strengthening of Soviet and Warsaw Pact military forces.

The Final Act adopted at the conclusion of the CSCE in 1975 in Helsinki can therefore be little more than an uneasy verbal compromise between widely divergent views on détente. It did not constitute a new charter for European cooperation, nor did it make any meaningful contribution to overcoming the political and ideological divisions in Europe. It did not lessen the military confrontation or influence the course of parallel negotiations on force reductions. It provided the Soviet Union with an argument to fasten its grip on Eastern Europe and to step up its subversive activities in Western Europe. In the West, it was hoped that human contacts would be facilitated and mutual political restraint exercised. The non-aligned and neutral European countries looked forward to progress in the field of arms control, troop reductions and continuing multilateral negotiations.

The Process of Détente: Images and Issues

Until 1975, détente stood for the political climate in which CSCE could be held. The Final Act was proclaimed to be the foundation for a new era to be marked by further changes and progress in mutual relations. But the fundamentally divergent policy aims pursued by East and West were re-emphasized almost from the day the leaders signed the document. The outcome of the Belgrade "follow-up" conference in 1977-78 made it clear that the participating states were unable to agree on anything but the dates of following meetings. Hence exacerbated discussions were referred to as the "thorough exchange of views," and the lack of any meaningful progress toward agreement as "the process of détente." The image evoked by the notion of détente came to bear less and less relation to the reality of deteriorating relations, except on the Soviet side, where the image has simply been incorporated into the lexicon of ideological fantasy.

At the same time, three issues emerged as paramount sources of conflict in the "process of détente": (a) Soviet policy outside Europe, and especially in Africa; (b) the arms race and disarmament talks; (c) human rights.

The Soviet-Cuban intervention in the Angolan civil war in the wake of the Portuguese withdrawal there inaugurated a new stage of active Soviet-sponsored military support for certain political movements in Africa. For the American administration, military involvement of this nature in African affairs was incompatible with Soviet-American détente.

The continuing and massive build-up of Soviet and Warsaw Pact military forces — more clearly discernible since 1975 — increasingly destabilizes the overall strategic balance upon which NATO had sought to develop its policy of arms control and troop reductions. As a consequence, the arms race has tended to accelerate and arms-control talks — SALT and MBFR — have made little or no progress. During the Belgrade conference, the Soviet Union resisted any attempt to improve or expand the agreement on confidence-building measures reached at CSCE.

More important still is the issue of human rights as a new source of conflict. The Final Act clearly made the protection of human rights and the improvement of cooperation in the humanitarian field a problem of mutual concern. The issue became crucial *not* because of the new emphasis given to it by the Carter administration, but because citizens of the Soviet Union and Eastern Europe asked their governments to apply at home what they had accepted internationally; it was not the West that tried to promote its image of human rights in the East. The crucial problem was that citizens of Eastern Europe demanded respect for fundamental human rights, in response to which their own regimes offered repression, vilification, harassment, imprisonment and condemnation. Détente has thus been undermined not by American concern, but by such flagrant Soviet violations as manifested in the trials of Yuri Orlov and Anatoly Shcharansky.

Since the Second World War, the issue of human rights can no longer be approached as an "internal" matter. In and of themselves, massive violations of human rights by totalitarian regimes are a threat to security and détente in Europe. A regime that deals with its own citizens as does the Soviet regime, which claims hegemony over other European countries and which professes the goal of extending its system of government over the world, cannot be considered a reliable partner for peace, reconciliation and détente.

Détente: Lessons and Illusions

As noted earlier, détente evokes associations of moving forward. The Belgrade review conference, even in the absence of any substantial agreement, concluded with the announcement that a thorough exchange had taken place on the deepening of mutual relations, the improvement of security, and the development of the process of détente in the future. All that had actually been agreed upon was to hold other such meetings. To put it differently, Belgrade in fact reduced détente from the concept of a climate in which to *make* progress to one in which multilateral exchanges of view continue *despite* the lack of progress. The process itself — CSCE, MBFR, SALT, etc. — has replaced progress.

Even in its reduced meaning, the concept risks becoming merely the reflection of an illusion, namely, nations that negotiate do not necessarily experience a deterioration in their mutual relations. East-West relations have deteriorated markedly over the last few years. The Soviet-American negotiating relationship has so deteriorated that the SALT talks are in a deadlock, and mutual hostility again predominates. Africa has become an object of East-West confrontation. The ideological lines of division are deepening, while Soviet subversion in Europe has increased markedly.

Comparing the image of détente with the reality of East-West relations, we must thus conclude that most of the objectives that should have been pursued under détente have now been given up: overcoming division, improving security, arms control, trust, and cooperation. We are left with a question: can continuous multilateral discussion prevent the persistent adversary relationship from sliding into military hostilities or a further shift in the balance of power in favor of the Soviet Union?

The outlook in my opinion is uncertain at best. At its present stage of development, the Soviet regime appears to be driven more by an arrogance of power and a desire to expand its influence than by a willingness to accommodate and cooperate, more geared towards exploiting Western weakness than accepting a world of diversity.

A relationship of détente with such a regime confronts democratic governments in the West with the perennial difficulty of maintaining adequate military strength, while concomitantly seeking agreements on easing tension. It confronts them with the necessity of supporting human rights while at the same time controlling crises that are bound to erupt as a result of the repression of human rights. It demands that they explain at home that every effort should be made to avoid war, although democratic and totalitarian regimes are unlikely partners for peace.

The internal, moral and political strength required for such a policy is more than most NATO members at present can muster.

Notes

* The text of this essay is based largely on material previously published by the author. See in particular: "Détente after Helsinki," in *The Yearbook of World Affairs*, 1978, Vol. 32; "From Yalta to Helsinki: Developments in International Law," in *The Netherlands Yearbook of International Law*, 1977, Vol. 8; "Security in the Seventies: Changes, Issues and Policies," in Czempiel and Rustow, eds., *The Euro-American System* (Frankfurt am Main: Campus Verlag, 1976); and *Uncertain Détente* (edited collection) (Alphen aan den Rijn: Sijthoff & Noordhoff, 1979).

Image and Reality in International Relations:
The Case of Eastern Europe

Andrzej Korbonski

The purpose of this essay is to make some random comments with regard to the problem of image and reality as it has affected international politics in Eastern Europe since the communist seizure of power in the region at the end of World War Two. "Image" in this context will be defined as a "popular conception" of a country or process as projected through various channels, while "reality" will be viewed as the actual state of affairs existing in the country or the area at a given point in time.

No attempt will be made here to delve more deeply into the meaning and theoretical implications of the concepts of image and image formation, perception and misperception, deception, rationality and irrationality; the pioneering research in this field has been done by Robert Jervis, and I have benefited greatly from it. Instead, I propose simply to concentrate on three components of international politics in Eastern Europe in order to determine the extent to which each of them has been influenced by the presence of images. The three components are:

1. The relations between Eastern Europe and the Soviet Union;
2. The relations among individual East European countries, excluding the USSR;
3. The relations between Eastern Europe and the West.

The above division suggests that the emphasis will be on foreign rather than domestic policy in the region and in some of the individual countries. It also means that the focus will be on policy-makers rather than on the populations at large. It follows that rather than dealing with national attitudes and perceptions, I shall limit the discussion to the views and judgments of the ruling elites, which may or may not differ from those held by the respective populations.

Relations Between Eastern Europe and the Soviet Union

It may be said that the communist takeover of Eastern Europe in the aftermath of World War Two, aided and abetted by the Soviet Union, was a historical accident not anticipated by many of the actors until the very onset of the actual seizure of power. In general, the overwhelming majority of the population throughout Eastern Europe, while welcoming the incoming Red Army as liberators from German occupation, did not expect it to stay (in some cases indefinitely) and did expect the return of the region to the *status quo ante bellum*. To be sure, a tiny minority, mostly communist party members in the various countries, might have hoped for the eventual incorporation of their respective countries into the USSR as Soviet republics; but most of the people — elites and masses alike — anticipated the return, with Western aid, of the old, established political, economic and social order.

That the reality proved to be quite different from the image was the outcome of several factors, lack of information undoubtedly being one. During the war, most of the countries — particularly those occupied by Germany, such as Czechoslovakia, Poland and, to some extent, Yugoslavia — were by and large deprived of news on the developments (especially on the military and diplomatic scene) that ultimately decided their future. While their respective governments-in-exile either knew or suspected that the postwar fate of their countries would be largely determined by Moscow, they were reluctant to impart their suspicions to their representatives at home for fear both of reducing local anti-German resistance and weakening their own political positions. After all, they expected or hoped to return home after the war to reassume power.

The countries that fought on the side of Germany — Bulgaria, Hungary and Romania — although probably better informed than their neighbors to the north and the west, were also reluctant to accept the reality of becoming a part of the Soviet sphere of influence. Almost to the end, they hoped for a miracle in the form of an Anglo-American military intervention and occupation that would eventually lead to the reimposition of the status quo.

In sum, because of the lack of information concerning the postwar plans of the "Big Three," the various East European countries had little choice but to engage in wishful thinking and false image formation, especially with regard to the West but also with respect to the Soviet Union.

In contrast to an almost uniform and usually highly favorable image of the West, the East Europeans' perceptions of the USSR varied sharply from country to country. Historical circumstances accounted for most of the variations, although some images were conditioned by geography and such factors as ideology and religion.

Thus Poland was clearly most hostile to the USSR, which projected a highly negative image to all strata of Polish society. Throughout history, but especially since the beginning of the seventeenth century, Tsarist Russia had been one of Poland's fiercest enemies and had made the largest gains from the country's numerous partitions. The uprisings of the nineteenth century, the Bolshevik revolution, and the Soviet-Polish war of 1919-20 only succeeded in strengthening that feeling of enmity; and the Ribbentrop-Molotov treaty of August 1939, which gave the signal for the Soviet "stab-in-the-back" attack on Poland some three weeks later, further blackened the Soviet image. The mass deportations of Polish citizens into the USSR and, last but not least, the revelation of the Katyn murders of Polish officers utterly condemned Russia for Poland.

While the above image was most likely shared by all social classes, there were additional factors that shaped the anti-Soviet attitudes of particular segments and groups in Poland. The peasants, who still accounted for about two-thirds of the Polish population on the eve of the takeover, had little or no use for Russia and communism, which more than anything represented forces opposed to the Catholic Church and the private ownership of land. The upper and middle strata of Polish society disliked communism for the same reasons, to which was added a strong dose of anti-Russian nationalistic feeling.

Hungary's similar attitude towards the Soviet Union reflected the fact that the two countries were very much alike in many respects. Moreover, Russia's leadership in partitioning Poland at the end of the eighteenth century was matched by its suppression of the Hungarian Revolution of 1848-49, and the Polish-Soviet war of 1919-20 followed by only a few months Bela Kun's abortive Hungarian Soviet Republic.

The third strongly anti-Russian and anti-Soviet country in the region was Romania, whose long-standing territorial conflicts with the Soviet Union (e.g., over Bessarabia) were influential in its decision to join Nazi Germany in attacking the USSR in June 1941.

For these three countries, the image projected by the Soviet Union was one of an aggressive and imperialistic power bent upon establishing its hegemony over all of Eastern Europe, if not beyond. This was a rather traditional image which, at least initially, was not substantially affected by the fact that post-1917 Russia was ruled not by a Tsarist but by a communist regime. For a brief period during World War Two this traditional image might have acquired a more favorable cast in light of the heroic Soviet resistance against the Germans; but once the tide had turned and the Red Army began to advance westwards, the old image again came to the fore, and with greater power.

The perception of the Soviet Union held by the other East European countries — Bulgaria, Czechoslovakia, and Yugoslavia — was quite different. Although none of these countries favored communism, they all maintained traditionally warm feelings towards Russia. It was, after all, Russia that had liberated Bulgaria from the Turkish yoke in the late 1870s and that soon thereafter raised the banner of Panslavism, proclaiming itself protector of all Slavs, and particularly the Balkan Slavs — the Serbs, the Macedonians, and the Bulgarians as well as the Czechs and the Slovaks. The historic links were in some cases further strengthened by the existence of close linguistic and religious ties with Russia.

Thus, on the eve of the communist takeover of Eastern Europe, it seemed clear that the fact that the seizure of power was led by the Soviet Union would elicit varying reactions in different countries, depending largely on their images and perceptions of Russia. By and large the assumption was borne out; the takeovers in Bulgaria and Czechoslovakia were easier than those in Hungary, Poland and Romania, the Yugoslav case being *sui generis*. In other words, the fact that communism was imposed from the East rather than from the West made considerable difference insofar as its acceptance in Eastern Europe was concerned: had it come from France or the United States rather than from Russia, it would have been much more palatable to the East Europeans. The stigma of the Soviet label clearly influenced the receptivity of the various countries to the system about to be imposed upon the region. Turning to the Soviet perception of Eastern Europe at the time of the takeover, it may be argued that it too was not uniform, in many instances the ultimate image of each country in the region being influenced by a mix of Marxism-Leninism and past history. Thus on the one hand, the Soviet Union saw itself not only as the liberator of the region, hence fully entitled to expect gratitude and reap material rewards, but also as a revolutionary power about to initiate a radical political and socio-economic transformation of the area. On the other hand, Moscow also seemed to view many of the countries in terms of traditional factors, implicitly or explicitly showing its greater affinity for Bulgaria, Czechoslovakia and Yugoslavia over Poland or Romania.

The seizure of power and the subsequent imposition of the Stalinist model did not essentially change the existing reciprocal national images and stereotypes, except of course for Yugoslavia and the Soviet Union, whose images of each other were not quite the same after June 1948. The Soviet-Yugoslav rift was actually an interesting case of misperception on both sides: Stalin believed that Yugoslavia would not resist and would eventually collapse and surrender to Soviet demands; and for several years after the break Tito was still firmly convinced that it was all a misunderstanding that would soon be cleared up, Yugoslavia once again being welcomed to the camp.

Stalin's death and the gradual dismantling of the Moscow-led monolith resulted in internal relaxation throughout the bloc. This, in turn, had considerable impact on the East Europeans' perception of ensuing changes, especially those affecting the relations between the center and the periphery. The key element in this matrix was, of course, the changes that came about in the Soviet Union's domestic and foreign policies. On the domestic scene, the arrest and execution of Beria and his accomplices, followed by the subsequent downgrading of the role and importance of the secret police, did not go unnoticed in Eastern Europe. Neither did the increasing calls for the return to the "Leninist norms" and the principle of collective leadership. These and other changes came to a head at the Twentieth Congress of the Communist Party of the Soviet Union.

In the international arena the changes were, if anything, even more dramatic. Malenkov's "New Course" and Khrushchev's "Peaceful Coexistence" came together at the summer 1955 summit meeting at Geneva. Shortly before that, Khrushchev's humiliating pilgrimage to Belgrade largely defused the Soviet-Yugoslav conflict, and his proclamation at the Twentieth CPSU Congress to the effect that the war between the two ideological camps was no longer inevitable, had major repercussions on Eastern Europe's attitude towards both the Soviet Union and the West.

As has been suggested by Brzezinski, perhaps the most telling aspect of the break-up of the communist monolith was the emergence of striking differences in the interpretation of, and reaction to, the above changes on the part of individual East European countries. Thus Hungary between 1953 and 1955 went through a series of major political and economic reforms that eventually paved the way for the revolt of 1956. The East Berlin riots of June 1953 can also be traced to the succession struggle in Moscow. On the other hand, some countries apparently formed a different image of what had been happening in the Kremlin and proceeded very cautiously with the dismantling of the Stalinist edifice, even after the Twentieth Congress, which in a sense put the official imprimatur on their plans.

The individual countries' reactions to the congress and to Khrushchev's secret speech form perhaps the most interesting example of the varying images and perceptions held by the different countries and their leadership. The history of the events need not be repeated here; suffice it to say that the individual countries interpreted both de-stalinization and the return to the doctrine of "many roads to socialism" differently. The ultimate outcome of those differing perceptions was the continued fragmentation of East European communism: Albania clashed sharply with Moscow and eventually left the camp; Hungary and Poland, respectively, went through a bloody and a bloodless revolution; and the other countries remained essentially unchanged. Albania's rulers apparently perceived both the Moscow-Belgrade reconciliation and de-stalinization as major threats to their survival and decided to seek Peking's protection. With regard to Hungary and Poland, it might be assumed that both of them viewed the officially sanctioned reintroduction of the doctrine of "many roads to socialism" as a granting of authority to conduct some far-reaching political reforms without having to secure Moscow's permission in advance. The remaining East European countries viewed and interpreted the changes in Moscow as having little or no relevance for their own situation.

One might speculate briefly about the other — i.e., the Soviet — side in the perceptual equation. It soon became obvious that in delivering his secret speech Khrushchev was guilty of a serious misperception of the deep crisis that some key countries in the region had undergone. Although the Soviet leader gave his blessing to de-stalinization and the doctrine of "many roads," he obviously assumed that the Kremlin's lead would be as closely followed as before. The events in Hungary and Poland in 1956, as well as the reactions of China and Albania to de-stalinization, thus took him by great surprise.

Since then, with one significant exception, the relations between the Soviet Union and Eastern Europe in the past fifteen years have tended to be less volatile and more stable. The one exception, of course, was the 1968 crisis in Czechoslovakia.

I am prepared to argue that the events of the "Prague Spring" and the Soviet intervention in August 1968 were a perfect example of false images, misperceptions and wrong inferences drawn by all sides to the dispute. A good case can be made that the Soviet leaders were largely misled about the changes in Czechoslovakia, which they perceived as threats to the survival of the communist system in that country. At least two of the leaders of neighboring states, East Germany and Poland, formed an exaggerated image of the Czechoslovak liberalization process spilling over into their own countries. And finally, the leaders of the Czechoslovak communist party, and especially Alexander Dubcek, badly misjudged Soviet attitudes and behavior and were therefore totally unprepared for the intervention. The great majority of the Czechoslovak people, as suggested earlier, have traditionally held warm feelings towards Russia and were also taken aback by the Soviet action. As a result of the invasion, the Czechoslovak attitude has changed dramatically and the popular friendship has turned to hostility.

The decade following the Prague Spring was mainly characterized by considerable stability, especially when contrasted with the preceding twenty years. It may be speculated that the actors on the scene, the Soviet Union and its junior East European allies, having learnt lessons and drawn inferences from the past, have been engaged in an attempt to reach some mutually satisfactory *modus vivendi*. The issue of perceiving each other's objectives and attitudes thus became crucial.

Insofar as Eastern Europe as a whole was concerned, the key problem was to determine the threshold of autonomy vis-à-vis the USSR — no mean feat when the Soviet Union is both player and umpire in a game whose rules are constantly changing and fuzzy, if they exist at all. It was up to the leaders of the individual countries to estimate the margin of freedom at their disposal to conduct foreign and/or domestic policy that might depart to a greater or lesser degree from the norm specified by the Kremlin. There were some striking differences in this respect among the various countries, once again testifying to the continuing disparities within the communist camp.

Hungary appeared to be the most emancipated member of the Warsaw Pact. Leaving aside the different systemic variables peculiar to the country itself, one might assume that the Hungarian leaders — for whatever reason — were more adept or skillful than their neighbors in correctly estimating the margin of Moscow's tolerance for different types of policies: Hungary's image of Soviet intentions and attitudes corresponded relatively closely to reality.

Poland, the number-two member of the Warsaw alliance, has had a mixed record in estimating or forecasting Soviet reactions to innovative foreign and domestic policies. During the fourteen years of Gomulka's rule (1956-70), the country was fairly successful in maintaining a modicum of autonomy in both the foreign and the domestic spheres. The so-called Rapacki Plan for a nuclear-free zone in Central Europe and the Bonn-Warsaw Treaty of December 1970 could serve as examples of the former, while the maintenance of the private sector in agriculture could illustrate the latter. For various reasons, the Gierek regime that replaced Gomulka's at the end of 1970 was more reluctant to test the ceiling. It may therefore be argued that the current Polish government could afford to liberalize its policies further without antagonizing Moscow. Romania, which in the mid-1960s appeared quite successful in challenging Soviet hegemony, was able to do so because it correctly assessed the Soviet reluctance to move against it in the face of the Sino-Soviet conflict and the progressing fragmentation of the international communist camp. It was only after the intervention in Czechoslovakia that Ceausescu appeared to assume a lower profile, although even today Romania behaves differently from most of the other East European countries. Here again, Romania's image as essentially Stalinist on the domestic front makes it easier for Moscow to tolerate its maverick behavior on the international scene. In contrast, Czechoslovakia's Stalinist domestic policy is not offset by a semi-autonomous foreign policy.

What has been the Soviet perception of Eastern Europe in the late 1970s? It would appear that over the years Moscow has learnt some lessons from the events of the 1950s and 1960s, and that at some point it began to see itself more as the leader of a conventional politico-military-economic alliance than as the *vozhd* of an ideological camp engaged in a sharp doctrinal struggle with the capitalist world. This new self-image meant that the Kremlin realized that the leadership of an alliance carried with it an obligation to provide aid and support for its members rather than the right to exploit them. Hence the Soviet willingness to supply the Warsaw Pact nations with oil at prices below those charged by OPEC, and to ship grain to Eastern Europe even when a poor Soviet harvest made such shipments highly burdensome.

To put it somewhat differently, it may be said that in the past few years the Soviet Union has become much better informed about the situation in the individual East European countries and, as a result, its perception of the various changes and processes in the region has acquired greater depth and sophistication. For example, Moscow has been aware for some time of the potential linkage between economic well-being and the system's legitimacy, and has provided economic aid to regimes unable to cope with economic diffficulties, such as Poland. There is also some evidence pointing to a somewhat greater tolerance on the part of the Kremlin towards the various dissident movements, if not at home then at least in some of the East European countries. Altogether it seems that Moscow has learnt some lessons from the Czechoslovak crisis and is doing its best to avoid a repetition.

There is one final aspect of Soviet-East European relations in which the problem of perception and images is crucial: the reliability of the East European armed forces in the event of an East-West confrontation, and the willingness of the East European military to resist a possible Soviet intervention *à la* Czechoslovakia. To assess either that reliability or that willingness is difficult. One might imagine that, in the event of an armed conflict between NATO and the Warsaw Pact, the East European armies might not be willing to fight their American or British counterparts but might possibly fire at the West Germans. This may be the Soviet perception of the Warsaw alliance, and might explain Moscow's reluctance to supply its junior partners with the most advanced weapons. The other question lends itself only to speculation. It has been hypothesized that one reason for the Soviet decision to intervene in Czechoslovakia in 1968 was the Kremlin's belief that the Czechoslovak government and armed forces would not resist. Similarly, the reluctance or unwillingness of the Soviet Union to intervene in Poland in 1956 and later, and in Romania in the 1960s, might well have been due to Moscow's realization that both countries would fight. The same seems to be true for Yugoslavia, which has long enjoyed the reputation of a country that would fiercely resist any Soviet attempt to intervene in the wake of Tito's death. This image of Yugoslavia may well prove decisive in determining that country's future.

Relations Among Individual East European Countries

As a general proposition, it may be stated that the relations among the individual East European countries have been governed by roughly the same factors that influenced the relations between Eastern Europe and the Soviet Union. In other words, the images and perceptions of one another formed by the different countries were conditioned mostly by history. The cognitive-affective balance played a very important role in guiding the policy vis-à-vis individual countries, some of which were clearly "liked" while others remained strongly "disliked."

One of the most striking aspects of contemporary Eastern Europe is the remarkable persistence of traditional images and perceptions, which continue to have an impact especially on bilateral but also on multilateral relations within the region. For example, the old friendship between Poland and Hungary, dating back some two centuries, was clearly responsible for an almost "special relationship" between the two countries in the mid-1950s and periodically since then. On the other hand, traditional antipathy for and distrust of the Czechs made any Polish support of the Prague Spring next to impossible, and few if any Poles mourned the demise of the Dubcek regime. The typical Polish image of the Czechs (but not of the Slovaks) was that of a cowardly and opportunistic people, unwilling to fight and ready to collaborate with the enemy, be it Germany or Russia. Needless to say, the behavior of the Czechoslovak army in August 1968 strongly reinforced this particular image.

There were other traditional conflicts in the area. The enmity between Hungary and Romania is well known and need not be discussed here. Neither is there much love lost between Hungary and Czechoslovakia, although there are indications that the old antagonisms may be fading. The conflict among nationalities in Yugoslavia has also been analyzed in great detail in the literature and will not be dealt with here.

East Germany is a special case. The East European countries that were conquered and occupied by the Third Reich perceived East Germany, at least initially, as virtually an enemy; even today the position and status of that country within the Warsaw alliance appears to be different from that of the others. On the one hand, some East European countries view East Germany as a continuation, if not of Nazi Germany, then of the characteristic Prussian state. On the other hand, nearly all the East Europeans tend to admire East Germany as the only state where communism works, and they attribute its success to the presence in East Berlin of a synthesis of Marx and Bismarck. Interestingly enough, there is evidence that the East Germans frequently repay the other East Europeans in kind by treating them with arrogance and contempt.

There is little doubt that the Soviet Union has been well aware of the existing antagonisms and that it has utilized them for its own purposes. Stalin in particular excelled in the policy of *divide et impera,* opposing any suggestions of regional union or other multilateral arrangements. As a result, his death found the region probably less united than before, despite the superficial appearance of an impregnable Stalinist monolith. While Khrushchev encouraged greater political, military and economic integration via the Warsaw Treaty and the resurrected Council for Mutual Economic Assistance, the results proved meager.

There are many reasons for the slow progress in economic and political integration. One of them is clearly the continued presence of traditional images, coupled with a striking ignorance of the actual situations existing in the various countries. It may be hypothesized that people, and especially elites, in Poland and Hungary today know more of what has been happening in Western Europe and the United States than in the Soviet Union and the rest of the Warsaw alliance. There are no signs that this information gap has narrowed despite a major increase in tourist traffic and trade. Until this gap is closed, the chances of the traditional images being abandoned and replaced by more realistic ones are slim.

What about the future? As suggested above, the persistence of traditional stereotypes in Eastern Europe has been largely due to an information gap. Whether this gap can be bridged, thus leading to a change in mutual perceptions, depends on such variables as the attitude of the USSR, the presence of strong nationalistic feelings, and the state of East-West relations.

Although the Soviet Union has always been deeply interested in the developments in Eastern Europe, it is difficult to say, at this moment whether the Kremlin today prefers close integration to a somewhat looser arrangement within which it can utilize the traditional enmities to play one country against the others for its own benefit. It may be argued that the absence of any Soviet pressure to forcibly integrate Eastern Europe may ultimately lead to a closer voluntary collaboration in the area. It may also affect the continued existence of strong nationalist tendencies: there are already some signs that the new generation in Eastern Europe may not be as nationalistic or chauvinistic as its predecessors. Finally, the continuation of détente and the relaxation of international tension may also work in the direction of closer cooperation, not only within Eastern Europe but also between Eastern Europe and the West.

Relations Between Eastern Europe and the West

In a sense, many of the questions concerning the impact of images and reality on the relations between Eastern Europe and the West have already been addressed. To a very large extent these relations were strongly influenced by the images and perceptions formed and held by both sides. As in the previous two cases examined, these perceptions were deeply affected by history and by the existence of a wide information gap between images and the realities.

The ignorance of the actual (and past) national objectives and attitudes has been quite striking, especially on the part of the West; this ignorance can be attributed, again, to reasons of history, as well as geography, culture, religion, and language. Geography was particularly relevant for the United States, but also played an important part in forming the images held by the major West European countries. One factor occasionally ignored is the relative newness of several East European states, which acquired independence only after World

War Two. Countries such as Czechoslovakia, Poland and Yugoslavia may have had a lengthy and glorious history spanning many centuries; but their modern statehood dated only to 1918. This in itself was partly responsible for the lack of correct information about the region in the West and the latter's reliance instead on traditional images, many of which bore little resemblance to reality.

As a result, the overall image projected by Eastern Europe (with the perennial exception of Czechoslovakia) during the interwar period was that of a collection of strange, non-democratic countries constantly quarrelling with one another and beset by economic difficulties. In the United States this image was frequently reinforced by the presence of emigrants from the area who did little if anything to correct it. Very frequently the Western perception of Eastern Europe was affected by the propaganda conducted by hostile states or ethnic groups such as Weimar Germany or the Ukrainians who, for example, were instrumental in denigrating further the image of Poland.

The wartime alliance between the three East European countries, Czechoslovakia, Poland and Yugoslavia, and Great Britain and the United States — essentially an accident — did relatively little to change the traditional image of the region held in London and Washington; and it soon became obvious that the future of Eastern Europe was of little concern to the two powers. In the final analysis, already by the end of the war the area was perceived by them as falling properly within the Soviet sphere of interest.

There is no doubt that this represented a major blow to most of Eastern Europe, which held totally different expectations and perceptions of Western intentions and its own future: the West had been viewed as being so opposed to the communist takeover of the area as to start a third world war on that account. It was assumed that the same West that had declared war on Hitler in defense of Poland would not let Poland be taken over by the communists. The same logic was applied to the other countries in the region.

The Western world's indifference to communist seizure of power elicited varying reactions in Eastern Europe ranging from a feeling of betrayal, to bitter disappointment, to an understanding of the Western predicament. However, there is little doubt that the shining image of the West, and of Britain and the United States in particular, became considerably tarnished in the process. The subsequent cold war enunciations of the doctrine of "liberalization" and "roll back" were not taken too seriously by the East Europeans, especially when the Hungarian revolution of 1956 received no material support from the West.

The failure of the West to come to the aid of the Hungarian revolt appeared to convince all in Eastern Europe that there was little point in counting on Western support. The perception of an essentially indifferent West was strengthened by the fact that by the late 1940s the Western powers had already lost interest in the various East European countries, which were viewed as Soviet satellites without any autonomy whatsoever. Since these countries were perceived as smaller copies of the Soviet Union, the West completely ignored the process of political and social change in the region after Stalin's death and was thus greatly surprised by the 1956 explosions in Poland and Hungary.

The relations between Eastern Europe and the West have improved considerably in the past decade or so, partly as a by-product of East-West détente and partly because of the growing volume of information each side has about each other. Nevertheless, Western behavior during the Prague Spring hardly departed from that during the Hungarian revolt, and the only difference between the two events was that no one in Czechoslovakia — or, for that matter, in Eastern Europe — even expected the West to do anything. The American involvement in Vietnam was subsequently interpreted as a sign of growing Western abandonment and the eventual "finlandization" of Europe.

All in all, it may be argued that the image projected by the West in the late 1970s was a rather disappointing one for East Europe. It perceived the West as a power losing its superiority over the Soviet Union, losing its will to fight and resist communist encroachments, and distracted by trivial and inconsequential matters. This image was strengthened by the 1975 Helsinki Conference, which was interpreted as a major Western surrender to Moscow. That this was not the case, and that the conference proved to be a major headache for the Kremlin, was largely unnoticed in the area. President Carter's advocacy and support of human rights was viewed hopefully, as a sign of America's return to not only political but also moral leadership; but the budding image soon faded with the West's lackluster performance at Belgrade. Time will tell whether the disappointing image of the West will be with us indefinitely.

Détente as a Source of International Conflict *

Kalevi J. Holsti

Most of the literature on perceptions in foreign policy focuses on decision-makers' views of their opponents' capabilities, intentions and possible actions in particular situations. While the impetus for those analyses has been better to understand how, to what extent, and why holders of authoritative foreign policy roles often misread the world around them, the policy implications are of only slightly less concern. The works of George, Jervis and others have explicitly studied ways of making decision processes more sensitive to the extent that opponents' motives and objectives are carefully weighed against the evidence, alternative courses of action are thought through to their probable outcomes and costs, and "signals" are carefully evaluated. No procedures can ensure against decisions that will have unanticipated results; but mechanisms to ameliorate stereotypic thinking, to check judgment, or to reduce pressures for group conformity can be constructed. In the past decade, work in this area has gone far and knowledge of the conditions under which poor decisions are likely to be made has increased significantly.

Whether for scientific or prescriptive purposes, almost all studies of perceptual phenomena in foreign policy-making have employed limited time, spatial and contextual domains. The days, and sometimes weeks, preceding the outbreak of a war have provided the data for these studies. When such short time spans and such limited units of analysis as perception of threat and perception of capability are examined, foreign policy behavior seems to contain little grand strategy or concern for long-range objectives. The spatial contexts are also limited to the actors directly involved. In a critical situation, policy-makers no doubt focus on immediate situations. But what of all the "background" factors, such as historical knowledge and political experience, that may deeply affect evaluations? Finally, foreign policy studies employ *crisis* as the context in which decisions are made. Such attention hardly needs justification. But it is fair to point out that crisis decision-making is not typical of decision-making in any government, and reveals virtually nothing about the major objectives and strategies of most governments in most situations. Major foreign policy undertakings — such as the Marshall Plan, SALT, the Europeans' efforts to create the EEC, and Iran's former aspirations to create a security zone in Southwest Asia — are probably of no less consequence to international politics than are crisis decision. Yet such programs and foreign policy projects have seldom been the object of systematic foreign policy inquiry.

The long-range expectations of policy-makers, the images of future states of affairs — new orders — that some statesmen seek to achieve, and the impact those images have on specific courses of action and diplomatic programs are phenomena that have received relatively less attention. They are concerned less with assessments of an opponent's objectives and intentions in a particular situation, and more with the general sources of its foreign policy, the links between domestic and international politics, the role of ideologies, and the opponent's own long-range plans. The roles and functions of many states, not just opponents, are also included. Many policy-makers, particularly those of small, non-involved states, concentrate on day-to-day affairs and have little time or inclination to try to identify, much less to control, regional and global trends or to construct models of new world orders. Others, such as Dr. Kissinger, or many Soviet officials, are more given to serious analysis of the future, and to a certain extent their day-to-day decisions are guided by long-range plans and certain expectations they develop concerning the regional or global structures they are attempting to construct.

Only a brief sketch of the theoretical background to the subsequent analysis of the discrepancies between images and realities in international politics can be presented here. The argument is that most policies of decision-making elites result not from perceptions of opponents in critical situations, but from more or less explicit theories or assumptions about general situations or problems involving, usually, many actors. Among such theories we might list some of the following, which have been popular in the diplomatic rhetoric of Western statesmen over the past three decades:

1. The USSR is strongly motivated to promote its version of revolution abroad and to use its economic, political and military strength to weaken the West.
2. Poverty creates political instability, which provides a fertile ground for communist penetration. Foreign aid programs can alleviate poverty and hence create political stability.
3. Virtually any international conflict can be resolved through patience, good will, and negotiations.

4. With proper policies, governments can create a world typified by a "just and lasting" peace.
5. Economic interdependence can help mute conflicts, even those between East and West.

Such assumptions or theories are critically important in forming policy-makers' *expectations* about the results of any particular diplomatic program. Consider a typical National Security Council study in the United States, for example. In addition to analyzing the nature and sources of a particular problem, it proposes alternative courses of action, estimates costs, and indicates expectations of results coming from the proposed actions. The expectations of results (or "image" of a future state of affairs) no doubt heavily influence the ultimate choice among competing alternatives. Finally, the expectations are themselves derived explicitly or implicitly from policy-makers' theories and assumptions. These comments can be formulated in the following diagram indicating the direction of influence or causality.

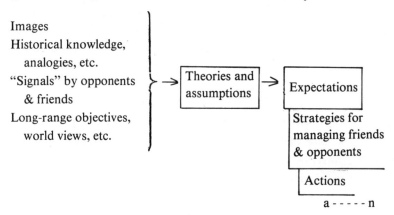

This paper explores the problem of expectations and predictions in the context of Western efforts to create a stable "zone of peace" in the European continent. It focuses on the Conference on Security and Cooperation in Europe (CSCE) which culminated, after more than two years of negotiations, in the "Final Act" signed by the heads of state or government of all the countries in Europe and North America (except for Albania) in Helsinki during July 1975. My thesis is that, while the leaders of the major powers did not believe that the CSCE and its resulting document would by itself build a secure structure of peace in Europe, they did anticipate that because it contained specific obligations that would increase contacts between East and West it would reduce the likelihood of confrontations, crises and war. Although expectations varied from government to government, most saw it as a significant step forward in the détente process.

But the record in the three years since the elaborate Helsinki ceremonies indicates that the expectations of the majority were not warranted, that some of the assumptions underlying the theory of détente were not examined critically enough, and that in some important respects the Final Act and its subsequent use by governments increased rather than decreased the levels of tension in Europe. Why has this been the case?

Before extending the argument, several caveats should be made. First, in developing the argument we will be taking methodological license by inferring *expectations* from behavior. Since full documentation on the Helsinki and Geneva negotiations is unavailable, we will have to assume that the Final Act expresses roughly the intentions and, implicitly, the expectations and foreign policy theories of those governments that were willing to spend more than two years in drawn-out negotiations.

Second, the discussion examines the expectations and objectives of the major powers and not those of Europe's small states. The Final Act has probably increased the sense of security of Finland, Austria, Yugoslavia, and Romania, and thus fulfilled some of their hopes. Some of the major points concerning non-intervention and non-interference were strongly supported, and in some cases proposed, by these states in the expectation that they could be used to hinder any future Soviet attempts to intimidate them during periods of strained relations. The code of behavior outlined in "Basket I" — as acknowledged even by Brezhnev — "erects a legal, moral, and political barrier in the way of those given to military gambles."[1] But whereas Brezhnev was alluding to the United States or West Germany, the neutrals of Europe, and Romania, had another major power in mind when they vigorously supported explicit strictures against any type of external pressures or interference in their internal affairs. Some have noted that two months prior to the Helsinki signing ceremonies, Kissinger already invoked Basket I in warning the Soviets to stop providing overt assistance to Alvaro Cunhal in Portugal.[2] No piece of paper is a guarantee of security, but the vulnerable small states of Europe have at least a potentially effective propaganda weapon they can use against various forms of intimidation.

Third, a good deal has been accomplished — but gone largely unnoticed — in some of the areas covered in the Final Act. Those countries (e.g., Canada) that in Geneva and Helsinki strongly promoted the sections dealing with humanitarian issues, such as family reunifications and easing the availability of exist visas, have quietly but consistently reminded the Soviets and the East Europeans of their obligations and have achieved positive results. Freedom of travel has certainly not been — and probably never will be — attained; but since 1975 about 10,000 East Germans have been allowed to settle in West Germany, as have many Poles.[3] Over 5,000 East Europeans and Russians have emigrated to Canada to rejoin their families. It is unfortunate that the Western press, in focusing almost exclusively on the human rights issue, has remained silent on these achievements.

The confidence building measures (CBMs) dealing with reciprocal observation of large troop maneuvers have little significance for the major powers, since the latter are presently capable of obtaining all the information they need through electronic and satellite means. But for the small states of Europe, which lack sophisticated intelligence capabilities, such measures may indeed reduce anxiety, particularly in crisis or near-crisis situations. One wonders, for example, whether the various "maneuvers" carried out by the Warsaw Pact forces in the spring and summer of 1968 to intimidate the Czechs would have taken place in the presence of NATO, Yugoslav or other observers.[4]

While acknowledging these positive results of the CSCE, it remains that many of the expectations of the major-power participants have not been achieved, and that the heavy focus on the human rights provisions of the Final Act has created a new dimension of conflict in East-West relations.

Dr. Kissinger, of course, was never an enthusiastic proponent of the multilateral diplomacy leading to the Final Act. The head of the American delegation to the negotiations was the ambassador in Czechoslovakia, which indicates something about the standing of the conference among Kissinger's diplomatic priorities. Yet many of the provisions of the Final Act give effect to Kissinger's (and many others') theory of détente. Stated briefly, that theory is a resurrection of the old "stake in society" argument in eighteenth- and nineteenth-century political thought: those who have economic and other interests to preserve will act reasonably in their politics and in their relations with their fellow men. The outcasts, the misfits and the property-less will always be the source of revolt and mischief. Hence the vote should be restricted to those in possession of some minimum amount of wealth. In brief, economic interests and interdependence create stable politics. At the international level, the theory argues that if you involve your opponent in a variety of interdependencies (and dependencies) through trade, cultural contacts, scientific collaboration, loans, credits, and the like, the concrete advantages he gains therefrom will impose restraints on other sectors of his foreign

policy behavior. What has been "given" in the form of bilateral and multilateral cooperative agreements can always be taken away if the opponent
does not behave properly.

The theory also borrows from the functionalist arguments of David
Mitrany and his successors. All the agreements and international technical
organizations will breed *habits* of cooperation and collaboration that will
eventually "spill over" into military, security, and diplomatic issue areas. This
hypothesis is carried on today, for example, in the thinking of Marshall
Shulman, Special Assistant on Soviet Affairs to the American Secretary of
State, who has argued that the "development of [Soviet] trade with the United
States and other advanced industrial nations can be a stabilizing factor in
Soviet policy in the world."[5] International involvement leads to restrained
foreign policy behavior.[6] Détente, then, is a strategy to manage the power of
the adversary, the CSCE being one important component. While state agreements will create the interdependencies, the free flow of people and ideas will
create the mutual understanding and empathy necessary to remove the distorted images resulting from decades of cold war.

It would be difficult to verify the assumptions and hypotheses contained in
this view of détente.[7] We might tentatively accept the general expectations
contained in the theory; but we must also recall that personality disorders, new
political movements, and ideologies have often driven policy-makers to forgo
economic and other concrete interests for the sake of achieving revolutionary
goals or some strong psychological or national need. In 1932 Germany was
reasonably interdependent with the rest of Europe; several years later Hitler
set about to destroy the system of diplomatic, economic and technical
cooperation so laboriously created after World War One. The depression, unanticipated by the Stressemans and Briands of Europe, also helped dash the
hopes of the optimists.

It is not stretching reality to argue, then, that while Kissinger was not an
enthusiastic proponent of the process leading to the Final Act, the Helsinki
document to a great extent expresses in concrete form the former secretary of
state's and other Western leaders' expectations or hopes about how to achieve
a stable Europe through détente. The preamble of Basket I, dealing with
diplomatic and security issues, states that the totality of the act will help in
"ensuring conditions under which [the peoples of the signatory states] can live
in true and lasting peace." The Final Act, it also suggests, "should promote
better and closer relations . . . and thus [overcome] the confrontation stemming from the character of their past relations."

The speeches by heads of state and government at the signing ceremonies reveal a good deal about expectations in foreign policy. Most of them were cautiously optimistic. Unlike certain news analysts who insisted on comparing the event with the Congress of Vienna, most of the speakers warned that the Final Act was not in itself sufficient to propel the process of détente; the critical matter was not resolution, but implementation. Western leaders clearly implied that if the norms and obligations in the document were observed and implemented, the predictions about behavior in the theory of détente would be proven correct. Prime Minister Wilson was perhaps the most optimistic of the major-power leaders. He did not believe that documents in themselves diminish tensions or insecurity. "But they do represent more than good intentions, more than the desire to set our relations on a new course. They are a moral commitment to be ignored at our mutual peril, they are the start of a new chapter in the history of Europe."[8] President Ford warned against expecting miracles but stated that "we can and do expect steady progress that comes in steps. Clearly the Final Act is a major step forward."[9]

Only Brezhnev hinted that seeds of conflict lay within the document. He must have recognized already in the Finnish capital the blunder his government had made in accepting the sections on human rights in return for guarantees against the use of arms to alter Europe's territorial configurations — guarantees that were unnecessary, given the fact that, with the exception of Greece and Turkey and a few minor disputes, no state in Europe has raised territorial issues since the West Germans relegated reunification to the level of dreams rather than practical possibilities. Hence, while Brezhnev generally praised the Final Act, he also emphasized that the cornerstone of the whole enterprise was the principle of non-interference in internal affairs.[10] It is unlikely that he would have spoken of one brief paragraph in a document of over 90 pages had he not already anticipated that the provisions of "Basket III" dealing with human rights were going to lead to diplomatic confrontations. His qualms were fully justified.

While there are numerous problems of translation and ambiguity in the Final Act, the main difficulty is that it combines two contradictory sets of norms: governments undertake to guarantee certain fundamental rights to their citizens, but no government may interfere in the internal affairs of another state. The document is not, of course, a treaty; but as a moral and political statement it provides benchmarks against which the signatories can (or even should) monitor each others' behavior. And unlike some interpretations of the U.N. Charter that state that the Security Council cannot take action unless a threat or breach to peace or an act of aggression has taken place, the review procedures of the Final Act provide no similar qualifications. Theoretically, any signatory can publicize or condemn any other European or North American governments' record in the field of human rights, even if that record does not impinge in any way upon the mutual relations of nations. On the other hand, the prohibitions against interference, direct or indirect, in each others' internal affairs make any discussion basically an exercise in rhetoric; no agreement on remedial action is possible, as the Belgrade review conference has demonstrated.

The human rights issue does not concern only individual freedoms. Basket I, in sections VII and VIII, includes guarantees of human rights for minorities and the right of self-determination. We already know the Soviet record on self-determination and minority policy, but there is nothing to stop the Soviets from hiding their own shortcomings by attacking Western countries for their treatment of minorities. What could be more futile or possibly damaging to détente than sterile debates about the land rights of Eskimos in North America, the Quebecois, the separatist movements in the Canary Islands, the Azores, and Madeira, to say nothing of the plight of the Basques, Bretons and Tyrolians? The targets of Soviet attack would have to defend themselves by falling back on the non-interference clause, which would obviously prove highly embarrassing, or by extending the debate to include Soviet nationality policies. Under such conditions, the rhetoric and diplomatic style of the cold war would very likely reappear.

It is difficult to know exactly what the proponents of the human rights clauses expected to obtain from the communist nations. Surely they could not have believed that the governments in the Soviet bloc would transform themselves into liberal democracies, or that they would actually conform to the standards of a non-treaty declaration when they do not even observe the meager rights outlined in their own national constitution.[11] The human rights issue has added a new dimension of conflict in East-West relations, and until the Carter administration recently decided to back off, the Soviets were beginning to make their own linkages: no progress on SALT and other security matters so long as the United States vigorously pursued its program of condemning the Soviet Union's already well-known record in human rights. There is little doubt, though some may argue the opposite, that the acrimony raised in this issue tilted the balance toward more conflict in East-West relations.

Other sections of the Final Act deal with increased communications between the signatories. The French delegation in particular prompted the expansion of cultural relations and other provisions that would open up East Europe and the Soviet Union to more Western correspondents, publications and tourism. While some limited progress has been made in these areas,[12] the realities of political life in the Soviet bloc countries suggest that their regimes will not move fast or far enough to please Western governments. They have welcomed trade expansion and technical cooperation, but they do not yet adequately trust the political reliability of the "new communist man" to allow free Western access to him. As Ieuan John has put it, the communist regimes "cannot let increased external relations interfere with internal conformity."[13] The unfettered flow of Western books, periodicals, magazines and films into the communist nations would constitute a form of penetration that no authoritarian regime could tolerate. It is one thing for the Soviets to allow politically reliable trade and scientific delegations to roam throughout the world, or to tolerate a certain amount of emigration; it is a different matter for Westerners to go freely into the communist nations, accompanied by all manner of literature, goods and films. The Soviets consider free access an open invitation to subversion from the West.[14]

Thus far the human rights issue has so dominated the review procedures that the area of increased communication has received little formal attention.[15] But it would be naive to believe that the communist regimes will suddenly open themselves to Western penetration. If this issue comes eventually to dominate East-West agendas, the acrimony will likely be only slightly less pronounced than it has been in the human rights area. Here, then, is another seed of conflict where the possibilities for cooperative enterprises are quite limited, and where expectations were unrealistically high.

The tone of the argument so far might seem to counsel excessive timidity on the part of Western governments in confronting the more unpleasant realities of communist life. Shouldn't these governments do everything possible to nurture the liberalization of communist societies? The argument is not that this is an unworthy objective, but rather that by including in the Final Act commitments and principles that have little or no chance of being observed or implemented, and yet insisting on immediate conformity, the level of diplomatic tension is likely to increase and be accompanied by a waning of public support for détente. And if the linkage theory is valid, increased diplomatic rancor in one area should have negative consequences on issues where there *are* some common interests and where possibilities for further agreements *do* exist. It is unlikely that if the United States vigorously condemns the Eastern countries for their human rights record, it will get SALT, a relaxation of repression, a satisfactory MBFR agreement, and open access to communist societies. If it pushes too hard in the areas involving core sensibilities, it may get no results elsewhere. A more sensible strategy might be to focus initially on areas where arguments are possible and, only after those have been fully secured in writing and practice, to turn to more ideologically sensitive issues. Only if the linkage hypothesis is incorrect could one take action on all fronts simultaneously and hope to get positive results across the board.

Some might argue that the major European nations and the United States had to get something important from the Soviet Union in return for recognizing the territorial changes resulting from World War Two. This was one rationale, it has been suggested, for the inclusion of the statement on human rights. The Final Act does not preclude territorial change and it does not legitimize Soviet conquests between 1939 and 1945. It merely states that the signatories cannot use force or threaten military action to rectify frontiers. It would be difficult to foresee any circumstance in which Finland might liberate Karelia, West Germany would use force to reunify the two Germanies, or Romania might threaten the Soviet Union with military action in order to regain Bessarabia. The Final Act symbolically heralded East Germany's full entry into the international community, but that result would have come to pass in any event. The Final Act's provisions on territorial arrangements confirmed the obvious; little of substance was forfeited. Indeed, it could be pointed out that in agreeing to the principles of non-interference and self-determination, the Soviets in effect abrogated the main lines of the Brezhnev doctrine — not an inconsiderable gain for the small states of Europe.

If the CSCE was even a minimally important step, one of many that might lead to new interdependencies and eventually to a "zone of peace" on the continent, in the short run few expectations along these lines were warranted. In fact, the conference and the resulting document did not address the fundamental source of conflict on the continent, which is that both sides — but particularly the Soviet Union — while temporarily accepting the status quo do not see it as a desirable long-range state of affairs.

Long-range Soviet objectives remain unchanged: they seek the departure of North American troops from the continent and the takeover of the bourgeois governments by the fraternal parties. They publicly declare that they will do whatever is feasible to achieve these objectives, for détente to them does not mean the end of socialist evolution (or revolution), but merely a set of norms that, they hope, will reduce the likelihood of wars and crises. To the Russians, détente may change the modalities of conflict, but it is not an alternative to conflict. For example, the May 1972 "Basic Principles of Soviet-American Relations" signed by Brezhnev and Nixon says nothing about the incompatibilities that produce conflicts, but only pledges the parties to prevent crisis and to do their "utmost to avoid military confrontations."[16] When Giscard D'Estaing visited Moscow three months after the signing of the Final Act, he publicly appealed for "ideological disarmament" on the grounds that constant propaganda harangues and Soviet involvement in Western European politics did not help relax tensions. Brezhnev contended that the continuation of the ideological struggle against the West was not inconsistent with the Helsinki Declaration, and indeed announced shortly thereafter that the struggle would intensify. As Yuri Andropov pointed out in an April 1976 speech:

> Our foreign policy is . . . a class policy because, while we pursue a consistent, continual, and sincere policy of peace, [we also] follow a firm position of proletarian internationalism and solidarity with the people struggling for freedom and social progress. There are no contradictions here. We do not expect in détente that the monopoly bourgeois . . . will side with the revolutionary struggle. . . . The Soviet Union makes no such demands on the West. But the West may make no demand on the Soviet Union to renounce its solidarity with those who are waging a struggle against exploitation. . . .[17]

With such views guiding Soviet policy-makers, we can argue that the essential reasons why there has been some diminution of tensions in Europe and the resulting development of some elementary "rules of the game" during the past decade has less to do with agreements or détente theories than with the development of a rough nuclear parity, the refusal of the United States to withdraw from Europe, and the dramatic changes in the complexion of Western Europe's communist parties. If the Soviets actually appeared to be making considerable progress toward their goals on the continent, it would most likely lead to a resumption of the cold war, not to détente.

In the face of the vast increase in WTO military capacity, there is no possibility — as there was several years ago — of the United States removing its forces from the continent. Soviet military policy has contradicted Russian diplomatic objectives, and there is little evidence to suggest that things will change in the near future.

Equally important, but more interesting, are developments with the communist parties of Western Europe. The June 1975 East Berlin summit of European communist leaders could have been little more than a debacle for the Soviet party's aspirations regarding the "victory of socialism" in Western Europe. Despite Brezhnev's insistence on including all the old shibboleths of the international communist movement, one after another the leaders of the non-bloc parties, as well as those of Romania and Yugoslavia, mounted the rostrum and rejected the sacred tenets. Ceausescu explicitly denounced the notion of a "center" for communist movements. Using almost religious metaphors, Carillo made the same point. Berlinguer demanded that all parties be considered sovereign and equal and claimed that no party had the right to interfere in the affairs of another. Tito repeated that point and went on to argue that non-alignment was a perfectly respectable foreign policy orientation for a communist state. The final communiqué was of course a compromise, but one in which the opposing parties did not meet halfway. The old concepts of proletarian internationalism, democratic centralism, dictatorship of the proletariat, the leading role of the CPSU — none of these appeared in the text. More recently, the Spanish party voted to disinherit itself from Leninism. Perhaps more significantly, actual debate and meaningful voting took place in the congress.

This is not the place to review the debate about communist participation in Western governments: anyone can quote selectively to prove a point. It is more clear, however, that a few portfolios held by party members would not necessarily signal a victory for Soviet interests or a defeat for the West; communists would insist on certain policy changes, to be sure, but we could not predict that those changes would somehow enhance Soviet influence or prestige in the Western countries. The Finnish experience and the communist-led local government history in northern Italy provide no cause for excessive pessimism. Would the Soviet party have reason to rejoice, then, if the Italian communist party (PCI), which has pledged fidelity to NATO (until both military blocs are disbanded) and the EEC were to participate in a cabinet in Rome? Indeed, if present trends in the Western parties continue into the future, it is possible to speculate that the Soviets would rather deal with the Schmidts, D'Estaings and Callaghans than with the leaders of some of the Western fraternal parties.[18]

Reversing the perceptions, would the Italian, Swedish or Spanish parties applaud the victory of the pro-Soviet factions in Yugoslavia after Tito's death? Or a new Soviet squeeze on Berlin? Or, for that matter, a withdrawal of American troops from the continent? Most of the Western communist parties, like the radical socialists and the socialists in France during the twentieth century, have become increasingly reconciled to political pluralism (if not yet within their own parties); the revolutionary tradition has been taken over by the anarchists, nihilists and terrorists, few of whom have earned the admiration of Moscow.[19] Overall, the situation of the leftist forces remains ambiguous;

but the trend seems to favor the perpetuation of pluralist societies more than a Soviet-style "victory of socialism."

Yet as long as the Soviet regime publicly commits itself to the eventual destruction of the present order in Europe, détente can be little more than an expression of moderation reflecting the facts of nuclear life. There has been an impressive burgeoning of East-West economic and technical relations, to be sure, but it is too early to judge whether the interdependencies and dependencies created through them will ever lead the Soviet regime to accept the present order as a desirable one.

Western aspirations towards the East are more ambiguous. They have ranged from Dulles' rhetoric about liberation to the Sonnenfeldt doctrine, which more or less accepts Soviet hegemony over Eastern Europe for the immediate future. Yet some of the sections of the Helsinki Final Act, combined with American and European economic incentives, indicate that a desirable order from the Western perspective is one in which the East European states enjoy considerable freedom from Soviet domination in their foreign and domestic policies, and in which they would open themselves to increased Western cultural, and possibly ideological, influence. To the extent that such an order is pursued aggressively, we could hardly expect the Russians to abandon their own commitment to ideological struggle. They do not see themselves as being only on the offensive and, whether erroneous or not, they continue to believe that the events in Czechoslovakia in 1968 were linked to Western (particularly West German) penetration.

Let us summarize the theme of the paper. After more than two years of painstaking negotiations in Helsinki and Geneva, thirty-five nations of Europe and North America became signatories to a lengthy document outlining appropriate modes of conduct in diplomatic relations, steps to increase communications, cultural and scientific contacts, and obligations with reference to human rights and humanitarian problems. The basic thrust, from the Western point of view, was to significantly increase the flow of people, goods and ideas between East and West. Basing their expectations on the spillover theory of détente, leaders of the major Western states anticipated that these increased flows, and the consequent interdependencies, would inhibit or deflect the Soviet Union from aggressive foreign policy behavior and encourage liberalization of the communist domestic orders. The Final Act would help break down the East-West barriers erected after World War Two and might eventually serve as the foundation for a pan-European system with few ideologial, diplomatic, or military cleavages.

Perhaps it is premature to judge the long-range consequences of the CSCE exercise, but if the three years that have passed since the Helsinki gathering are any guide, then results have lagged far beyond most governments' expectations. The hypotheses contained in détente theory have not yet proven correct, and there is little or no trend indicating that they will be. Despite some impressive results in the humanitarian field, the possible increase in the sense of security among some of Europe's small states, and the potential deterrent role of the Final Act, the preparatory and review conferences exacerbated rather than diminished East-West tensions. Some of the sections of the act contained the roots of new types of conflict; apparently Brezhnev was the only one to recognize this. Thus, as the Carter administration pushed hard on the human rights issue, the Soviets became more obstreperous in other areas.[20] In brief, attempts to seek fulfillment simultaneously of all the undertakings in the Final Act halted or slowed progress in some areas critical to the construction of a more stable and less threatening international system. The media's almost total concentration on the human rights issue and particular trials in the Soviet Union significantly reduced public and American congressional enthusiasm for further agreements with the Soviet Union.

What, then, are some of the lessons of the CSCE experience? First, any agreement that is designed to improve relations between normally hostile opponents has a greater chance of being implemented if it does not include provisions that allow and even encourage the parties to attack each others' core values. Elements that have not the slightest possibility of being implemented may become confused with areas where interests overlap and where cooperative enterprises may be constructed. While from a purely moral perspective it may be admirable to pay lip service to human rights, prudent diplomats would not emphasize issues in which the values at stake are diametrically opposed. The international community cannot, and should not, ignore severe deprivation of human rights. But if governments wish to pursue these matters with full vigor, they cannot expect accomodating behavior in other issue areas. A case can be argued that the most effective pressure on the Soviets has come not from American governmental posturing — particularly at Belgrade — but from the actions of thousands of individuals and professional, scientific and cultural organizations in the West that have taken up the cause of communist dissidents.

A second lesson is that documents that do not go to the roots of conflict cannot by themselves create zones of peace out of cold war areas. What they can do is identify areas where interests between opponents converge, and set in motion those bureaucratic and other procedures that will lead to the establishment of more interdependencies. Whatever the shortcomings of the theory of détente, as a guide to policy it is probably less fraught with danger than the Dulles position that you can tame an opponent by isolating him from the rest of the international community. The Helsinki Final Act may thus prove of some value for the peripheries; but so long as the Soviet government is committed to a vision of a communized Western Europe, and if the Western states aggressively pursue their vision of weaning East Europe away from Soviet tutelage, we cannot expect the continent to become a genuine zone of peace or, in Deutschian terms, a "security community" where hostile armies do not face each other and where there is no expectation of armed conflict. The crisis-prone system of the cold war probably no longer exists; and few men demonstrate much interest in returning to the certainties of that era. Yet the type of regional system envisaged in the Final Act is a long way from realization, and the pursuit of some objectives to the exclusion of others has probably put the ultimate goal even further in the distance.

A third lesson is that a document as comprehensive as the Final Act may create diplomatic and bureaucratic indigestion. Some expectations have had to be reduced simply because the CSCE tried to do too much. It covered everything from pollution in the Mediterranean (thanks to Malta's last-minute blackmail of the conference) to exchange of films, tourism, the use of force, non-interference, business law, trade, investment, athletics, and many other subjects. The review conferences are supposed to monitor behavior and assess progress — or lack of it — in the bilateral and multilateral relations of thirty-five states. Despite press treatment to the contrary, the Final Act is not solely an East-West document. In theory, at least, the cultural relations between Austria and Portugal are as noteworthy as those between West Germany and Poland. Can the review conferences actually fulfill the roles assigned to them? The Belgrade exercise suggests they cannot. The debates revealed clearly that blocs continue to exist as the fundamental fact of European diplomatic relations. Despite a few mavericks like Romania and Yugoslavia, the breakdown of cleavages required for the development of a genuine pan-European system has not yet begun to take place.

The history of the CSCE and its results suggest that Western policy-makers' expectations about the progress of détente were based on overly optimistic assessments of the possibilities of liberalization in the communist bloc, on an underestimation of the continuing Soviet commitment to ideological and revolutionary goals in Europe and elsewhere, and on an inadequate appreciation of the extent to which communist regimes fear Western ideological penetration. The Final Act thus contains objectives and standards of conduct that will probably not be achieved or met in the next decade or longer. These are not problems confined to perceptions or misperceptions as those terms have been used in most of the international relations literature. What is involved is broader than the evaluation of an opponent's intentions or behavior in a particular set of circumstances.

This paper has not delved into the intellectual origins of the theory of détente. It has sought instead to demonstrate that diplomatic actions—in this case the Helsinki and Geneva negotiations — are sometimes undertaken to fulfill certain expectations arising out of broad-gauge theories or assumptions of international politics. The theory of détente is designed to manage or influence the foreign policy behavior of an adversary in the hopes of establishing a zone of peace in Europe. The theory contains numerous assumptions about the effects of increased international communication and interdependence, assumptions that have not been tested rigorously either in diplomatic practice or in quantitative studies of international policies. Several years after the signature of one of détente's major achievements, the Final Act, the level of tensions in U.S.-Soviet relations appears to be higher today than it was in 1975. We can conclude that the theory of détente gave rise to certain expectations about (a) the possibilities of liberalizing regimes in the communist bloc, (b) the consequences of increased interaction and interdependence on security issues, and (c) the effects of multilateral transactions and communications on breaking down stereotypes, cold war reflexive actions, and some of the ideological barriers that have existed between East and West since World War Two.

Despite its positive points, the theory overlooks some of the persisting and fundamental incompatibilities between Western and communist societies and contains overly optimistic assumptions about the effects of communication on behavior. Hence Western expectations about modifying Soviet diplomacy became overly elevated, with the result that Soviet transgressions of the code of conduct in the Final Act have led to a strong erosion of Western public support for the overall objective of normalizing relations with the Soviet Union. It is hard to say that Western policy-makers in this case have "misperceived" an opponent; rather, important theoretical constructs containing numerous assumptions have remained unexamined. If one is to understand the origins and playing out of the grand design called détente, we need more than information about perceptions of threat, capabilities or opportunities. The historical and intellectual roots of détente, as seen from the West, are located in our culture, public opinion and the reigning liberal ideology, and are not to be found only in policy-makers' utterances preceding an international crisis.

Notes

* Some of the points developed in this paper were presented initially in a lecture to the Korean Institute of International Affairs in Seoul, Korea, July 9, 1977.

1. Speech of Leonid Brezhnev to the Central Committee and the Supreme Soviet on the 68th anniversary of the Socialist Revolution, reprinted in *Survival*, January/February 1978, pp. 32-35.

2. James Reston, "Portugal and Détente," *The New York Times*, June 6, 1975.

3. Ieuan G. John, "The Helsinki-Belgrade Connection," *International Relations* 5 (November 1977): 149.

4. The record of implementing the CBM measures has been reasonably good, although the Western states have been more forthcoming in issuing invitations to maneuvers than have the communist states. WTO members have usually invited only neighboring military officials to observe their maneuvers and have usually rejected invitations to attend NATO operations. See Johan Holst and Karen Melander, "European Security and Confidence-Building Measures," *Survival*, July-August 1977, pp. 146-154.

5. Statement to U.S. House of Representatives Committee on International Relations, Subcommittee on Europe and the Middle East, October 26, 1977, reprinted in *Survival*, January/February 1978, pp. 25-31.

6. The theory underlying American-Soviet relations is outlined by a former high official in the State Department under Kissinger. See Helmut Sonnenfeldt, "Russia, America and Detente," *Foreign Affairs*, January 1978, pp. 275-294.

7. Kjell Goldmann and John Lagerkranz present data that show a diminution of hostile East-West verbal behavior coinciding with a decline in economic polarity on the continent. Such evidence would support the linkage hypothesis, but the direction of causality — if there is any — has not been established entirely, and there is the possibility of other variables being involved as well. See "Neither Tension nor Detente: East-West Relations in Europe, 1971-1975," *Cooperation and Confict* 4 (1977): 251–264. The assumption that increased communication creates understanding and thus reduces conflict is open to serious question. In many instances increased communication raises nationalism, awareness of fundamental differences between people and their societies, and intergroup conflict. See Walter Connor, "Nation-building or Nation-destroying?" *World Politics* 24 (April 1972): 319-355.

8. *Keesing's Contemporary Archives* 27308, September 1-7, 1975.

9. Ibid.

10. Ibid.

11. It is probably too early to evaluate what impact the publication of the Final Act in the communist countries has had on dissidents. Some have argued that it gave them new hope — and a new weapon. Others have pointed out that the new agitation has forced the communist regimes to become even more harsh. While this is an important matter, it is not the subject of this paper.

12. For example, Hungary recently abolished the requirement for Austrians to obtain visas in order to travel in the communist country.

13. "The Helsinki-Belgrade Connection," p. 148.

14. For example, Mikhail Suslov claimed in 1972 that the "main forces of bourgeois propaganda are directed toward planting poisonous seeds of political indifference, an attitude of anarchistic self-assertion, petit bourgeois money-grubbing, chauvinism, and nationalism in the ideological soil of socialist society." Quoted in Lothar Metzl, "The Ideological Struggle: A Case of Soviet Linkage," *Orbis* 27 (Summer 1973): 373.

15. The review conference discussed all aspects of the Final Act, but it is clear from some of the documentation that most of the discussion focused on ideologically sensitive questions, namely, human rights, communication, and liberalizing Western access to East Europe. See U.S., Department of State, "The Belgrade Followup Meeting to the Conference on Security and Cooperation in Europe, October 4, 1977–March 9, 1978," Special Report No. 43, June 1978.

16. Text in *International Legal Materials* 11 (July 1972): 756-60.

17. Quoted in Daniel S. Papp, "National Liberation During Détente: The Soviet Outlook," *International Journal* 32 (Winter 1976-1977): 95.

18. At the Moscow celebration of the 60th anniversary of the Bolshevik Revolution, Enrico Berlinguer claimed that his party believed in the historic, universal precepts of democracy, in the non-ideological character of the state, in the coexistence of different political parties, and pluralism in society, culture and ideology. The Russians would not permit Senor Carillo to address the meeting. Although facing considerable opposition internally, the French communist party still adheres to its Leninist and pro-Soviet tradition.

19. The press has speculated about connections between Italy's Red Brigades and Czechoslovakian financial and possibly armed support. At the time of writing no evidence has been published.

20. Other factors in the worsening Soviet-American relations were of course involved. The presidential transition in 1976 was one.

Globalism vs. Localism: National Security Perceptions in American Foreign Policy

Abraham Ben-Zvi

Introduction

The ongoing debate over the premises from which were derived a number of critical decisions in American foreign policy has been permeated with dichotomic concepts and interpretations. Concentrating on several emotion-laden issues such as the outbreak of the Pacific War, the origins of the cold war and the roots of American intervention in Vietnam, a large number of scholars have produced a voluminous, highly polemic literature on the subject. In many of the analyses, the tendency has been to view American diplomacy as either "realistic and self-interested to the point of rapaciousness," or "naive, overly idealistic, and moralistic."[1]

Alongside the welter of simplistic, one-dimensional explanations, another group of scholars has sought a more integrated, multifaceted interpretation of U.S. foreign policy and of the mechanism of human behavior in times of crisis and ambiguity. For example, although Gaddis's comprehensive account of the U.S. and the origins of the cold war is essentially a non-revisionist analysis, it does incorporate various "radical" themes and concepts into a multidimensional explanatory design.[2] Similarly, according to a recent inquiry into the dynamics of decision-making processes in crisis,[3] it has been implied that U.S. foreign policy is seldom shaped by a single factor or trend. Rather, it has been the outcome of a constant competition between two distinctive types of political actors who differ widely in their basic perceptions of world politics in general and of the origins and the nature of the crises confronting them in particular. Snyder and Diesing label these divergent types: the "hard-liner" and the "soft-liner" decision-makers. According to their analysis, the hard-liner tends to perceive the relations among nations as fundamentally conflictual: "nations, particularly adversary nations, are engaged in a virtually Hobbesian pursuit of power." Consequently, he is acutely sensitive "to power-strategic considerations, to the potential aggressiveness of other states, and to the need to preserve or improve the power and security position of his own state." Committed to the notion that the opponent is pursuing virtually unlimited expansionist objectives (and can only be contained through unadulterated coercion), this type of political actor usually advocates utmost firmness and irreconcilability in crisis situations as the optimal way of deterring and restraining adversary statesmen.[4]

By comparison, the soft-liner's overall perspective towards international affairs stresses harmony rather than conflict. Perceiving the opponent's long-run objectives as limited and specific, he believes that conciliatory gestures are likely "to give rise to mutual efforts to compromise," whereas harsh, coercive measures can only elicit retaliatory, recalcitrant behavior on the part of the adversary. Convinced, unlike the hard-liner, that the opposing camp is always a heterogeneous entity, the soft-liner is confident that, if implemented, his preferred strategy of conciliation will strengthen the moderate faction in the rival state and thus pave the way toward accommodation. Thus, perceiving the opponent as a differentiated unit whose enmity is transient and remediable, the moderate decision-maker differs sharply from the hard-liner, whose intransigent behavior in crisis situations derives from the belief that conflict is perpetual and animosities are permanent.[5] To be sure, Snyder and Diesing are fully aware that basic images and beliefs do not always have short-term, direct behavioral ramifications. They maintain that although the policy-maker's fundamental beliefs rarely change significantly within the confines of a specific conflict situation, his immediate perception of the adversary's behavior may occasionally be decoupled from his general image of the opponent's operational code and long-range objectives. They argue that as a given situation unfolds, the "rational bargainer" may react increasingly to the immediate conflict pattern and less to his basic perceptions, which gradually subside into the background. The "irrational bargainer," on the other hand, is characterized by a rigid belief system that always dominates his behavior.[6]

Seeking to proceed beyond the level of the incessant quarrels over who is to blame for a particular national catastrophe, these and other recently published studies indeed succeed in developing a coherent conceptual framework for the analysis of decision-making processes in crisis situations. And although they do not necessarily concentrate exclusively on American statesmen and diplomats, their analytical categories help replace some of the crude interpretations that abound in the literature surveying American diplomatic history. However, for all this theoretical innovativeness and tendency to analyze pertinent issues and decisions in American foreign policy in a comprehensive, multidimensional fashion, there still remains a question as to the *precise* roots of both the recalcitrant and the conciliatory patterns of behavior in specific conflict situations. The intense rivalry between these divergent types of decision-makers is a recurrent characteristic of many a crisis, yet it is not entirely clear where the divisions originate. Do they indeed derive from general, incompatible attitudes to human nature and the essence of social life, or from more specific perceptions of the contemporary international system?

Theoretical Framework: Presentation

In order to better elucidate this question and further differentiate between the factors determining intransigent and moderate attitudes in a number of crisis situations, this analysis concentrates on two distinct patterns by which the concept of "national security" has been referred to and defined by several high-ranking American decision-makers since the outbreak of World War Two. It is argued that while a number of policy-makers who advocated dichotomic policies in certain bargaining situations did hold several components of their belief systems in common, they nonetheless differed widely in their respective definitions of the bounds of American national interests. Indeed, incompatible national security perceptions occasionally overshadowed initial perceptual congruity, thus leading political actors to support irreconcilable postures in specific conflict episodes.

These two pervasive conceptions of that "vital interest" the U.S. was called upon to maintain and defend, which were the source of divergent policy recommendations, may be termed (a) the globalist-realist conception, and (b) the localist-realist (or nationalist-pragmatist) conception.

The category of globalism-realism is predicated on an all-inclusive definition of the parameters of American national security. According to this concept, virtually every development in the world is perceived as potentially crucial. Convinced that events halfway around the globe have an automatic, direct impact on America's core interests, globalist-realists decision-makers are predisposed to view any adverse turn of events anywhere as endangering the United States.[7] Consequently, desirable foreign policy goals are translated into issues of national survival, and the range of threats becomes limitless. Believing that international crises are seldom isolated phenomena but are merely elements within a wider context, namely, the worldwide effort (initiated by the forces of fascism or "international communism") to disrupt the global balance of power and thereby to threaten the security of the U.S., the globalist-realists underscore the need to stand firm and resist any attempt at encroachment, whatever its origin or location. This proclivity "to translate local situations into the starkest global terms" and to assimilate local occurrences into universal frameworks and patterns (by definition generalized and undifferentiated) has repeatedly led the globalist-realists to presume any opponent to be an inherently aggressive, expansionist entity and an integral part of the unfolding conspiracy to threaten America's security. Committed to a global design to challenge the existing status quo, the adversary could therefore be restrained only by a demonstration of American resoluteness.[8]

This globalist-realist insistence on the broad parameters of national security precluded any attempt to analyze local crises on their own merits. Perceived as but one facet of a larger pattern whose significance lay beyond the regional boundaries within which it unfolded, the local event was *a priori* stripped of whatever particular characteristics it may have possessed.

As has already been implied, the distinction between globalist-realist and localist-realist decision-makers has not necessarily derived from dichotomic world views. Indeed, most localist-realists consistently approach the international arena in terms of power considerations rather than moral or ideological premises. Nor are they motivated by visions of harmony and cooperation that might have obscured the sources of cleavage and tension among nations. Far from being hopelessly naive or optimistic, this group of political actors is acutely aware of the dangers of encroachment posed by ambitious, aggressive adversaries. However, unlike the propensity of the globalist-realists to incorporate any local disturbance into a worldwide, highly threatening complex, the localist-realists tend to focus on the regional parameters and intrinsic characteristics of unfolding crisis situations. Thus, while the globalist-realists are predisposed to see any conflict situation as inherently threatening, the localist-realists defer judgment until their analysis of the event in question has firmly established a direct link between that crisis and the immediate physical security and vital interests of the U.S. Committed to a narrow concept of "self-defense," they assert that the role of the United States in the world "should be primarily an expression of its objective position (size, wealth) and no more, and that there are severe limits to what even the most powerful nation can and should expect to accomplish."[9] In other words, while the globalist-realists tend to perceive American national security as an all-inclusive, limitless concept, the localist-realists advocate a "limitationist position," which is predicated on the notion that only those crises that pose an immediate threat to a narrowly defined cluster of vital interests should motivate the U.S. to act vigorously and resolutely.[10]

Given this "limitationist approach" and reluctance to automatically apply to the local theater certain preconceived concepts and interpretations, it is clear why there have been unbridgeable gaps between the policies promulgated by the globalist-realists and the postures advocated by the localist-realists. Despite the occasional similarity between the two in certain basic images of the world, the incompatibility of national security perceptions resulted, in a number of cases — including the Far Eastern crisis of 1941, the Korean crisis and the Vietnam War — in fundamentally different policy recommendations. It is to the analysis of these crises that we now turn.

Theoretical Framework: Applications

The U.S. and the Far Eastern Crisis, 1941
American policy towards Japan during the months preceding the Pearl Harbor attack was not formulated by a single cohesive group of decision-makers; it was rather the outcome of competition between two divergent groups enjoying varying degrees of power and which adhered to widely different conceptions of national security. However, one group appears to have played a dominant role during most of the "decision games" prior to the outbreak of the Pacific War. This group, the globalist-realists, included Secretary of War (from July 1940) Henry L. Stimson, Secretary of the Treasury Henry Morgenthau, Jr., and Stanley K. Hornbeck, political adviser to the State Department.[11]

These men perceived American national interests in the Far East as only one facet of a broader problem: the worldwide effort of Germany, Italy and Japan to disrupt the global balance of power and thereby threaten the security of the United States. This effort demanded American opposition in close cooperation with Britain, whose survival as a nation and empire was considered essential to the preservation of the European and Pacific balance of power. Indeed, the various political and military moves initiated by Japan, particularly after 1937, coupled with political developments in Europe and the German victories of 1939-40, led Stimson and Morgenthau to believe that a link did exist between concurrent developments in Europe and Asia. This belief was reinforced by the conclusion of the Tripartite Pact between Germany, Italy and Japan in September 1940, enabling those nations to collectively menace world peace.[12]

As the 1930s approached their end, it became clearer to Stimson, Morgenthau and Hornbeck that the East Asian crisis was not an isolated phenomenon, but part of a developing world crisis. They were convinced too that the survival of England and the British Empire was essential to forestall the frightening vision of the United States' encirclement by a formidable combination of hostile forces.

Since Japan was perceived by the globalist-realists as an integral part of the coalition seeking to "challenge the democracies and conquer the world," the attributes that characterized the behavior of all forces of change were applied to her. Japan was therefore viewed as an inherently aggressive power whose "diplomatic record was that of a highway robber."[13] Given this image of Japan, it is hardly surprising that the globalist-realists advocated a firm, uncompromising policy line towards her. Thus they strongly supported the imposition of comprehensive economic sanctions as the best means of deterring Japan and reducing the threat of a Pacific confrontation.

Indeed, the policy advocated by this group in 1940 and 1941 was based on the conviction that the imposition of sanctions such as a complete embargo on pretroleum and scrap iron would constitute the most effective deterrent measure available to the United States. They assumed that Japan, impressed by the United States' firm stance, would yield to pressure and adopt a much more moderate and conciliatory policy.

It is thus evident that the irreconcilable posture advocated so vehemently by Stimson, Morgenthau and Hornbeck was *not* the outcome of pre-existing belligerent attitudes and drives, but a single manifestation of a cluster of globalist-realist beliefs that revolved around the necessity to restore the balance of power in the Pacific as well as the Atlantic.

The group of decision-makers who sought in vain to prevent at least some of the drastic economic sanctions advocated by the globalist-realists did not adhere to a harmonious world view that might have led them to minimize the sources and severity of the Far Eastern crisis. Including President Roosevelt (who eventually yielded to the pressures exerted by the globalist-realists) and America's ambassador to Japan Joseph Grew, as well as a number of army and navy officials, this faction of localist-realists had no doubts as to the gravity and complexity of the unfolding crisis in the Pacific. For example, perceiving Japan as an "unstable, aggressive country with long-range plans to establish a vast empire and with no compunctions against defying the desire of the world for peace and disarmament,"[14] the president consistently demonstrated a deep hostility towards the Japanese. Notwithstanding these basic perceptions, it is clear that they did not affect the president's actual behavior during most of the period preceding the Pearl Harbor attack.

A cluster of localist-realist considerations overshadowed Roosevelt's initial stereotyped vision of the Japanese as "the Prussians of the East, and just as drunk with their dreams of domination," leading him to pursue a flexible, pragmatic policy in the Far East.

In essence, President Roosevelt and the rest of the localist-realists tended to perceive American-Japanese relations in 1940 and 1941 within the framework of considerations relating to the maintenance and protection of American national interests. Because they were preoccupied with the immediate maintenance and protection of those interests, the localist-realists were aware of "the tremendous burdens which a two-ocean war would impose."[15] They viewed the repercussions likely to result from an Axis victory in Europe as far more dangerous to the security of the United States than those resulting from further Japanese expansion in Southeast Asia. Thus Roosevelt and Grew tended to recommend a flexible, cautious policy towards Japan, to the extent that they expressed a willingness to conclude a "truce" or a *modus vivendi* agreement with the Japanese in order to avoid a diversion of American military power to the Far East. In this stand they differed sharply from the globalist-realists, who were determined to oppose any nation that in their view participated in the worldwide effort to disrupt the global balance of power.[16]

Similarly, the army's perspective and frame of reference were focused on the impact that political and military developments, wherever they might occur, might have on the immediate security and vital interests of the United States.

Thus, once a number of army officials, as well as Ambassador Grew, arrived at the conclusion that a German victory over Britain (followed by a German victory over Russia) would constitute a threat to the United States that would far outweigh any danger resulting from Japanese expansion, then the implications for the Pacific were clear. They sought to pursue a defensive strategy which, coupled with a restrained policy towards Japan, would enable the United States to concentrate its forces in the Atlantic.

Furthermore, whereas the globalist-realists regarded both Germany and Japan as the major initiators of the global effort to menace world peace, the president and the rest of the localist-realists believed that Japan's policies and military maneuvers in 1940 and 1941 were purely opportunistic.[17] Indeed, the localist-realists projected a picture of Japan's relations with its Axis allies that was much more dynamic, complicated and open to change than the one adhered to by Morgenthau, Stimson and Hornbeck, whose image of Japan was undifferentiated and inseparable from that of its Axis partners. As a result, members of the group, who clearly recognized the various factors that strained Japanese-German relations, tended to recommend certain broad policies designed to deepen Japanese-German cleavages.

However, President Roosevelt's preoccupation with many other issues, such as developments in the European war, prevented him from systematically and forcefully directing U.S. policy towards Japan. In addition, the president was continuously subjected to pressures exerted not only by several members of the cabinet, but also by a number of prominent public figures, various organizations and pressure groups, public opinion leaders, as well as several members of his own family, who urged him to harden American policy towards Japan. Toward the end of 1941, these pressures proved to be effective, as Roosevelt gradually abandoned his initial and moderate recommendations.[18] Despite the president's awareness of the possible repercussions of economic sanctions, American policy was characterized by increasing inflexibility.

Thus, the policy actually implemented by the U.S. in the Pacific was an intransigent one, ignoring the fluctuations and shifting dynamics that characterized the Japanese domestic scene. The globalist-realists remained totally unresponsive to the groups and factions in Japan that opposed war with the United States, and felt that conciliatory American moves (such as the relaxation of the embargo imposed on shipments of scrap iron, oil, and other materials to Japan) would not strengthen those groups' relative position vis-à-vis their powerful opponents in Tokyo who argued that war with the United States was inevitable.

Clinging to their fixed national security images, Stimson and Morgenthau did not react to and take advantage of tensions among the Axis powers. Despite the real conflicts that shadowed the relations among the members of the Tripartite Pact, these officials persisted in holding on to a vision of unity and harmony among the three aggressor powers cooperating in their united effort to conquer the world.

The tendency of the globalist-realists to perceive American-Japanese relations during 1940 and 1941 as one local element within a defined global conflict even led them to transplant such terms as "appeasement" and "Eastern

Munich" from the European context into the Far East.[19] It further led them to misunderstand certain occurrences and specific developments that took place in 1941 on the American-Japanese scene, such as the Japanese proposal for a summit meeting between Premier Konoye and President Roosevelt.

The gap between the hard-line posture advocated by the globalist-realists and the moderate, pragmatic policy promulgated by the localist-realists did not originate in any dichotomic systems of belief in incompatible images of the Japanese opponent. Motivated by divergent national security considerations, members of the administration, who in some cases held similar images of Japan, supported (with varying degrees of consistency and determination) widely different policy lines in the Pacific.

In the final analysis, the coercive means chosen by the dominant decision-makers, the globalist-realists, to achieve their objective of containing Japan contributed to the outbreak of the Pacific War. Thinking chiefly in terms of the military capabilities of Japan vis-à-vis the United States, Stimson, Morgenthau and Hornbeck failed to recognize the danger of war inherent in their hard-line diplomacy.

Ignorance of the psychology of the Japanese people (and especially of the middle-echelon officers) prevented them from perceiving the Japanese predisposition to give priority at crucial moments to nationalistic, ideological and psychological factors over purely military considerations, and consequently to make high-risk decisions.

Thus the globalist-realists remained oblivious to the spate of messages sent by Ambassador Grew on the eve of Pearl Harbor, as well as to the numerous memoranda submitted by a number of army officers, such as General Lee Gerow, warning against the assumption that continued economic sanctions would automatically force Japan into adopting a restrained policy towards the U.S.

Despite these mounting reliable warnings, the globalist-realists remained, almost to the very end, committed to their belief that Japan would not dare to directly challenge the U.S. in the Pacific.[20] Thus, when John Emmerson (a junior embassy officer in Tokyo) warned the State Department that Japan might launch an attack out of sheer desperation, he was rebuked by Hornbeck who replied: "Tell me of one case in history when a nation went to war out of desperation."[21]

The U.S. and the Korean War

The surprising outbreak of the Korean War in June 1950 momentarily united

Washington's high-policy elite. Faced with the northern aggression, *all* members of the Truman administration were convinced that military steps must be taken by the U.S. in order to repel that offensive and restore the status quo. However, although in agreement with regard to the measures called for to cope successfully with the Korean challenge, several policy-makers differed from one another in their perceptions of the exact origins and significance of the Korean War. Thus behind the initial facade of unanimity in the administration, two divergent interpretations existed of the roots and possible repercussions of the Korean invasion. The dominant view was the globalist-realist one, which maintained that Korea was part of the systematic attempt, initiated by the forces of "international communism," to disrupt the global balance of power and thereby to "constantly threaten, in both Europe and Asia . . . world peace."[22] According to this perception, Korea was merely one front, one aspect "of the global challenge by the Soviet Union to the postwar international system."[23] Convinced that "Communism was acting in Korea just as Hitler, Mussolini, and the Japanese had acted ten, fifteen and twenty years earlier,"[24] President Truman and Secretary of State Dean Acheson had little doubt that "if South Korea was allowed to fall, Communist leaders would be emboldened to override nations closer to our shores."[25] This perception of the crisis "as a first step in a new campaign of conquest" which, if allowed to go unchallenged, threatened to embroil the U.S. in "a third world war,"[26] *a priori* dictated certain derivative policy lines towards Korea. Exposing the inadequacy and irrelevance of certain preconceptions formally adhered to on the eve of war (e.g., that South Korea had no strategic significance for the global patterns of American security), the outbreak of hostilities along the 38th parallel led the globalist-realists to adopt a stronger posture of containment. In this respect, the events of June 1950 provided an impetus for accelerating the ongoing process of re-evaluating the U.S. global strategy in the face of the intensification of the cold war in Europe and the communist victory in China.[27]

By virtue of its dramatic impact, the sudden invasion served as a "trigger" convincing the president and his chief foreign policy advisers of the need to act swiftly and decisively in order to contain the onslaught and thus "deter new actions in other portions of the world."[28]

The decision to resist the northern invasion was supported by the entire policy-making machinery. However, while they endorsed the military steps eventually implemented in order to repel the invasion, a group of localist-realist officials differed from the globalist-realists in their basic interpretation of the origins and significance of the Korean crisis to American security. Subdued and latent as these differences remained throughout the initial phase of the war, they surfaced with vehemence once the possibility of expanding the war to the north had become a viable political option in the wake of MacArthur's spectacular landing at Inchon.

In essence, members of the localist-realist faction, and primarily George Kennan (who headed the State Department's Policy Planning Staff during the period immediately following the outbreak of war), challenged the prevailing globalist-realist assumption that the North Korean attack constituted "merely the first move in some 'grand design' . . . on the part of the Soviet leaders to extend their power to other parts of the world by the use of force."[29] Although highly suspicious in general as to Soviet intentions and *ultimate* cold war objectives, the localist-realists argued that the immediate origins of the Korean crisis must be sought within the isolated parameters of the Far East.

Specifically, Kennan and Charles Bohlen surmised that several American statements and decisions, and above all "our recent decision to proceed at once with the negotiations of a separate peace treaty settlement with Japan, to which the Russians would not be a party, and to accompany that settlement with the indefinite retention of American garrisons and military facilities on Japanese soil,"[30] may well have prompted the Soviets to initiate the move against the south. Seeking to impress Japan and deter her from embarking on an anti-communist course, the Soviet Union, according to the localist-realist interpretation, planned the military offensive against a nation neighboring Japan, which was closely associated with the U.S., thus hoping to challenge American credibility in the Pacific.[31]

Evidently, while Kennan and Bohlen, like the globalist-realists, believed that the Soviet Union was deeply involved in North Korea's preparations for war, they analyzed the Korean invasion in terms of Soviet concerns and fears in the face of the adverse developments anticipated on the Japanese front, rather than as a manifestation of the inherent "demonic and monstrous"[32] communist drive for world domination.

For all their sensitivity to the regional context and, above all, to the acute perception of threat that permeated Soviet behavior given the U.S. policy towards Japan, the localist-realists' initial policy recommendations did not differ from those supported by the globalist-realists. Convinced that a vigorous American reaction was necessary in order to encourage Japan to further consolidate relations with the West, Kennan and Bohlen strongly argued for the mobilization of American troops "to repel this attack and to expel the North Korean forces from the southern half of the peninsula."[33]

However, this early intra-governmental consensus quickly evaporated. As soon as it became clear to the localist-realists that the globalist-realists had abandoned the original war aim of restoring the status quo in Korea and had embarked, after MacArthur's victories in August, on a new strategy designed to "liberate North Korea," the gap between the two approaches became fully manifest.

As has already been noted, that gap did not originate in incompatible world views. As an experienced observer and analyst of the Soviet Union, Kennan frequently emphasized fundamental Soviet hostility towards the West as well as its inherent expansionist drives. The United States, Kennan pointed out, was confronted with "a political force committed fanatically to the belief that with [the] U.S. there can be no permanent *modus vivendi,* that it is desirable and necessary that the internal harmony of our society be broken, if Soviet power is to be secure."[34] "Soviet pressures against the free institutions of the western world," he concluded in his famous "X" article, is "something that can be contained by the adroit and vigilant application of counterforce. . . ."[35] Committed as he was to the *principle* of containment, Kennan, unlike the globalist-realists, continuously underscored the need to differentiate among various regions and crisis situations in terms of their relative importance to American security and vital interests. Convinced that the U.S. had to define the main task of containment as "one of seeing to it that none of the regions (except the Soviet Union) where the sources of modern military strength could be produced in quantity fell under Communist control," Kennan stressed the need to "firmly contain Soviet inherent expansionist tendencies only as they affected such vital areas as "the United Kingdom, the Rhine valley with adjacent industrial areas... and Japan."[36]

This "limitationist" approach to the parameters of American national security, which was predicated upon the premise that "we are not necessarily always against the expansion of Communism, and certainly not always against it to the same degree in every area," was clearly evident throughout the summer of 1950. Believing that the U.S. should confine its military efforts to the south of Korea, Kennan repeatedly warned against "an emotional anticommunist fervor" which "would ignore the value to ourselves of a possible balance between the existing forces on the Asiatic continent, [and] would force everyone to declare himself either for us or against us. . . ."[37] Thus once the U.S. had signalled its determination to resist "by force of arms" the North Korean incursion, the localist-realists saw no need to persist in the military drive beyond the former demarcation line along the 38th parallel. Such a posture, Kennan and Bohlen predicted, could "prod China and/or the Soviet Union into a war."[38]

This determined effort on the part of the localist-realists to prevent an expansion of the Korean War proved abortive. Ignoring numerous warnings that the drive to occupy the north and approach the Chinese border along the Yalu River would lead to a full-scale Chinese intervention, the globalist-realists remained committed to their notion that the march to the Yalu would restrain China. Hoping to create "situations of strength" that would help implement effectively the global posture of containment, Truman and Acheson ignored the fact that the Chinese communists were more highly motivated to prevent American troops from occupying North Korea than U.S. leaders were to carry out the occupation against Chinese opposition. Overlooking the possibility that the enemy might not follow a similar train of thought, they failed to cross the conceptual boundaries that separated them from their opponent.

Once again, then, one is faced with an unbridgeable gap in the policy recommendations, derived from incompatible national security perceptions. On the one hand, the globalist-realists, who integrated the Korean crisis into their dichotomic vision of the world, viewed American security as directly threatened by the northern onslaught. On the other hand, the localist-realists, concentrating on the specific regional circumstances, were capable of recognizing "the finer distinctions of the psychology of our adversaries."[39] The global perspective led Truman and Acheson to generalize and form "historical lessons" in an extremely simplistic and superficial manner; the localist-realists fully appreciated the many differences that separated past events from the occurrences of 1950.

Furthermore, while the globalist-realists adhered to a vision of unity and harmony within the communist camp, maintaining that the "Chinese Communists were Russians satellites,"[40] the localist-realists were acutely sensitive to the tensions and misunderstandings that clouded relations between the Soviet Union and communist China. Consequently they advocated a pragmatic, conciliatory posture towards China, in the hope of "splitting the Chinese Communists from the Russians on issues of real importance."[41]

No such posture was implemented by the U.S. during the early phases of the Korean War. Clinging to the notion that "the Soviet Union was behind every one of the Chinese and North Korean moves and that we had to think of all that happened in Korea as world matters,"[42] U.S. policy-makers refused to reconsider the premises of their strategy in Korea. Ultimately, it became clear that the coercive hard-line strategy pursued in Korea in the summer of 1950 helped improve the heretofore strained relations between the Soviet Union and China, thus transforming the vision of a cohesive, united opponent into a reality.

The U.S. and the Vietnam War

As in the previous cases, an analysis of the decision-making process with regard to Vietnam between 1964-65 indicates that the two major factions competing for power did not differ from each other in their respective images of the world. While all the policy-makers involved perceived the crises of their era in terms of certain realistic categories and concepts, they differed widely in their definitions of the bounds of American national interests. Furthermore, as in the events of 1941 and 1950, the intra-governmental debate between the two groups, the globalist-realists and the localist-realists, was resolved in favor of the more powerful globalist faction. And although not all the globalist-realists supported the posture of gradual escalation in Vietnam with the same degree of conviction, they were all motivated by the same set of considerations.

Thus beyond certain differences in nuance and emphasis, all the globalist-realists viewed the Vietnam War as one local "battlefront" fully integrated into the global patterns of the cold war. Perceiving Vietnam as one manifestation of the worldwide communist attempt to disrupt the balance of power and thus threaten American national security, the globalist-realists applied to the Far Eastern theater "the lessons of the thirties" that stressed the need for utmost firmness as the most appropriate means for deterring any aggressor.[43]

Like President Truman during the Korean crisis, President Johnson repeatedly elaborated on the global parameters of American national security: "The challenge that we face in Southeast Asia today is the same challenge that we have faced with courage and that we have met with strength in Greece and Turkey, in Berlin and Korea, in Lebanon and Cuba. . . . If we ran out on Southeast Asia, *I could see trouble ahead in every part of the globe — not just in Asia but in the Middle East and in Europe, in Africa and in Latin America.* I was convinced that our retreat from this challenge would open the path to World War III."[44]

Thinking in global terms, the president and the rest of the globalist-realists were convinced that the Vietnam conflict had enormous implications "for the security of the United States and the free world."[45] Believing that the forces of revision and totalitarianism "have chosen to make South Vietnam the test case for their particular version of the so-called 'wars of national liberation'," they assumed that a communist success in the south would lead "to the same kind of aggression in other parts of the world wherever the existing governments are weak and the social structures fragmented."[46]

As in the Far Eastern crisis of 1941 and the Korean crisis of 1950, the global framework into which Vietnam was integrated obscured the cleavages and divisions that strained relations within the adversary camp. Insensitive to the intense rivalry and widening split between the Soviet Union and communist China, the globalist-realists clung to their vision of a hostile, coordinated power bloc bent on world conquest. Indeed, as the president's advisers appraised the world situation in 1965, the Soviets and the Chinese still seemed to be in full pursuit of bellicose, expansionist policies across the globe, and still quite ready and able to join in the support and manipulation of proxies for purposes inimical of those of the U.S.[47] On those occasions when the globalist-realists were faced with ironclad data indicating that relations between the Soviet Union and China were charged with tension, they tended to underestimate the intensity and severity of the cleavage, maintaining that these divisions reflected nothing more than disagreement over tactics.

As in the previous cases analyzed, the global perspective adhered to by such policy-makers as President Johnson, Secretaries Rusk and McNamara, and advisers McGeorge Bundy and Walt Rostow led them to support — with varying degrees of determination — hard-line positions at various phases of the Vietnam War. In 1964 and 1965, this preference for irreconcilability was manifested in connection with the "Rolling Thunder" operation. While members of the globalist-realist group differed considerably in their estimates of the intensity of the bombing effort that would "signal to the Communist enemy the firmness of U.S. resolve" and consequently would "influence Hanoi's will to continue its aggression,"[48] they all shared the expectation that the strategy of air strikes against the north would strengthen confidence and cohesion in the south, thus providing the U.S. with "substantial bargaining leverage."[49]

It is indeed clear that all the globalist-realists assumed that the leaders of North Vietnam would not risk the destruction of the industrial plant they possessed. Bound to a seemingly national, albeit ethnocentric, model of decision, they failed to recognize the asymmetry of motivation that existed between the parties to the conflict. Thus they could not conceive that their northern opponent, while militarily weaker, might be willing to take greater risks and accept greater costs than expected. And indeed, in retrospectively appraising the success of the "Rolling Thunder" operation, analysts of the

CIA and DIA (Defense Intelligence Agency) recognized that there was no sign that bombing the north, either on its own or in combination with other U.S. actions, had brought about any greater readiness to settle on any terms other than Hanoi's.[50]

Thus in the same way that Stimson, Morgenthau and Hornbeck did not believe that their punitive policy towards Japan could provoke her to retaliate and directly challenge the U.S. in the Pacific, and in the same way that Truman and Acheson could not grasp the prospects of China's intervention in Korea, so the globalist-realist in 1964-65 failed to appreciate that a direct, frontal attack on a society could strengthen the social fabric of that nation, increase popular support for the existing government, and enhance the determination of both the leadership and the populace to fight back.[51]

As in the cases of Pearl Harbor and Korea, the dominant decision-makers formulating American policy in Vietnam in 1964-65 were the globalist-realists. And while localist-realist members of the administration such as Undersecretary of State George Ball consistently criticized the posture pursued by the U.S. in Southeast Asia, they were in no position to modify American diplomacy and strategy.

In analyzing Vietnam, Ball's frame of reference was similar to that of Grew and Kennan. Concentrating on the local and regional dimensions of the conflict as it unfolded rather than on the global parameters of the cold war, Ball was capable of distinguishing between South Vietnam and Western Europe in terms of their relative importance to American security. Maintaining that "our commitment to the South Vietnamese people is of a wholly different order from our major commitments . . . to Berlin [and] to NATO," he urged the administration to "begin a process of differentiation." Highly critical of the prevailing tendency to "give the South Vietnamese struggle an exaggerated and symbolic significance,"[52] Ball argued that "the conflict in South Vietnam [was] essentially a civil war within that country" which as such was devoid of any cold war significance. Thus viewed "as a guerrilla war . . . between Asians," the Vietnam War was only a distracting factor preoccupying the U.S. at the expense of other responsibilities in areas crucial to American security. While such globalist-realists as Secretary Rusk claimed that the U.S. could not abandon South Vietnam "without disaster to peace and to our interests throughout the world,"[53] Undersecretary Ball was confident that by extricating itself or at the very least reducing its "defense perimeters in South Vietnam to accord with the capabilities of limited U.S. deployment," the U.S. could concentrate its resources and attention on "such vital points as

Berlin."[54] Fearing that a sustained bombing program could stiffen Hanoi's determination to continue the war, Ball warned that "the bombing of the North cannot win the war, only enlarge it."[55] As an alternative to the bombing program, Ball advocated a moderate, flexible approach which would seek "a compromise settlement" in Vietnam.[56] Criticizing, as Grew did twenty-five years earlier, American inflexible attitudes and negotiating tactics, Ball recommended: "Now is the time to start some serious diplomatic feelers looking towards a solution based on some application of a self-determination principle. . . . If the initial feelers lead to further secret talks, we can inject the concept of self-determination that would permit the Viet Cong some hope of achieving some of their political objectives through local elections or some other service."[57]

No such feelers were forthcoming in 1965. For all his experience and merits as a veteran diplomat and statesman, Ball — like Grew and Kennan before him — was completely unsuccessful in his plea for a "compromise solution" in Vietnam. Rivetted to their preconceptions, the globalist-realists continued to believe that only "a show of force could convince Hanoi to come to the bargaining table," and that "no small power could possibly resist America's sophisticated technology and enormous military strength."[58]

Conclusion

The foregoing analysis of American attitudes in three crises in terms of two incompatible national security conceptions has not professed to be illustrative of all the prevalent patterns of crisis behavior in U.S. foreign policy. For example, although in all the cases discussed, ideological and moral considerations either merged with or were outweighed by realistic notions, there is no doubt that they were instrumental in the shaping of a welter of foreign policy decisions of great magnitude in the history of American diplomacy. Furthermore, at least one category of acute international crisis, namely, direct superpower confrontation, by definition precludes any distinction between the global and the local patterns of realistic perceptions. Confined mainly to the periphery or the "gray areas" of the contemporary international system, this typology of U.S. decision-makers should be viewed as a tentative attempt to underscore the role of national security concepts in determining actual policy recommendations in specific bargaining situations. It is therefore hoped that the distinction drawn above between two widely different forms of political realism will lead to further conceptualization and differentiation of the problem of perception and action, and will thus pave the way toward a better understanding of human behavior in times of crisis and ambiguity.

Notes

1. Gerald A. Combs, *Nationalist, Realist, and Radical: Three Views of American Diplomacy* (New York, 1972), pp. 3, 25.

2. John Lewis Gaddis, *The United States and the Origins of the Cold War 1941-1947* (New York, 1972). For another comprehensive and insightful analysis see Alexander L. George and Richard Smoke, *Deterrence in American Foreign Policy* (New York, 1974).

3. Glenn H. Snyder and Paul Diesing, *Conflict Among Nations* (Princeton, 1978).

4. Ibid., pp. 297-299. See also Charles Lockhart, "Problems in the Management and Resolution of International Conflicts," *World Politics* 29 (1977): 381.

5. Snyder and Diesing, *Conflict Among Nations,* pp. 298-299; and Lockhart, "Problems in the Management of Conflicts," p. 382. See also, in this connection, Jervis's analysis in Robert Jervis, *Perception and Misperception in International Relations* (Princeton, 1976), pp. 58-113.

6. Snyder and Diesing, *Conflict Among Nations,* pp. 333-339.

7. James Forrestal, cited in Daniel Yergin, *Shattered Peace: The Origins of the Cold War and the National Security State* (Boston, 1977), p. 196. See also Klaus E. Knorr, "Threat Perception," in idem, ed., *Historical Dimensions of National Security Problems* (Lawrence, Kansas, 1976), p. 93.

8. Ibid. See also Wolfgang Friedman, "Interventionism, Liberalism, and Power-Politics: The Unfinished Revolution in International Thinking," *Political Science Quarterly* 83 (1968): 174; Seyom Brown, *The Faces of Power: Constancy and Change in United States Foreign Policy from Truman to Johnson* (New York, 1968), pp. 15-27, 37-42; and Bernard Brodie, *War and Politics* (New York, 1973), pp. 346-349.

9. Alan Dowty, "Observations on the American Conception of International Relations," paper prepared for the Adlai Stevenson Institute Meeting of Fellows, November 1971, pp. 11-12. See also Abraham Ben-Zvi, "American Preconceptions and Policies Toward Japan, 1940-1941: A Case Study in Misperception," *International Studies Quarterly* 19 (1975): 235.

10. Dowty, "Observations on the American Conception," p. 12.

11. Ben-Zvi, "American Preconceptions and Policies," pp. 231-233.

12. Ibid. See also: Akira Iriye, *Across the Pacific: An Inner History of American-Asian Relations* (New York, 1967), p. 203; and Knorr, "Threat Perception", p. 93.

13. Henry Morgenthau, Jr., memorandum to President Roosevelt, 1938, cited in Ben-Zvi, "American Preconceptions and Policies," pp. 235-236.

14. Stephen E. Pelz, *Race to Pearl Harbor* (Cambridge, 1974), p. 75.

15. William L. Neumann, "Ambiguity and Ambivalence in Ideas of National Interest in Asia," in Alexander DeConde, ed., *Isolation and Security* (Durham, North Carolina, 1957), p. 152.

16. Ben-Zvi, "American Preconceptions and Policies," p. 235.

17. U.S. Congress, Joint Committee on the Investigation of the Pearl Harbor Attack, *Pearl Harbor Attack, Hearings* (Washington, D.C., 1946), Vol. XIV, p. 1358.

18. See, for example, Paul W. Schroeder, *The Axis Alliance and Japanese-American Rela-*

tions, 1941 (Ithaca, 1958), pp. 55-57; and William L. Langer and Everett S. Gleason, *The Undeclared War, 1940-1941* (New York, 1953), pp. 697-708.

19. See, in this connection, Stanley Hoffmann, *Gulliver's Troubles, or the Setting of American Foreign Policy* (New York, 1968), p. 135; and Ernest R. May, *"Lessons" of the Past: The Use and Misuse of History in American Foreign Policy* (New York, 1973), *passim.*

20. Roberta Wohlsetter, *Pearl Harbor: Warning and Decision* (Stanford, 1962), pp. 349, 354.

21. Chihiro Hosoya, "Characteristics of the Foreign Policy Decision-Making System in Japan," *World Politics* 26 (1974): 353.

22. Harry S. Truman, *Memoirs*, Vol. II, 1946–1952 (New York, 1965), p. 421.

23. Akira Iriye, *The Cold War in Asia* (Englewood Cliffs, 1974), p. 180.

24. Truman, *Memoirs*, Vol. II, p. 379. See also May, *"Lessons" of the Past*, pp. 80-82; and Glenn D. Paige, *The Korean Decision* (New York, 1968), p. 178.

25. Truman, *Memoirs*, Vol. II, p. 372. See also Dean Acheson, *Present at the Creation* (New York, 1969), pp. 404-405; and David S. McLellan, "Dean Acheson and the Korean War," *Political Science Quarterly* 83 (1968): 16-39, *passim.*

26. Truman, *Memoirs*, Vol. II, p. 379.

27. George and Smoke, *Deterrence in American Foreign Policy*, pp. 146-152; 171-172.

28. Truman, *Memoirs*, Vol. II, p. 386.

29. George F. Kennan, *Memoirs, 1925-1950* (Boston, 1967), p. 497.

30. Kennan, *Memoirs, 1925-1950*, p. 498. See also George and Smoke, *Deterrence in American Foreign Policy*, p. 152.

31. George and Smoke, *Deterrence in American Foreign Policy*, p. 152.

32. Kennan, *Memoirs, 1925-1950*, pp. 497-498.

33. Ibid., p. 486. See also Charles E. Bohlen, *Witness to History, 1929-1969* (New York, 1973), p. 290.

34. Cited in Gaddis, *The United States and the Origins of the Cold War* , p. 303.

35. George F. Kennan ("X"), "The Sources of Soviet Conduct," *Foreign Affairs* 25 (1947): 566-582.

36. John Lewis Gaddis, "Containment: A Reassessment," *Foreign Affairs* 55 (1977): 877.

37. Kennan, *Memoirs, 1925-1950*, p. 495.

38. Bohlen, *Witness to History*, p. 293.

39. Kennan, *Memoirs, 1925-1950*, p. 499.

40. Truman, *Memoirs*, Vol. II, p. 458.

41. Kennan, *Memoirs, 1925-1950*, p. 491.

42. Truman, *Memoirs*, Vol. II, p. 440.

43. May, *"Lessons" of the Past*, p. 101.

44. Lyndon Baines Johnson, *The Vantage Point* (New York, 1971), p. 117 (emphasis added).

45. *The Pentagon Papers: The Defense Department History of United States Decision-Making on Vietnam*, Vol. IV (Boston, 1972), p. 633.

46. Ibid.

47. Townsend Hoopes, *The Limits of Intervention* (New York, 1969), p. 12.

48. *The Pentagon Papers*, Vol. III, p. 220.

49. Ibid.

50. Ibid., Vol. IV, p. 56.

51. Ibid., p. 119.

52. Ibid., p. 610.

53. Ibid., p. 23.

54. Ibid., p. 51.
55. Ibid., p. 52.
56. Ibid.
57. Ibid., pp. 616-617.
58. Doris Kearns, *Lyndon Johnson and the American Dream* (New York, 1976), p. 276.

Presidential Strategies and Character:
The Eisenhower and the Nixon Administrations

Shmuel Sandler

Introduction

One of the outcomes of World War Two and of the cold war was the mobilization of the public and the elites in America in support of the foreign policy advocated by the incumbent president, resulting in unparalleled presidential supremacy over the conduct of foreign affairs. The emergence of a complex and threatening international system promoted the idea that only the president was equipped with the sophisticated means for the effective conduct of foreign policy. On two occasions, however, this process of presidential accumulation of power was threatened: American intervention in Korea and, later, in Vietnam. At both times presidential authority was threatened and the possibility of a restored role for Congress in the conduct of foreign affairs seemed imminent. In the wake of what were perceived as presidential blunders in both areas, two related lines of criticism emerged. One was that the president had abused his powers and dragged the nation into an unnecessary war. The second was the expression of doubt about presidential wisdom in foreign policy-making. While the behavior of Congress and the public in the aftermath of World War One and on the eve of World War Two was regarded as a sign of ignorance, American involvement in Korea and Vietnam indicated that the executive branch too was not immune to mistakes. Consequently, the strengthening of controls over presidential power and the development of an enlarged role for Congress in foreign affairs were deemed healthy for the country and its political system.[1]

It was against this similar background that two presidents entered the White House during two different periods in American contemporary history. Upon assuming office, the Eisenhower and the Nixon administrations were faced with situations in which the unsuccessful execution of foreign policy in a marginal area threatened to inhibit the continuation of the broader framework of American foreign policy established during and after World War Two.

Domestic intolerance of direct American participation in protracted small wars was accompanied by revisionist disapproval of the extent of presidential power. Consequently alongside a strategic framework that would preserve the U.S. global interests, both presidents also adopted definite albeit less explicit domestic strategies designed to restore and ultimately even increase the powers of their office.

In comparing the two presidential strategies we must take into account two factors. The first is the different atmospheres prevailing in 1953 and 1969; the second is the dissimilarity in the characters of the two presidents. Our contention will be that these variations were decisive in influencing the different modes of behavior that each president followed in his domestic strategy, yet despite these differences both tried to advance the supremacy of the executive in foreign affairs.

Before embarking on the analysis of presidential strategies we must identify the various components of the domestic political system. If we take the presidency as the focus of our analysis, there are five major institutions with which the executive branch must interact in the process of foreign policy-making: Congress, competing elites, the news media, the machinery of governmental bureaucracy, and public opinion. The intensity of this interaction and the direction it takes, however, depend on circumstances and on the character of the issues that dominate the political scene. American involvement in Korea and Vietnam restored the confidence of Congress in the establishment of the legislature's power in foreign affairs. Every president must contend with competing elites, but Korea and Vietnam elevated certain elites who challenged the basic principles of both incoming Republican administrations. The news media and the governmental bureaucracy also acquired more power in foreign affairs, particularly during Vietnam. Every president must be concerned with public opinion, but the Eisenhower and the Nixon administrations inherited situations in which the public's attention was more strikingly aroused than at any other time.[2] The behavior of each president vis-à-vis each situation will be analyzed in this essay.

Eisenhower's Presidential Strategy: Ascendancy Through Conciliation

When General Dwight D. Eisenhower took office in 1953, it seemed unlikely that the presidency would continue to accumulate power as it had since the end of World War Two. The legacy of the Korean War, the ascendancy of the right-wing Republican elite that was ideologically opposed to the aggrandizement of the chief executive (even when the White House was occupied by a Republican), and the personal beliefs of the incoming president all seemed to indicate that presidential influence over foreign affairs would be limited to the point it had now reached, and probably even reduced. In reality, however, the presidency under Eisenhower continued to accumulate power. When the next administration came to power it inherited an even stronger institution than the one that had been given the Republicans in 1953.

Two interrelated external factors contributed significantly to Eisenhower's presidential strategy. The cold war atmosphere which had assisted Truman to acquire power for his office became even more intense during the Eisenhower-Dulles years, promoting a crisis atmosphere that justified a strong executive. In addition, the various devices that the Eisenhower administration had adopted in its foreign policy strategy required and also seemed to license the centralization of power in the White House. The United States' ability to carry out a strategy of massive retaliation and its corollaries was based on the assumption that the commander-in-chief could independently regulate the various instruments of American foreign and defense policy.[3]

But there were other forces at work influencing the president's route to supremacy in foreign policy-making, factors too weak to neutralize the external realities or the inherent requirements of the Eisenhower foreign policy, but influential enough to affect the style and the mode of operation of the Eisenhower presidency. The style that emerged may best be described as aggrandizement through conciliation.

Eisenhower's military background and his Whig persuasion gave him great respect for the traditional concept of the separation of powers.[4] As a soldier he strongly upheld loyalty to the constitution and to the institutions governing his country; as a Republican he was "committed to the Whig theory of partnership between President and Congress."[5] These traditional ideas were particularly strong in the Republican Party after it had been out of power for twenty years, during which time the Democrats had increased the power of the executive to an unprecedented level in American history. Having criticized the Democrats on this issue for twenty years, it was inconceivable that the Republicans would change their attitudes swiftly once they took over the White House. Furthermore, the fact that the Republican victory did not bring the "old guard" into the executive branch, while it did become well entrenched in Congress, did not help either to reconcile the tensions between the two branches of government or to moderate the attitudes of the right wing. A certain element of opposition persisted even after the Republican candidate had won the election.[6]

Another aspect in Eisenhower's world outlook pertinent to his behavior in office was his perception and understanding of leadership. Emmet Hughes, one of Eisenhower's advisers, recalled the president's oft-repeated credo: "You do not *lead* by hitting people over the head." Leadership, according to Eisenhower, "is *persuasion* — and *conciliation* — and *education* — and *patience*. That's the only kind of leadership I know — or believe in — or will practice."[7] These remarks were made in relation to Congress, particularly the conservative faction in the legislature, and seemed to indicate that the president, despite his military past, preferred conciliation to confrontation. Perhaps the fact that he had spent most of his life in the military — and this mostly as a staff officer — rather than in political struggles contributed to this attitude. Likewise, his relatively short contest for the presidency and his assumption of office as a national hero may have contributed to his moderation. And the fact that most of his opposition originated within his own party provided a further impediment to public confrontation with Congress.[8]

Eisenhower's presidential strategy should be examined from four aspects: his relations with the "old guard" in the Republican Party, his relations with Congress in general, with the media and in terms of informing the public, and the administration and the execution of foreign policy.

The adoption of the strategy of massive retaliation provided Eisenhower with a framework which, at least on the surface, could be regarded as a victory of the conservative elements within the Republican Party. The emphasis on sea and air power in American defense had always been recommended by conservatives such as Herbert Hoover and Robert Taft. Massive retaliation also suggested a certain element of "disengagement which could be interpreted by the right wing as a denunciation of certain commitments abroad made by the previous administration."[9] Samuel Lubell has defined this strategy as a "slow double turn"; "Eisenhower himself . . . turned somewhat to meet the 'isolationist' viewpoint in the Republican party, while the disillusionists . . . turned somewhat more to meet him."[10] Thus Eisenhower's removal of the Seventh Fleet from the Formosa Straits, the unleashing of Chiang Kai-Shek, and Dulles' firm warnings to Red China were additional gestures towards the "Asia first" wing of the Republican Party.[11] The secretary of state's anti-communist rhetoric and the budgetary and economic concerns of the new president also matched the expectations of Eisenhower's internal opposition.[12]

Finally, Eisenhower refused to intervene in the nomination process of key positions in Congress, leaving most of the positions to be taken by conservative leaders.[13]

However, most indicative of Eisenhower's solicitous treatment of the right wing was his attitude and behavior towards McCarthyism. His first overt move of conciliation came in Milwaukee in 1952 when Eisenhower agreed to delete from a campaign speech a passage praising General George Marshall, one of McCarthy's prime targets.[14] Throughout his first two years at the White House, while McCarthy was storming through Washington, denouncing the Voice of America, demanding censorship of American embassy libraries overseas, and terrorizing government officials, Eisenhower refused to launch a frontal attack on the senator from Wisconsin. He enacted Executive Order 10650, which in effect institutionalized the McCarthy-initiated purge of the State Department and related agencies. At times, Dulles or Vice President Nixon were used to appease McCarthy or to demonstrate that the administration was as anti-communist as the right wing wanted it to be.[15] Even when McCarthy attacked the president's personal choice for a major diplomatic post — Charles E. Bohlen, nominated as ambassador to Russia — and Eisenhower and Dulles were obliged to defend the administration's candidate, the behavior of the secretary of state and of the president was far from courageous.[16] Likewise, when McCarthy initiated his attack on the army, an institution with which Eisenhower maintained a special relationship, the president refused to oppose the senator from Wisconsin personally. And finally, when McCarthy supporter Senator Pat McCarren charged that McLeod, McCarthy's delegate detailed with "cleaning up" the State Department, had been "unable to clear" Bohlen because of Dulles, the secretary of state was ready to fire McLeod. He was dissuaded by Bedell Smith, one of Eisenhower's intimates, who felt the president "did not want an open break with the right wing."[17]

During Eisenhower's first two years in office, his policy towards the Democrats was far from conciliatory. "The concerted effort to bridge the foreign policy gap within the Republican party prevented Eisenhower and Dulles from putting external affairs on a bipartisan basis."[18] In the course of the two years in which the Republicans controlled Congress, the Eisenhower administration attacked the Democrats, charging them with past subversion. During the 1954 campaign Eisenhower endorsed Nixon's ugly attacks on the Democratic party, and also warned the country that a Democratic victory would mean a "cold war" between the legislature and the executive. And significantly, no Democrats were appointed to important policy-making positions in the State Department, nor were those long experienced in foreign affairs ever consulted.[19]

However, once the Democrats gained control of Congress, Eisenhower's policy changed. At his press conference the day after the Democratic victory, Eisenhower retreated from his statement of "cold war" between Congress and the executive.[20] The following day Eisenhower suggested in a cabinet meeting that the administration offer its cooperation to the majority party and endorse bipartisanship in foreign affairs.[21]

This behavior accorded with Eisenhower's broad domestic strategy. So long as Congress was controlled by the Republicans, and the Republican Party — at, least in Congress — was dominated by the right wing, Eisenhower attempted to pursue his foreign policy goals and their domestic counterparts by appeasing the right wing. And indeed Senator Everett Dirksen led the fight for mutual security legislation, while people like Senator William Knowland assisted him in defeating the Bricker Ammendment, designed to reduce the president's power in foreign affairs.[22] Once the Democrats became the majority party and the "old guard" lost its power both in Congress and within the Republican Party, the president offered the Democrats bipartisanship.

The relations between the president and the new Congress were immediately put to the test. When the situation in the Formosa Islands deteriorated, Eisenhower sent to Congress what later became the Formosa Resolution. In his message the president requested a joint resolution to cover any possible American intervention in the vicinity of Formosa. Although Eisenhower did not repeat Truman's unilateral decision-making in Korea, he still pointed out to Congress that authority for "some of the actions which might be required would be inherent in the authority of the Commander-in-Chief."[23] He made it clear that he was asking for a congressional resolution in order to "clearly and publicly establish the authority of the President to act in whatever fashion it might be necessary."[24] Under the leadership of Senator Lyndon B. Johnson and Representative Sam Rayburn, Congress overwhelmingly — 410 to 3 in the House, 85 to 3 in the Senate — voted for a resolution which authorized the president to employ the armed forces "as he deems necessary" for the purpose of securing and protecting Formosan and "related positions and territories of that area now in friendly hands."[25] Furthermore, the resolution included a paragraph stating that the resolution "shall expire when the President shall determine that peace and security of the area is reasonably assured by international conditions."[26]

Thus Eisenhower involved Congress in responsibility for a potential intervention in a local war, without conceding any of his powers as chief executive. Congress was responsible for a possible fiasco, despite the fact that the president would be under no obligation to consult with it if the decision for an actual intervention was taken. Congress had in effect handed the president a blank check.

Eisenhower's views on the dissemination of information did not include any feelings of obligation to court either the press or the public. According to Emmet Hughes, the president disliked public appearances before the press or on national television. During the early weeks of his administration he grumbled and argued against holding press conferences, "deploring their establishment by Roosevelt as a fixed form of presidential communication." He tried to "break away from the formula of direct address to his audience, in favor of informal 'discussion,' with Dulles or other Cabinet members joining the 'presentation'."[27] He reduced the number of press conferences in comparison to his predecessors; Roosevelt had held an average of 6.9 conferences per month; Truman an average 3.5; and Eisenhower cut that figure to 2.0.[28] Although in his memoirs Eisenhower tried to project a sensitivity towards the press and towards informing the public, there is no doubt that he did not feel that cultivating a positive relationship with the press was one of his highest priorities. It is true that on certain issues he tried to influence public opinion vigorously; but at the same time he was passive on other topics, leaving the initiative to the press. This indifference was at least partly the result of the fact that Eisenhower enjoyed public popularity even before entering office, and his standing in public opinion remained strong throughout his presidency.[29] He did not need the help of the media in fashioning a strong public image.

The most far-reaching innovation of the Eisenhower administration in the field of publicity was with respect to Congress. This policy was concentrated in the doctrine of "uncontrolled discretion" in releasing information, or, as it was later termed, "executive privilege." Confronted with McCarthy's inquisitorial hearings, the administration posited an absolute presidential right to withhold information from Congress. This policy was revolutionary in the sense that it extended the right to secrecy to the entire executive branch. While presidents since Jackson "had claimed their own conversations and communications with their aides and with cabinet members as privileged," this privilege was not extended to "everybody in the executive branch."[30] "The historic rule had been disclosure, with exception; the new rule was denial, with exception."[31] Even though this doctrine was developed as a defense against the

McCarthy investigations, the fact remains that Eisenhower extended to his administration, and thereby to future administrations, the right to withhold information from Congress and the public; Congress and the media went along with this line of thinking.[32] As in the Formosa Resolution, Eisenhower enhanced the power of the presidency without the need for conformation with the two institutions affected most by it, Congress and the press. Through conciliation and agreement Eisenhower the Whig had surpassed all his "imperial" predecessors.

Finally, we have to examine the administration and execution of foreign policy in the Eisenhower years, and particularly the attempts of the Eisenhower government to increase its control over the implementation of foreign policy. In general, the attitude of the administration towards the bureaucracy conformed with its overall strategy of increasing presidential power in foreign policy-making.

In the summer of 1952 Truman remarked that, in the event that Eisenhower won the election, "He'll sit here, and he'll say, 'Do this! Do that!' *And nothing will happen.* Poor Ike — it won't be a bit like the Army. He'll find it very frustrating."[33]

The impact of Eisenhower's military background has been taken into account by most students of the Eisenhower era, who considered it the source for the organizational principle which dominated the process of policy-making. W.W. Rostow has argued rightly that "these conceptions of leadership and organization were, evidently, the product of a military career — but of a particular kind of military career. He never intimately commanded units in combat."[34] It is also correct that although "Eisenhower was able to find and to install a kind of chief of staff for domestic affairs in the person of Sherman Adams.... in military and foreign affairs, however, no equivalent post or function emerged."[35] Nevertheless, the president was concerned about the fact that decisions were not implemented, or were implemented wrongly. Consequently, he established an Operations Coordination Board designed to ensure that the president's decisions were in fact carried out.

Despite the central role that Dulles played in foreign policy-making and implementation during his years as secretary of state, it should be noted that Eisenhower promoted the role of the National Security Council (NSC) as the central organ for dealing with foreign and military affairs. He created the position of "Special Assistant to the President for National Security Affairs," who was also chairman of the NSC Planning Board. Testifying before the Jackson Subcommittee on National Policy Machinery, General Robert Cutler, the first such special assistant, confirmed that the NSC was the president's central organ of foreign policy-making. He disclosed that during its first two years, the council met fifty-two times each year, an average of one per week.[36] Furthermore, while the NSC was the central organ of policy-making, coordination and control over implementation was carried out by the OCB, an interdepartmental committee on the under-secretary and agency-director level.[37] The creation of this organ, later abolished by President Kennedy, indicated the Eisenhower administration's intention to ensure that the bureaucracy implemented the president's decisions, with the OCB being to policy follow-up what the NSC Planning Board was to policy development. Thus the Eisenhower administration was engaged in promoting the power of the president vis-à-vis the bureaucracy, a development that would become more salient during the Nixon years. Whether or not this mechanism succeeded is not under investigation here; the fact is that the Eisenhower administration was involved in increasing the control of the executive over the implementation of foreign-policy decisions. Certainly this policy was another aspect of the general attempt to enhance the power of the executive.

Richard Nixon's Presidential Strategy: Ascendancy Through Confrontation

The circumstances under which Richard Nixon took office were even less favorable for the "imperial presidency" and continued American globalism than were those of 1953. While the intervention in Korea seemed to a certain degree justified in the light of Soviet-Chinese expansion and the general cold war climate, the war in Vietnam was more difficult to vindicate. In a less dangerous environment, in which the image of the enemy was changing, it was harder to justify the continued need for American intervention in various conflicts. The frustrating course of the war, the split in the communist camp, and a variety of other developments promoted a profound revisionist movement directed against both globalism and presidential power in American politics. Under these circumstances it was only natural to anticipate that various segments of the American polity would be less inclined to accept the dominance of the executive over the conduct of foreign affairs.

The major dissimilarity between Eisenhower and Nixon lay in their personal characters and perceptions of leadership. To use James Barber's classification tools, Eisenhower was a passive president, Nixon an activist one.[38] Despite the negative feelings that both presidents shared with respect to their post, there were significant differences in their attitudes. Nixon's course of action prior to his becoming president, his ambitions, his aggressive feelings, and his desire for power were in direct opposition to Eisenhower's make-up and style. Whereas the passive president, by definition, waits for a crisis to occur and then responds, the active one anticipates and tries to avert it. "Nixon is a special variant of the active-negative character," Barber has concluded. His remarkable flexibility with respect to issues and ideologies provided him with strength not to feel personally threatened when certain policies were defeated several times. However, "threats to his independence in particular — the sense that he is being controlled from without because he cannot be trusted, because he is weak or stupid or unstable — will call forth a strong inner response. For Nixon, the prime form of the active-negative command 'I must' is this: I must make my own way."[39]

The interaction between this power-oriented personality and an environment geared towards reducing presidential power influenced Nixon's style in the domestic setting of policy-making. The environmental threats to internationalism and to the presidency clashed with Nixon's personality and world view, and thus intensified the new president's resoluteness and commitment to consolidate the power of his office. His belligerent nature and style, as revealed in his early campaigns for congress and later with Eisenhower, impelled him to pursue his goals through confrontation with the menacing forces around him. For a person who had not hesitated to advance his personal power by falsely accusing people of being communists, sensitivity to congressional power or the thought of sharing power with other forces was impossible. "The President thrives on opposition. . . . It is a form of stimulation for him," Margaret Mead has remarked.[40] The struggle for power was an integral part of Nixon's political nature and style.

In addition, we must consider the impact of the experience of his immediate predecessor on Nixon's conception of his office. Here was Johnson, a president elected by a landslide, with a legislature controlled by his own party, initially enjoying fair relations with the press, surrounded by a Democratic bureaucracy, and experienced in Washington politics — and yet forced to relinquish power in the face of domestic opposition. Nixon, lacking most of Johnson's advantages but still determined to maintain the leadership of the United States in global affairs, could not hope for a more favorable domestic environment than that of his predecessor.

Johnson's ordeal taught Nixon that despite the strength of the executive in foreign policy-making, and despite the multitude of devices at his disposal for controlling the domestic environment, the American president remains subject to domestic accountability for his international behavior. The high cost of globalism fostered the creation of a coalition among the attentive public, Congress, the news media, and certain elements in the bureaucracy, a coalition strong enough to counterbalance presidential power and threaten the president's independence in foreign policy-making. A partial solution was the reduction of the costs of global involvement, which formed the external aspect of the Nixon strategy. But it was no less important to relieve the executive of these domestic restraints altogether, and this formed the essence of the Nixon domestic strategy. Given that the various elements in the domestic setting would not relinquish power voluntarily, the Nixon strategy intimated a confrontation between the presidency and competing institutions.

One of the main targets of Nixon's strategy was the liberal opposition; it was decided to disarm this group by removing its central weapon. By demonstrating to the public that it was determined to end American involvement in Vietnam and that the era of global confrontation was over, the administration sought to diminish public support of its ideological and political critics — a goal successfully achieved, as witnessed by the overwhelming defeat of the liberals in the 1972 elections. Clearly, the Nixon administration did not adopt these policies *solely* to disrupt its opposition, but this consideration certainly played a significant role. A similar logic guided Eisenhower's massive retaliation policy: the central theme of the strategy and the verbal style used to "sell" it were designed for both external and domestic rivals. But whereas in the case of Eisenhower the administration attempted to mobilize the opposition on behalf of its policies, the Nixon administration tried to remove the opposition from the emerging consensus. While Eisenhower tried to conciliate his ideological opposition, Nixon confronted it head-on.

In order to accomplish this goal, Nixon appealed to that element in the American polity least knowledgeable and interested in the essence of foreign policy issues — the general public. He sought to build a direct and special relationship with the force that had the least part in the actual political struggle for power, but the most decisive vote in determining the results of that struggle. The objective was to destroy the coalition that emerged during Vietnam by diminishing public support for Congress and the news media. By promising the public the termination of American involvement in Vietnam as rapidly as military conditions would allow, by reducing the human cost of the war, and by appealing to American honor, he hoped to satisfy the basic needs of the public and to increase support for himself and his policies. Thus Vietnamization and the withdrawal of American forces, and détente as well, were not simply elements of an external policy, but also domestically oriented devices designed to bring the American people over to the side of the president. By committing himself to ending American involvement in Vietnam and by taking initiatives with the Soviet Union and China, Nixon portrayed himself as a president dedicated to peace, thus satisfying the basic desires of the American people.

Nixon's "populistic" policy included another device, the appeal to the "silent majority." Not only did he select the public over the elites, but within the public he chose the less informed and more nationalistic sector. In his radio-television address of November 1969, after presenting his Vietnamization plan and his peace initiatives, he appealed to "real America" and asked for the support of "the great silent majority of [his] fellow Americans." He coupled his appeal for unity and support with a nationalistic motive: "Let us also be united against defeat," he declared. "Because let us understand: North Vietnam cannot defeat or humiliate the United States. Only Americans can do that."[41] The last comment was undoubtedly directed against the anti-war coalition.

A third segment of the American political system to receive "special treatment" at Nixon's hands was the news media. Nixon had always blamed the press of being unfair to him personally, an attitude that reached a climax in the famous "last press conference" held after Nixon's defeat to Governor Pat Brown in California, where he accused the news media of having carried out a personal vendetta against him for years. Nixon's perception of the press did not change significantly when he finally became president of the United States.

Moreover, the Nixon administration perceived the press as liberal and thus anti-Nixon by definition. In this sense the press was considered and treated like a competing elite. The concentration of control over the national press in the hands of a few families, most of them centered in the East Coast (Boston-New York-Washington), fanned the flames of general suspicion towards the "Eastern liberal establishment" which Nixon implanted in his administration. From the beginning, the general view was that the Nixon administration could not expect fair treatment from the media.[42]

Most important was the fact that, in the wake of the Vietnam experience, the media emerged as the president's leading adversary, evolving into an institution competing with the executive. It was the media that succeeded in producing alternative sources of information to the official ones that had been controlled by the executive branch. It was the press that possessed the information that permitted it to question the administration's reports about Vietnam and underscored the "credibility gap" between what the administration knew and what it chose to divulge to the public. The press competed with the president in the sphere of public opinion; it claimed to represent the American public; it tried to shape public opinion; and it was the connection between the American people, their president, and the outside world. For this administration, such a role could not be entrusted to any independent elite, especially a liberal and loudly anti-Nixon press.

The tactics employed against the media followed the patterns of the general framework of the Nixon's administration's domestic strategy. The general idea was to diminish the role of the press in the American polity and eventually to remove it from the domestic setting of foreign policy-making as is evident in the coordinated attack launched on the media during the fall of 1969.[43] Following the President's November 3 broadcast to the nation, Herbert Klein, Nixon's director of communications, pointed to the discrepancy between the degree of public support enjoyed by Nixon's policies and the criticism of those policies voiced by television and radio networks' news commentators. "Credibility isn't just the problem of the government," he remarked. "I think it is a problem with the media as well."[44] At about the same time, Vice President Agnew delivered his famous "media speech," in which he drew the public's attention to the fact that a small group of un-elected persons "wield a free hand in selecting, presenting and interpreting the great issues of our Nation. We would never trust such power over public opinion in the hands of an elected government," the vice president declared; "it is time we questioned it in the hands of a small and un-elected elite."[45] In his December 8 press conference, Nixon endorsed his vice president's line of attack.[46]

The Nixon administration's verbal attacks on the media's right to express independent views and to criticize his foreign policy were accompanied by the down-grading of the traditional role of the presidential news conference. Nixon had fewer press conferences than any modern president; during his first term in the White House, he held a total of thirty-one, an average of less than eight a year, or one conference per one and a half months — about a third of the average of his three predecessors, or a tenth of Roosevelt's yearly average.[47] The role of the press secretary was considerably diluted; the appointment to that post of a twenty-nine-year-old advertising man with no experience in Washington or journalism rather than Herb Klein, Nixon's veteran secretary, the creation of the competing position "Director of Communications for the

Executive Branch," to which Klein was appointed, and certain early announcements by Haldemann—all would seem to suggest that the role of the presidential press secretary may originally have been slated for abolishment.[48]

Moreover, the Nixon administration was actively involved in reducing the routes of information to the public through the press, and thus the status of the press, by diminishing access to the sources of information. In court, General Attorney John Mitchell attacked the right to privacy of reporters' sources (an act generally seen as inimical to the First Amendment).[49] He tried to censor *The New York Times* and *The Washington Post* when they attempted to publish the Pentagon Papers. During Nixon's first term, also, the famous "plumbers" took form, set up to stop government leaks to the press. At the same time, the administration tried to intimidate certain reporters with the help of governmental agencies like the FBI and the IRS.[50] Finally, in March 1972 Nixon issued Executive Order 11652, which strengthened Eisenhower's Executive Order 10501 and expanded the government's right to secrecy and its right to prosecute unauthorized disclosure.[51]

However, the preceding analysis should not lead us to the conclusion that the Nixon administration disregarded the importance of publicity and dissemination of information to the public. On the contrary, the Nixon administration was very sensitive to public communications. No administration invested so much in public relations as did the Nixon government. Besides the press secretary and the "communications director," in fact, a third apparatus emerged, headed by Charles Colson, and designed to invite public support for the president's policies and serve as a general supervisory office for public relations. In addition, John Scali, a diplomatic correspondent of the ABC broadcasting network, was hired to handle "foreign policy image-making."[52] Henry Kissinger was appointed by the president to conduct background briefings to reporters, but his name was not permitted to be disclosed by them, nor could members of the Senate Foreign Relations Committee get copies of the briefings for a long time.[53] The press thus became a tool in the hands of the administration to advance its views on foreign-policy issues. Certain news editors understood the implications of this strategy and consequently stopped their participation in it.[54]

As a final note, it should be mentioned that Nixon surrounded himself with an unprecedented number of men from the advertising field and that the Nixon public relations staff numbered at least sixty people.[55]

Nixon's treatment of the fourth factor in the domestic setting of foreign policy-making, the bureaucratic apparatus, could be related to a certain degree to several factors in the president's psychological make-up. The general belief that national security bureaucracy had played a leading role in bringing about American involvement in Vietnam,[56] the questionable loyalty of Washington bureaucrats to a Republican administration,[57] the personal distrust felt by both Nixon and Kissinger towards bureaucrats in general,[58] all influenced Nixon's policy of reducing the power and the role of the traditional national security bureaucracy in foreign policy decision-making. Other relevant factors in Nixon's decision to centralize control over foreign policy-making in the White House were his preference for secrecy in the handling of foreign affairs,[59] and particularly his desire to break away from the cold war atmosphere in which the current Departments of State and Defense were formed.

The attempted phasing-out of the foreign policy bureaucracy was advanced on both the organizational and the functional levels. By promoting the role of the NSC and his Special Assistant for National Security Affairs in foreign policy-making, and by substantially increasing the number of White House employees inv lved in foreign policy, the president effectively under-cut the bureaucracy's traditional place in national affairs.[60] Going further still, Nixon denied them central functions in making and implementing policy concerning cardinal issues of American interest.[61] The policy towards China, the SALT talks and the question of détente with the Soviet Union, and even negotiations with North Vietnam — all were directed and managed almost entirely from the White House, in particular through Henry Kissinger. Of the major issues, the State Department was left with the Middle East, and even here the White House interjected its own efforts during the 1970 Jordanian crisis and its aftermath.[62]

On the operational level, the administration instituted the Kissinger-chaired NSC Review Group, to whom the Interdepartmental Groups (IGs) and the Under-Secretaries Committee (USC) had to report, thereby greatly increasing Kissinger's influence and scrutiny over the planning and the preparation of NSC policy papers. Crisis management was brought under the direct control of the White House by the establishment of the Washington Special Action Group (WSAG), again chaired by Kissinger.[63] Through this unit Kissinger could intervene directly in the Jordanian crisis in 1970 and the Indo-Pakistani war in 1971. During the Cambodian incursion, Kissinger handled both policy decisions and military operations decision.[64] Furthermore, major diplomatic missions were taken away from the State Department and given to the personal envoy of the president. The NSC staff numbered fifty-two members in April 1971, three times as many as Rostow's staff at its peak.[65]

Finally, the Nixon domestic strategy was also directed at reducing the power of Congress. If the other segments of the domestic system constituted actual centers of power resulting from the pluralistic nature of the American polity and the global interests of the United States, Congress was intrinsically the constitutional adversary of the presidency. It was here that a large part of the opposition to American involvement in Vietnam was concentrated. It was Congress that suffered most from the emergence of the imperial presidency, and it was the legislature that, under the Constitution, controlled appropriations for the war in Vietnam and defense spending in general. It was natural, therefore, that Nixon try to reduce the power of this institution.

Nixon's relations with the Congress were complex. In contrast to Eisenhower's conciliatory policy towards the isolationist wing in Congress, Nixon confronted the anti-war coalition in the legislature, including the liberals of his own party, very aggressively.[66] Instead of appealing to the opposition by holding up to them his own policies of détente and retrenchment, thus promoting a consensus in the legislature (for the internationalists would have supported him anyway), he preferred to rely solely on a coalition of conservative Republicans and Democrats. In addition, he tried to use the conflicts of institutional interests between the House and the Senate to contain anti-executive legislation.[67] In the House he could rely particularly on House Speaker Carl Albert, Majority Leader Hale Boggs, and Chairman of the House Foreign Affairs Committee Thomas Morgan, along with the regular Republican leadership, including people like Gerald Ford.[68] He ignored the criticism of Republican senators like John Sherman Cooper, Mark Hatfield and Jacob Javits, who joined or initiated anti-war resolutions or restrictions on the executive's war powers.[69] Thus with the help of conservative members of both parties, and institutional conflicts in the legislature, Nixon attempted to contain the opposition on Capitol Hill to his foreign policy and preserve the dominant role of the executive in formulating this policy.

But, as was the case with the other segments of the American political system, Nixon's grand design was not limited to the containment of Congress and the preservation of executive power vis-à-vis the legislature. "The Nixon revolution was aimed at reducing the power of Congress at every point along the line and moving toward rule by presidential decree."[70] First, his administration attacked legislative privilege to obtain information on the activity of the executive branch "without risking criminal prosecution."[71] At the same time, he revived Eisenhower's executive privilege thesis with respect to the right of the president to deny Congress access to executive information.[72] Executive Order 11652, which was primarily directed against the news media, also affected the flow of information to Congress. Likewise, the administrative changes in the process of foreign policy-making also diminished Congress's power. The concentration of foreign policy power in the hands of the president and his de facto secretary of state, who ran United States foreign policy directly from the White House and was thus immune from testifying before Congress, reduced even further the legislature's control over foreign policy-making, and especially curtailed the access of Congress to foreign issues and information. By shielding his foreign policy maker and his staff from Congress, Nixon minimized the legislature's information about international affairs. All in all, by reducing the information available to the media, excluding the accountable bureaucracy from important foreign policy issues, and attempting to halt the leaks from the White House, Nixon further weakened the contacts between Congress and the international political system.

Finally, Nixon planned to reduce the power of Congress through an unprecedented landslide victory in the 1972 presidential elections, which was more important to him than a Republican Congress. In an interview with Theodore White, Nixon clearly indicated that he was looking for a "new majority," not a "new coalition" or a "new Republican majority."[73] He told White that he needed this mandate for the effective conduct of foreign affairs, and that a landslide similar to that of Eisenhower in 1956 was not sufficient. "In the foreign field, the President leads and Congress follows," he claimed.[74] When White suggested that, on the eve of the American Bicentennial, there might be a need to change the Constitution in order to grant the president wider powers, the president replied that he did not need formal changes in order to accomplish the results that he desired. He preferred a "change that works." "We don't want too violent a change," the president asserted. Considering past experience and the abilities of "Erlichman's crowd" and "Kissinger's crowd" in accomplishing their goals, Nixon felt that after his victory "we're going to be in a position to present to the country changes in the system that will work."[75] Undoubtedly, Nixon anticipated that after his landslide, whatever powers Congress had still retained or regained in foreign affairs would have been further reduced.

Conclusion

In comparing the presidential strategies of the Eisenhower and the Nixon administrations it seems clear that the character of each president determined his mode of behavior. Eisenhower, the passive-negative president and accommodating personality, pursued the interests of his office through conciliation. Nixon, the active-negative president who perceived politics in terms of crisis and conflict, pursued presidential power through confrontation. Both presidents inherited comparable domestic environments hostile to the continued dominant role of the executive, particularly in foreign affairs; but each pursued a different course in his attempt to restore the powers of his office. The interaction between the cold war climate of the early 1950s, a climate that was conducive to presidential authority, and the president's personality contributed to the accommodating style of Eisenhower. In contrast, the combination of a détente atmosphere, in which it was more difficult to justify presidential discretion in foreign policy, and Nixon's belligerent character intensified his confrontationist style in presidential politics.

The question that remains to be resolved is why Eisenhower succeeded in restoring the status of the presidency while Nixon, in the final analysis, failed. This is particularly important in the face of Nixon's substantial scores in the international arena. How do we explain the fact that he could not — although he certainly tried to — use his international achievements to save his presidency? Does the comparison between the two experiences indicate that a conciliatory approach towards domestic elites "pays off" more so than a confrontationist one?

Perhaps this is indeed so. The American political system is ultimately one dominated by elites, and since the Nixon strategy was aimed at eradicating the power of these elites, it was only natural that, at the first opportunity that presented itself, these elites would try to dispose of him. In the final analysis, it was these elites that counted, and not the masses whom he tried to court, in determining the outcome of the power struggle in Washington. On the other hand, and not in contradiction to our first, hesitant, "yes," the reduction in international tension affected the legitimacy of presidential supremacy in international affairs. Therefore, while Eisenhower could justify presidential ascendancy on account of the international situation, Nixon's strategy had no justification. Détente brought about a decline in the importance of foreign policy issues in the mind of the American polity, and when a presidential crisis occurred, Nixon could not seek salvation in his international achievements.

If the second answer is in fact pertinent, this may signal a considerable change in the status of the presidency in the future. If relaxation of tension with the communist powers continues, and public attention focuses more on domestic issues rather than on foreign policy issues, then future presidents will find it more difficult to legitimize the broad powers held by the executive. The brief experience of President Gerald Ford and President Jimmy Carter's experience to date point in this direction. It may be too early to speak about the end of the imperial presidency; however, a more pluralistic system may well be in the making.

Notes

1. For further analysis, see Francis E. Rourke, "The Domestic Scene," in Robert E. Osgood et al., *America and the World* (Baltimore: The Johns Hopkins Press, 1970), pp. 149-150; and Francis E. Rourke, "The Domestic Scene: The President Ascendant," in Robert E. Osgood, *Retreat from Empire* (Baltimore: The Johns Hopkins Press, 1973), pp. 79-80.

2. For a comparative analysis of public opinion during Korea and Vietnam see John E. Mueller, *War, Presidents and Public Opinion* (New York: John Wiley & Sons, 1973).

3. For another analysis of the relationship between the external environment and Eisenhower's presidential strategy, see Arthur M. Schlesinger, Jr., *The Imperial Presidency* (Boston: Houghton Mifflin, 1973), pp. 163-168.

4. Robert J. Donovan, *Eisenhower: The Inside Story* (New York: Harper & Brothers, 1956), p. 87.

5. Clinton Rossiter, *The American Presidency* (New York: The New American Library, 1963), p. 162.

6. Donovan, *Eisenhower,* p. 84.

7. Emmet Hughes, *The Ordeal of Power; Political Memoir of the Eisenhower Years* (New York: Atheneum, 1963), p. 128.

8. Ibid., p. 128.

9. Samuel Lubell, *The Revolt of the Moderates* (New York: Harper & Brothers, 1956), pp. 96-97.

10. Ibid., p. 97.

11. Norman Graebner, *The New Isolationism* (New York: The Ronald Press, 1956), pp. 127-130. See also Ronald J. Caridi, *The Korean War and American Politics: The Republican Party as a Case Study* (Philadelphia: University of Pennsylvania Press, 1968), pp. 256-259.

12. Graebner, *The New Isolationism,* pp. 130-132. See also Donovan, *Eisenhower,* chap. 4.

13. Hughes, *The Ordeal of Power,* pp. 128-129. See in addition the tactics that Eisenhower used in order to appease Senator Taft in Donovan, *Eisenhower,* chap. 7.

14. Ibid., p. 244. See also Hughes, *The Ordeal of Power,* pp. 41-43.

15. Lubell, *The Revolt of the Moderates,* p. 87. See also Marquis Childs, *Eisenhower: Captive Hero* (New York: Harcourt, Brace and Co., 1958), p. 181.

16. Townsend Hooper, *The Devil and John Foster Dulles* (Boston: Little, Brown, 1973), pp. 158-160.

17. Childs, *Eisenhower,* p. 186. See also Donovan, *Eisenhower,* pp. 250-256.

18. Graebner, *The New Isolationism,* p. 143.

19. Ibid., p. 143.

20. *Public Papers of the Presidents of the United States: Eisenhower, 1954* (Washington, D.C.: National Archives and Records Service, 1960), pp. 1012-1013.

21. Donovan, *Eisenhower,* pp. 282-283.

22. Ibid., p. 238; and Hughes, *The Ordeal of Power,* p. 126.

23. Dwight D. Eisenhower, *Mandate for Change 1953-1956* (New York: Doubleday & Co., 1963), p. 468.

24. Ibid.

25. Ibid., p. 608.

26. Ibid.

27. Hughes, *The Ordeal of Power*, p. 131.

28. Elmer C. Cornwell, Jr., *Presidential Leadership of Public Opinion* (Bloomington: Indiana University Press, 1965), p. 178.

29. Mueller, *War, Presidents, and Public Opinion*, pp. 179-184, 233-237.

30. Schlesinger, *The Imperial Presidency*, pp. 157-158.

31. Ibid., p. 390.

32. Ibid., pp. 161-163.

33. Cited in Richard E. Neustadt, *Presidential Power* (New York: The New American Library, 1960), p. 22.

34. W.W. Rostow, *The United States in the World Arena* (New York: Harper & Row, 1960), p. 389.

35. Ibid., p. 390.

36. Robert Cutler, "The National Security Council Under President Eisenhower," in Henry Jackson, ed., *The National Security Council* (New York: Frederick A. Praeger, 1965), p. 119.

37. Jackson, *The National Security Council*, p. 37.

38. James David Barber, *The Presidential Character* (Englewood Cliffs, N.J.: Prentice-Hall, 1972), pp. 156-163 and chaps. 10-12.

39. Ibid., p. 442.

40. Cited in ibid.

41. Council on Foreign Relations, *Documents on American Foreign Relations, 1968-1969* (New York: Simon and Schuster, 1970), pp. 44.

42. This notion is elaborated in Theodore H. White, *The Making of the President, 1972* (New York: Atheneum, 1973), chap. 10.

43. The encouragement given to this campaign by the president is confirmed by Rowland Evans, Jr., and Robert D. Novak in *Nixon in the White House: The Frustration of Power* (New York: Frederick A. Praeger, 1965), p. 317; and by David Wise, *The Politics of Lying: Government Deception, Secrecy and Power* (New York: Random House, 1973), p. 231.

44. Cited in ibid., p. 232.

45. Cited in Evans and Novak, *Nixon in the White House*, p. 316.

46. *Public Papers of the Presidents of the United States: Nixon, 1969*, p. 1004.

47. James E. Pollard, *The Presidents and the Press, Truman to Johnson* (Washington, D.C.: Public Affairs Press, 1964), pp. 87, 105 and Wise, *The Politics of Lying*, p. 246.

48. During the post-election period, Haldeman announced that "there will be no Sherman Adams, no Jim Hagerty," adding that there will be no press secretary in the "traditional sense." See Wise, *The Politics of Lying*, p. 140.

49. White, *The Making of the President, 1972*, p. 264.

50. See for instance the cases of CBS's Daniel Schwepp and of *Newsday* in ibid. See also Wise, *The Politics of Lying*, pp. 218-225.

51. For further analysis of the expansion of the right to secrecy over the Eisenhower order, see Schlesinger, *The Imperial Presidency*, pp. 333-336. In this connection, notice Nixon's Official Secrets Act.

52. Wise, *The Politics of Lying*, p. 197.

53. Ibid., p. 300.

54. This group included Benjamin C. Bradlee, the executive editor of *The Washington Post*, and A.M. Rosenthal, the managing editor of *The New York Times;* see ibid., p. 302.

55. Ibid., p. 198.

56. See for instance Richard J. Barnet, *Roots of War* (New York: Atheneum, 1972). For a more balanced view, see Francis E. Rourke, *Bureaucracy and Foreign Policy* (Baltimore: The Johns Hopkins Press, 1972).

57. Rourke, "The President Ascendant," p. 95.

58. Marvin Kalb and Bernard Kalb, *Kissinger* (Boston: Little, Brown, 1974), p. 80. See also Henry Kissinger, "Domestic Structure and Foreign Policy," in *American Foreign Policy* (New York: W.W. Norton, 1969), pp. 17-26.

59. Rourke, "The President Ascendant," pp. 96-97.

60. For further analysis of Nixon's organizational changes with regard to national security affairs, see I.M. Destler, "Can One Man Do?"; and John P. Leacacos, "Kissinger's Apparat," *Foreign Policy* V (Winter 1971-72), pp. 3-40.

61. Rourke, "The President Ascendant," p. 98.

62. Kalb and Kalb, *Kissinger,* chap. 8.

63. The analysis of the White House bureaucracy relationship is based on I.M. Destler, *Presidents, Bureaucrats and Foreign Policy* (Princeton: Princeton University Press: 1972), pp. 118-153; and Leacacos, "Kissinger's Apparat."

64. Destler, *Presidents,* p. 139; and Kalb and Kalb, *Kissinger,* chap. 8 and pp. 257-262. Kissinger's behavior during the Jordanian crisis was described as that of a general and an admiral; see ibid., pp. 201-202.

65. Destler, *Presidents,* p. 126.

66. Nixon's attitude and treatment of the liberals in his own party are further elaborated in Evans and Novak, *Nixon in the White House,* pp. 107-108.

67. Rourke, "The President Ascendant," pp. 91-92.

68. Ibid., pp. 91-92; and Henry Brandon, *The Retreat of American Power* (New York: Doubleday, 1973), pp. 147-148.

69. Consider, for example, the Cooper-Church amendment to forbid the use of funds to maintain American combat troops in Cambodia; followed by the McGovern-Hatfield amendment forbidding the use of funds to keep American troops in Vietnam after December 31, 1971; the Javits-Dole bill spelling out the circumstances in which the president, as commander-in-chief, could use the armed forces; the War Powers Act sponsored by Senator Javits and the conservative-hawkish Senator Stennis limiting presidential intervention capability without congressional approval to thirty days. See Francis O. Wilcox, *Congress, the Executive, and Foreign Policy* (New York: Harper & Row, 1971), pp. 32-38; and Brandon, *The Retreat of American Power,* p. 150.

70. Schlesinger, *The Imperial Presidency,* p. 239.

71. Ibid., p. 240.

72. Ibid., p. 241.

73. White, *The Making of the President, 1972,* p. 299.

74. Ibid., p. 302.

75. Ibid., p. 303.

On Memories, Interests and Foreign Policy: The Case of Vietnam

Michael Nacht

In Graham Greene's *The Quiet American,* a fictional account of love and war in Southeast Asia, the following exchange takes place between Fowler, a skeptical, opium-smoking English war correspondent, and Pyle, a bright, young, confident American intelligence officer:

Fowler:	Sometimes the Viets have a better success with a megaphone than a bazooka. I don't blame them. They don't believe in anything either. You and your like are trying to make a war with the help of people who just aren't interested.
Pyle:	They don't want communism.
Fowler:	They want enough rice. They don't want to be shot at. They want one day to be much the same as another. They don't want our white skins around telling them what they want.
Pyle:	If Indochina goes —
Fowler:	I know that record. Siam goes. Malaya goes. Indonesia goes. What does "go" mean? If I believed in your God and another life, I'd bet my future harp against your golden crown that in five hundred years there may be no New York or London, but they'll be growing paddy in the fields, they'll be carrying their produce to market on long poles, wearing their pointed hats. The small boys will be sitting on the buffaloes. I like the buffaloes, they don't like our smell, the smell of Europeans. And remember — from a buffalo's point of view you are a European too.
Pyle:	They'll be forced to believe what they are told; they won't be allowed to think for themselves.
Fowler:	Thought's a luxury. Do you think the peasant sits and thinks of God and democracy when he gets inside his mud hut at night?[1]

Greene's work was first published in 1955, a full ten years before the United States introduced large numbers of combat troops into South Vietnam. His words were prescient, for the conversation between Fowler and Pyle was repeated with slight variations in Vietnam and in the United States for almost twenty years thereafter. What was the United States doing in Vietnam? What were American objectives? What were the aims, hopes and aspirations of the South Vietnamese people? How did American intervention differ from French colonial rule? What was the nature of the threat — to South Vietnam? to Asia? to the United States.

Americans and others debated these questions *ad nauseum,* particularly from the time U.S. troops assumed a major role in the war in Vietnam until the collapse of the South Vietnamese government almost a decade later. The answers to these questions differed then and now because of variations among us in our views of what is central to American foreign policy and what is peripheral, because we cannot agree on the appropriate means to achieve specific ends, and because we even choose to read the historical record differently in order to reinforce our own notions of what was a success and what was a disaster.

But these variations notwithstanding, a dominant view has taken hold. It is now commonly agreed that the Vietnam War was a disaster, both for the South Vietnamese people and for the United States, and that it should not be repeated. "No more Vietnams" is a sentiment most Americans can and do endorse, even if they are not fully able to articulate what this slogan really means. What has prompted this dramatic shift in attitude from the views expressed by Pyle to the willingness to equate Vietnam with everything that is undesirable in American foreign policy? Clearly, Americans held certain views and retained certain images in the early 1960s about international politics and about themselves which they no longer accept. The agony of the Vietnam experience has produced this change.

It is the purpose of this paper to explore in a preliminary fashion the manner in which images of international politics are formed, to then review the principal elements of the American world view which led, in my judgment, both naturally and easily to the American military intervention in Vietnam, and to conclude with an assessment of contemporary American images of international politics in the wake of the Vietnam experience. The central question under investigation is: What has been the effect of the Vietnam War on the American self-image and on the role of the United States in the world?

Some Thoughts on Images

Because of the inherent complexity of human affairs, individuals continuously derive "images" of the physical world that surrounds them. Among other definitions offered by Webster, images can be defined as "mental conceptions held in common by members of a group and symbolic of a basic attitude and orientation." Social scientists, however, have had great difficulty either explaining how particular images are formed or identifying the conditions that lead to their transformation. This difficulty has persisted with reference to individuals, to small groups and to national governments. And with respect to the conduct of international relations, few scholars have been able to make much headway in developing a theory or set of theories that convincingly explain behavior among states.[2]

It may not be necessary, though, to set for ourselves the arduous task of theory formulation in order to gain insight into the role of images in international relations. I would submit that the work of two scholars — one a philosopher of science and the other a social psychologist — provide compelling arguments that can be extremely useful in the analysis of international politics, although neither is a specialist in this field, nor have they themselves applied their theoretical concepts to such phenomena. The former, Thomas Kuhn, has set down his views most comprehensively in a work aimed at explaining how scientific progress is made. The latter, Leon Festinger, has written at length on how individuals cope with information that runs counter to their firmly held set of beliefs.[3]

A brief sketch of each theory will suffice. Kuhn argues that when someone new comes to the world of science he or she finds an existing set of rules of how to think about problems, a collection of shared assumptions, and a common belief in the location of the frontiers of the discipline. Kuhn labels these rules and norms the "paradigm" that governs and dominates thinking in the discipline. According to Kuhn, at any point in time there is a paradigm that is widely, though never universally, accepted in the field. How then is scientific progress achieved? Kuhn answers thus: A young person or someone new to the field discovers, perhaps by accident, a phenomenon that cannot be readily explained by the existing paradigm. The phenomenon is almost always characterized as an "anomaly" by senior people in the field and is dismissed as a trivial variation from the norm rather than a reason to doubt the universal applicability of the paradigm. But further research reveals that there is not one but rather a whole class of activities that the paradigm cannot explain adequately. Over perhaps many years, even decades, a search is undertaken to develop a new set of norms and guidelines that explain these recently discovered phenomena. Eventually a competing paradigm is formulated which challenges much of the thinking of the established paradigm. If the new paradigm cannot withstand the critical challenges posed by its doubters, it disappears in short order. But if it can, it polarizes the field and, after some time, a transfer of allegiances begins to take place from the old paradigm to the new. Eventually, all but a few die-hards have deserted the old paradigm and the new one becomes the established set of rules for the discipline. The process is then repeated in turn with still another paradigm arising to replace the now established paradigm. And, given the cumulative nature of scientific inquiry, this process of paradigm replacement is, according to Kuhn, how scientific progress is made.

The second formulation, Festinger's theory of cognitive dissonance, can best be illustrated by example. Suppose a man who greatly enjoys gastronomy finds that he is grossly overweight. His physician informs him that the extra weight he is carrying is highly detrimental to his health and advises him to adopt a strict diet, eliminating virtually all his culinary delights. What choices does the man have? He may of course follow his physician's advice, stick to the diet and lose the weight. But he has several other options as well. He can continue his gastronomic activities without curtailment, justifying his action on several grounds. First, he could argue that "eating is part of his life," that he enjoys it greatly and that he would rather live a shorter, happier life eating what he wishes than be healthy but miserable. Second, he could cite Winston Churchill, who lived past ninety, as a counter-example to the notion that an overweight condition necessarily leads to a shortened life span. "It won't happen to me," he could say. Third, he could argue that to follow the dietary restriction proposed by his physician would be so stressful that he might develop ulcers or high blood pressure as a consequence, or have to resume smoking cigarettes just to "cope," each of these being equally or more detrimental to his health than his overweight condition. Or fourth, he could claim that he would prefer to "take his chances" with his condition. "One cannot avoid all the dangers in life anyway; you can get hit by a car crossing the street too, you know."

The man is torn between doing something he wishes to do and facing unpleasant consequences if he does it, or forgoing the activity. Festinger terms the unpleasant consequences "dissonance"; he asserts that the existence of dissonance, being psychologically uncomfortable, motivates the person to reduce the dissonance by avoiding situations or information that would increase it. In his own laboratory work Festinger observed a number of additional modes of behavior:

1. Following a decision, there is active seeking out of information that supports the action taken ("cognitive consonant" information).

187

2. Following a decision, there is an increase in the confidence in the decision. Individuals find the chosen course of action far more attractive
than the alternatives that were rejected.
3. Once the decision is made, it is very difficult to reverse the decision.
4. Characteristics 1-3 vary directly with the importance of the decision.
The more important the decision, the more pronounced are these effects.

While it would be unjustified and even foolish to claim a tight explanatory
fit between the theories of Kuhn and Festinger and American policy in Vietnam — certainly such a fit cannot be demonstrated rigorously — a strong
argument can be made that both theories enrich our understanding of how the
United States could find itself bogged down in Vietnam, and even shed some
light on current American images derived from the Vietnam experience.

The Containment Paradigm

There is no question that by 1950, if not earlier, the United States had adopted
"containment" as the cornerstone of its foreign policy and as the principal
guideline for dealing with the Soviet Union. The containment policy had, of
course, been articulated publicly by George Kennan in his famous "X" article
in *Foreign Affairs*[4] and had previously been espoused by Kennan and others
inside the government. Kennan argued that in the postwar period Soviet expansion was the principal threat to the Western world, and he called for a
"long-term, patient but firm and vigilant containment of Russian expansive
tendencies." Most often quoted was Kennan's observation that:

> Soviet pressure against the free institutions of the Western world is something that can be
> contained by the adroit and vigilant application of counterforce at a series of constantly
> shifting geographical and political points, corresponding to the shifts and maneuvers of
> Soviet policy.

Kennan argued that successful application of the containment approach
would not only thwart Soviet foreign policy goals, but would eventually lead
to a reform of Soviet domestic political institutions as well, which would in
turn modify the Soviet Union's expansionist tendencies.

The containment policy was appealing on several grounds. The principal
lesson that American policy-makers had derived from World War Two was

that appeasement of potential aggressors only brought on aggression. The Munich experience could never be repeated. In the aftermath of the war, with the consolidation of Soviet control over much of Eastern Europe, the threatening character of Soviet rhetoric, and the intransigence of Soviet negotiating behavior, it was the Soviet Union that loomed as the sole threat to Western institutions. The United States had emerged from the war as the world's strongest nation, both militarily and economically, and with the anticipation of the disintegration of the British and French colonial empires, the Truman administration moved to define the American national interest in terms of anti-communism and assigned itself the role of leading the defense of the West.[5] The containment policy, though remarkably vague as stated in Kennan's *Foreign Affairs* article, was consistent with the memories and interests of American policy-makers and provided a general guide for the conduct of U.S. foreign policy. Though it was criticized by Walter Lippmann and some others for permitting American foreign policy to be determined by Soviet initiatives, containment provided a framework more compelling than any alternative offered by its critics.

In his published work Kennan did not distinguish between political and military means to implement the policy, nor did he identify specific geographical regions where it was to be applied and others where it was to be avoided.[6] But the press of events led successive American administrations to apply the policy with a universality that was not particularly sensitive to the idiosyncrasies of geography and to rely most heavily for its implementation on the military instrument. Indeed, this sense of the global applicability of containment was in evidence by 1950 when a major review of America's national strategy made the following point:

> Our position as the center of power in the free world places a heavy responsibility upon the United States for leadership. We must organize and enlist the energies and resources of the free world in a positive program for peace which will frustrate the Kremlin design for world domination by creating a situation in the free world to which the Kremlin will be compelled to adjust. Without such a cooperative effort, led by the United States, we will have to make gradual withdrawals under pressure until we discover one day that we have sacrificed positions of vital interest.[7]

By the time John Kennedy assumed the presidency in 1961, the containment policy had a proven track record. A combination of economic assistance, military presence and alliance-building by the United States in Western Europe had halted Soviet westward expansion at the frontiers of Eastern Europe. The Truman Doctrine maintained the pro-Western orientation of Greece and Turkey.[8] Even the painful Korean War experience could be legitimately judged to be a success in that American military intervention established the *status quo ante* and maintained a non-communist government in South Korea. Clandestine operations in Iran and Guatemala and the use of the Marines in Lebanon all served to thwart communist expansion in the 1950s. Moreover, the network of bilateral and multilateral alliances established by the United States during the Eisenhower administration provided the policy with international political legitimacy. Except for the triumph of communist forces in China, which remained a highly contentious issue in American domestic politics, and the Castro victory in Cuba, which from the Washington perspective was not initially thought to be a communist success but rather one of nationalism, the containment policy had an unblemished record.

Recall, then, the stirring words of John Kennedy's inaugural address:

> Let every nation know, whether it wishes us well or ill, that we shall pay any price, bear any burden, meet any hardship, support any friend, oppose any foe to assure the survival and the success of liberty.
> In the long history of the world, only a few generations have been granted the role of defending freedom in its hour of maximum danger. I do not shrink from this responsibility — I welcome it.
> To those people in the huts and villages of half the globe struggling to break the bonds of mass misery, we pledge our best efforts to help them help themselves, for whatever period is required — not because we seek their votes, but because it is right.[9]

The president's words were the quintessential endorsement of and commitment to the containment paradigm — an open-ended pledge to prevent the spread of communism anywhere it chose to spread. By 1961 containment was the established orthodoxy of American foreign policy, with broad and deep support in the Congress, in the bureaucracy, in the business, labor and academic communities, in journalistic circles, and throughout the body politic.[10] Given containment's entrenched position, it would take highly significant contradictory evidence to dislodge it.

Paradigm Adjustment

Kuhn argues that most scientists spend their careers adjusting, refining and extending the existing paradigm rather than seeking its replacement. This is not to denigrate the worth of such efforts, but rather to suggest that paradigm criticism is not the norm but very much the exception in scientific research. Perhaps the same can be said of political-military analyses that tend to argue for the adoption of new techniques or for a reorientation of priorities without challenging fundamental assumptions of policy. In the 1950s in particular, there was a substantial amount of creative intellectual work performed in the service of tailoring American foreign and defense policy to the changing international environment. From Kuhn's theoretical perspective, however, this work would have to be defined as paradigm adjustment, since it focused on techniques of policy implementation rather than on presenting formal challenges to the existing containment policy. Three conceptual developments proved to be especially relevant to the Vietnam policy subsequently adopted in the 1960s: limited-war theory, theories of coercive diplomacy, and theories of counter-insurgency.

Limited-war theory was essentially an outgrowth of American experience in a limited war in Korea, as well as an intellectual reaction to the weaknesses of the doctrine of massive retaliation that had been first enunciated by Secretary of State John Foster Dulles at a meeting of the Council on Foreign Relations in New York in January 1954. The Korean War had been a frustrating experience because the United States had deliberately refrained from widening the conflict in order not to provoke a war between the United States and the Soviet Union or, at the very least, a full-scale war between the United States and the People's Republic of China on the Chinese homeland. The Korean War was a precedent-setting limited war in three respects. First, after several policy reversals, it was fought by the United States with the specifically limited objective of ensuring that South Korea was not ruled by a communist government. Second, it was waged in a geographically limited area, with the extension of the war to Chinese territory expressly forbidden by President Truman despite the protestations of General Douglas MacArthur. And third, it was fought with limited use of weaponry, particularly the lack of deployment of nuclear weapons.

In the aftermath of the Korean War, several American civilian strategists — Bernard Brodie, William Kaufmann, Robert Osgood, Henry Kissinger — felt that future wars would similarly be limited in terms of objectives, geography and weaponry, and were particularly concerned when the Eisenhower administration adopted a policy of planning to use, or at least threatening to use, nuclear weapons "at a time and place of our own choosing" to counter communist aggression in Europe or in "gray areas" that were not dominated by either the Soviet Union or the West. The civilian strategists found the policy of massive retaliation wanting because, they argued, it was not credible to our adversaries, our allies or ourselves.[11] It was inconceivable that the United States would in fact initiate nuclear war with the Soviet Union in response to a border incursion in Southeast Asia. The strategists went to great lengths to spell out the importance of credibility in making a policy of deterrence work, and stressed the need for the United States to acquire capabilities to match those of its adversaries if America wished either to deter aggressive acts taken by these adversaries or defeat them on the battlefield should deterrence fail.[12] Osgood in particular warned, however, that the United States was likely to be moving into an age of limited war that would not sit well with the American people unless American objectives were explained carefully and convincingly.

Many of these ideas were in turn adopted and amplified by Maxwell Taylor in a book published before Kennedy took office and of sufficient impact on the new president that Taylor was appointed Kennedy's personal adviser on military affairs. It was in Taylor's work that the term "flexible response" was coined: "the need for a capability to react across the entire spectrum of possible challenge, for coping with anything from general atomic war to infiltrations and aggressions such as threaten Laos and Berlin."[13] Thus Kennedy brought with him not only a reaffirmation of containment, but an intellectual commitment to acquire the capabilities to implement the policy more effectively than had previously been the case.

Techniques of coercive diplomacy were also part of the intellectual inheritance accepted by the Kennedy administration. Sensitivity to the importance and subtleties of signalling, to the psychology of threat, and to the significance of tacit agreements; the ability to distinguish between deterrence (punish the opponent *if* he acts) and compellence (punish the opponent *until* he acts); and the application of a strategy of controlled escalation to a conflict to indicate to an opponent the punishment that he will receive if he continues to pursue his goals — these were among the important concepts superbly articulated by strategists Thomas Schelling and Herman Kahn.[14] Although neither Schelling nor Kahn had any direct connection to U.S. policy in Vietnam, a number of key officials in the Kennedy (and then the Johnson) administration were familiar with their ideas, and there is fragmentary evidence to suggest that some of these concepts were embraced in the formulation and execution of U.S. strategy in Vietnam.[15] Whether it was the intention of the authors or not — and it must be stressed that neither Schelling nor Kahn publicly advocated that their strategic theories be applied by the U.S. government in the prosecution of the war — the net effect appears to have been to induce a sense of confidence among U.S. policy-makers that they could manipulate the conduct of the war far more effectively than they actually could.

This sense of confidence was no doubt bolstered by the experience of the Cuban missile crisis in October 1962, which was taken by members of the Kennedy administration to be a validation of the efficacy of coercive diplomacy. It demonstrated that by making use of the carefully controlled threat of force, America could make the communists back down. It indicated that by keeping lines of communication open, making unambiguous signals about one's intentions, and leaving clearly labelled "outs" for the opposition, the United States could prevail. That the success of this formula in a Soviet-American confrontation might not necessarily imply a similar success in Southeast Asia was not widely appreciated in Washington before 1965.

Because of the growing sense in Washington in the early 1960s that insurgent warfare was the principal tool of communist expansionism that the United States would have to confront, the Kennedy administration was able and willing to move energetically to develop counter-insurgency capabilities as a principal element of U.S. military force posture. Soviet Premier Khrushchev had articulated as early as January 1961 that "wars of national liberation" were "just" wars that he endorsed "wholeheartedly and without reservation."[16] The impression in Washington was that "the Khrushchev speech, though sufficiently tough, confined its bellicosity in the main to the underdeveloped world; and here, as Kennedy understood, the Russians were confronted by opportunities which they could not easily resist."[17] That the United States needed effective military forces to counter rebellion, subversion and guerrilla warfare was an unchallenged assumption in the early days of the Kennedy period, and it drew particular support from Robert Kennedy, then Attorney General; Walt Rostow, then Deputy Assistant to the President for National Security Affairs; and Roger Hilsman, then Director of the Bureau of Intelligence and Research in the Department of State.

The literature on counter-insurgency techniques was developed primarily by military officers and others who had had first-hand experience confronting guerrilla warfare in Malaya, the Philippines, Greece and elsewhere. Samuel

Huntington, one of the few American scholars to take interest in the subject, offered the following observations in introducing a collection of essays on guerrilla warfare:

> Revolutionary warfare is the struggle between a nongovernment group and a government in which the latter attempts to destroy the former by some or all of the means at its command, and the nongovernmental group attempts by all the means at its command to replace the government in some or all of its territory. The post-World War II struggles in Indochina, Malaya and Algeria were revolutionary wars. . . . Guerrilla warfare is a form of warfare by which the strategically weaker side assumes the tactical offensive in selected forms, times and places. . . . To win a revolutionary war, it is necessary to carry on a prolonged campaign for the support of a crucial social group. Guerrilla warfare and counterguerrilla warfare must be directed to this goals. Thus, the immediate problem of the United States is to develop a doctrine of counterguerrilla warfare as one element in a broader politico-military strategy of counterrevolutionary war.[18]

Huntington's plea was heeded even before his words had been published. In the first year of the Kennedy administration, the Special Warfare Center at Fort Bragg, North Carolina, was charged with the mission of training special forces to fight in the jungles of less developed countries; additional centers were established at Camp Pendleton, California, in Panama, Okinawa and West Germany; and a Counterinsurgency Committee directed by Maxwell Taylor was established to oversee the development of this military capability.

In the early years of the Kennedy administration the containment paradigm was not only reaffirmed, it was adjusted to accommodate strategies of limited war, concepts of coercive diplomacy, and techniques of counter-insurgency. Each adjustment made American military intervention that much more likely and easier to justify. In the early 1960s it was very difficult to see, at least from Washington, that Vietnam would be anything other than another successful application of the paradigm.

Defending the Paradigm

If Kuhn tells us something about paradigm development and adjustment, it is Festinger who provides insight into paradigm defense and into the process by which allegiances are transferred from the old paradigm to the new. Those with a vested interest in the old paradigm seek information and individuals to support their view and screen out, avoid or ridicule sources of dissonance that tend to undermine their position. This pattern was followed with respect to Vietnam policy as well.

When President Kennedy entered office he was warned by Eisenhower that

Laos was in deep trouble and could not afford to be lost to the communists. In the talks between the two men during the transition period between their presidencies, Vietnam was not mentioned except as an area that would be threatened if Laos fell. In January 1961 the American presence in Vietnam was limited to a 685-man Military Assistance Advisory Group. But by the time of Kennedy's death in November 1963, there were more than 16,000 U.S. personnel in the country, President Diem of South Vietnam had been overthrown, the political scene in Saigon was one of acute instability, and the military situation in the countryside vis-à-vis the communists was deteriorating rather than improving.

These developments may be defined in Kuhn's terms as anomalies, phenomena that were not readily explained by the existing paradigm. Some observers felt immediately that the United States was headed for trouble, that the old rules were not applicable to Vietnam, that American priorities were becoming distorted. But in Washington policy circles this was clearly a minority view that carried very little weight.

In succeeding Kennedy, Lyndon Johnson reaffirmed the American commitment to containment and to its applicability in Vietnam. He approved several steps to promote American military pressure against North Vietnam and used the Gulf of Tonkin incident in August 1964 to obtain from the Congress (by a vote of 88 to 2) blanket approval and support of "all necessary measures to repel any armed attack against the forces of the United States and to prevent further aggression." Johnson justified his need for the powers provided by the congressional resolution in the following terms:

> The challenge that we face in Southeast Asia today is the same challenge that we faced with courage and that we have met with strength in Greece and Turkey, in Berlin and Korea, in Lebanon and in Cuba. And to any who may be tempted to support or to widen the present aggression I say this: There is no threat to any peaceful power from the United States of America. But there can be no peace by aggression and no immunity from reply. That is what we meant by the actions that we took yesterday.[19]

To be sure, there was by this time some hesitancy among individuals in the government and outside it concerning the direction of U.S. policy in Vietnam; but this attitude can only be described as a mixture of hope and concern and in no way an abandonment of the containment paradigm. Perhaps *The New York Times* summed up the American mood most aptly with this editorial published August 8, 1964, the day after the passage of the Gulf of Tonkin resolution:

> President Johnson . . . now has proof of a united Congress and a united nation: he has demonstrated his own capacity for toughness. And the Communists have been left in no

doubt about American determination. This is a position of strength from which the Administration can and should now demonstrate that it is as resolute in seeking a peaceful settlement as it is in prosecuting the war.

Within the next twelve months the United States undertook extensive bombing of North Vietnam and began the process of placing large numbers of American combat troops on the ground in the south (the number rising from 125,000 men in July 1965 to 550,000 men by January 1968).

During this period of escalation, spokesmen for the administration — perhaps Secretary of State Dean Rusk most frequently and most articulately — presented the case for American military involvement in Vietnam. There were at least eight reasons offered to justify American actions:

> — To contain communism and prevent confirmation of the domino theory that predicted that the fall of Vietnam would lead to the sequential fall of all the independent states of Southeast Asia, much like a row of falling dominoes
> — To contain Chinese expansion
> — To honor American commitments to the Southeast Asia Treaty Organization (SEATO)[20]
> — To repel aggression from North Vietnam
> — To permit South Vietnam the right of self-determination
> — To demonstrate that the United States keeps its word
> — To satisfy South Vietnam's request for American assistance
> — To prove that wars of national liberation cannot succeed

The costs, risks and benefits of these interrelated objectives were never fully spelled out, but collectively they were judged by the American people to have sufficient merit that the policy was widely supported for a very long time.

In the early period of American military involvement, the only high-level official openly skeptical of the policy was George Ball.[21] Ball argued that the costs of a widening military involvement in Vietnam outweighed the potential benefits of retaining a non-communist government in the south. He rejected those arguments which drew an analogy between the Korean War and the Vietnam War. He was particularly concerned that American overinvestment in Vietnam would have deleterious effects on the United States position in Europe. Consequently he urged that the president seek a political solution to the conflict which would avoid deeper American military involvement.

But Ball was arguing from a position of weakness. He was a European expert and not an Asian specialist. He was alone in his opposition. And much of his case rested on unproven assertions of what would happen if the focus on American military policy were maintained; the reading of the historical record by most of his colleagues failed to support Ball's contentions. Moreover, it is probably the case that Ball's criticisms served Lyndon Johnson well, because Johnson, who was committed to the policy and in total disagreement with Ball's views, could justify to himself and to others that he was being exposed to the full range of policy options.[22]

The Transfer of Allegiances

There was no single event that completely transformed American opinion about the war in Vietnam or that shattered American confidence in containment. Rather, it was a slow, gradual process, an accumulation for almost fifteen years of information that was all of the dissonant variety. Different individuals and groups, with different stakes in the policy, withdrew their allegiance from the paradigm at different times, stimulated by different events. It took many years for the weaknesses of the paradigm to become widely recognized. Recall that it was not until 1968 that public opinion polls in the United States showed that more than 50 percent of the American public was opposed to military intervention in Vietnam. Note that until 1973 the Congress, despite its deep division over the war, remained passive and never rescinded the Gulf of Tonkin resolution or adopted any other measures indicating unequivocal dissatisfaction with American policy. Even the presidential election of 1972 between Nixon and McGovern — in many ways a plebiscite on U.S. policy in Vietnam — demonstrated the unwillingness of the American people to admit failure and to demand the withdrawal of all forces from the area unconditionally.

What can be noted, however, are several of the key developments that led to important defections from the ranks of the paradigm supporters. They may be summarized as follows:

Gulf of Tonkin Revelations — Senator William Fulbright, chairman of the prestigious Senate Foreign Relations Committee, who steered the Gulf of Tonkin resolution through the Senate, learned in 1965 that the administration had provided a highly incomplete and misleading account of the events that led to the incident. Feeling that he had been a victim of the Johnson administration's duplicity, he became an outspoken critic of

American policy. His criticism was particularly important because it broke the bipartisan consensus in the Congress on U.S. foreign policy that had been in evidence since the days of Arthur Vandenburg and the Truman administration. Fulbright's eloquent and vigorous attacks, while ridiculed by Johnson, had the effect of providing a prominent Southern establishment figure as a rallying point for the developing anti-war movement.

Discriminatory Draft — It became evident by the mid-1960s that Americans doing the fighting and dying in South Vietnam came disproportionately from black and other minority groups, with large numbers of middle-class white youths able to avoid the draft through deferments. Eventually this led important members of the civil rights movement, including Martin Luther King, Jr., to become vigorous opponents of the war.

Sino-Soviet Split — As early as the late 1950s, a few American analysts detected that the Soviet Union and the People's Republic of China were in open disagreement because of ideological differences, boundary disputes, competition for influence in the less developed countries, personal animosity between Mao Tse-tung and Khrushchev, and other reasons. As the appreciation of this split spread among American intellectuals, it undercut the argument that the United States was confronted by a monolithic communist movement and severely weakened the strategic rationale for American intervention.

Criticism by Southeast Asian Specialists — There was little expertise on Southeast Asia in the United States. But the few notable authorities, particularly Bernard Fall and Robert Shaplen, emphasized the differences between the reality of the situation as they saw it and the premises of American policy: the heroic figure of Ho Chi Minh to the Vietnamese people; the historical animosity between the Chinese and the Vietnamese and between the Vietnamese and the other peoples of Southeast Asia; the non-democratic traditions and apolitical interests of the Vietnamese peasantry; the cleavages between the Catholic, French-speaking urban elite in Saigon and the Buddhist peasants in the countryside; and the innate corruption of the successive Saigon regimes in comparison with the more effective organizational techniques of the Viet Cong. These observations tended to undermine the arguments that the war was about

Chinese expansion or about South Vietnamese self-determination, and served to blur the distinctions between the evils of South and North Vietnamese communists and the evils of corrupt South Vietnamese anti-communists.

Deleterious American Domestic Effects — The mounting criticism of the war, particularly among the young, intellectual and minority groups, led to substantial upheaval in the form of demonstrations, sit-ins and boycotts. Television coverage of the war brought the conflict into the homes of millions of Americans on a nightly basis. American casualties, starting to mount toward 50,000, became a potent issue and galvanized additional opposition to the war. Expenditures of $30 billion annually to finance the war effort began to produce inflationary effects in the economy as well. By 1968 social upheaval was quite widespread and had itself become a tangible cost of the war, leading previous supporters of the policy to change their views. Alastair Buchan, for example, a sage and highly respected British observer of the American scene and a specialist on European-American relations, was forced to conclude in 1968 that "the Vietnam War is the greatest tragedy that has befallen the United States since the Civil War."[23]

Defection of Kennedy Administration Officials — Key members of the Kennedy administration who stayed on to work for President Johnson became progressively disillusioned about the effectiveness and appropriateness of the policy. The disillusionment started as early as 1965 and was quite pronounced by 1966. The sense of asymmetry between the limited war waged by the United States and the total war waged by the communists; the ability of the North Vietnamese to absorb vast amounts of punishment; and the inability of the United States to transform the South Vietnamese government into an effective, less authoritarian, and widely supported regime brought on the resignations of McGeorge Bundy, George Ball, Robert Kennedy and others. Robert McNamara and John McNaughton also turned against the policy and, although they stayed on in the Johnson administration (McNaughton was killed in a plane crash in 1967 and McNamara was eased out by Johnson in late 1967), they lost much of their influence with the president. Johnson interpreted these desertions as being motivated by the animosity of members of the Eastern establishment toward a Texas-born president and by their desire to see him replaced by Robert Kennedy.

Criminal Acts By the American Military — Further erosion of support for the policy was produced when it was documented that criminal acts had been committed by the American military in Vietnam, thus obscuring the previously held image of the American hero in conflict with the communist villain. The massacre at My Lai, the bombing of hospitals in North Vietnam, the falsification of body counts in order to satisfy quantitative measures of effectiveness, and the subsequent cover-up of these acts by high-level U.S. military officials generated the view that considerable corruption permeated the American war effort.

Tet Offensive — Perhaps more than any other single event, the Tet Offensive demonstrated a gap between the American public's perception of the war and the military reality. President Johnson and his colleagues had spent much of 1967 building the case that most hamlets and cities in South Vietnam were safe from communist attack and that the war was being won. But on January 31, 1968, forces of the National Liberation Front attacked every town and city in the country as well as virtually every significant American military base. Although communist forces ultimately suffered great losses, American policy had been dealt a grievous political blow.

Open criticism of American policy spilled onto the pages of major American news magazines and was endorsed by leading figures in broadcast journalism. For many Americans, it was Tet that led to their transfer of allegiances away from the containment paradigm.

Lack of Allied Support — With the transfer of allegiances away from the policy quite pronounced by early 1968, Johnson replaced McNamara with Clark Clifford, who had been a strong supporter of military intervention. Clifford went on a fact-finding tour of the region, expecting to be bolstered by allied support for the U.S. war effort. He found instead only the mildest expressions of support and an unwillingness on the part of the nations of the Asian Pacific region, except for South Korea, to contribute more than a token military presence to Vietnam. This lack of enthusiasm was crucial in changing Clifford's mind about the policy, and his change of mind was perhaps the decisive blow that led President Johnson to halt the escalation of the war and to decide not to run again for the presidency.

Widening of the War Effort — Despite the criticism of the application of containment to Vietnam, the Nixon administration sought to disengage from Vietnam only under conditions that would permit the South Vietnamese government to continue to function for several years. This led to the decision to intensify the war effort by invading Cambodia (to rid the communists of sanctuaries) and increasing the frequency and destructiveness of the bombing, even while reducing the total level of U.S. combat troops in the area. These actions led some to believe that American military involvement might not end without congressional action. A substantial impetus was thus provided for the passage of the War Powers Act to constrain the ability of the president to wage war without congressional authorization.

The cumulative effect of these experiences was to transfer allegiances away from the containment paradigm to the point of destroying its legitimacy. And with the publication of *The Pentagon Papers* and the subsequent documentation of presidential wrong-doing in several areas by Kennedy, Johnson and Nixon, a substantial dose of skepticism now pervades American attitudes concerning whatever policies the current president chooses to adopt.

Toward a New Paradigm?

In the aftermath of the Vietnam experience, no new paradigm has emerged to replace containment. A transfer of allegiances has taken place away from containment without moving toward any single alternative. In this sense Kuhn's description is not applicable and instead, during the years since the fall of Vietnam, we have witnessed an unsuccessful search for a new set of guidelines to govern American foreign policy. At this juncture three schools of thought can be distinguished: paradigm defenders, paradigm adjusters, and paradigm deniers.

The paradigm defenders argue essentially that the premises of containment are correct and that the United States failed in Vietnam only because its own domestic political processes prevented the proper execution of the policy. According to this view the United States made only one crucial error during the war: it abandoned South Vietnam. In addition, the United States applied its military force in too limited and too gradual a fashion, permitting North Vietnam to adjust to the incremental changes in military pressure. Future American intervention should still be guided by the objective of containing communism, and particularly Soviet expansionism. But U.S. strategy should emphasize the rapid application of maximum military force. Adherents of this view emphasize that South Vietnam was ultimately defeated by conventional forces from North Vietnam and not through communist victories in guerrilla warfare. They note that the domino theory was proven correct, that Cambodia and Laos have fallen, and that Thailand is now gravely threatened. The principal concern of the paradigm defenders is that, as a consequence of Vietnam, the United States has lost the will to conduct an active foreign policy. Too many lessons — and the wrong lessons — will have been learned.

The paradigm adjusters argue that the Vietnam experience should teach us a good deal. We should now understand that communism is a movement that in and of itself does not threaten vital U.S. interests. Indeed, the United States can conduct economic relations with communist regimes and can play balance of power politics among communist states. The Vietnam conflict was essentially a civil war in which American intervention and the containment paradigm should have played no part. The Vietnam experience should teach us that the United States cannot be the world's policeman, that it is of crucial importance to understand indigenous political, cultural, economic and historical patterns of behavior in formulating particular regional policies, and that we must remember who our close allies are — Western Europe, Japan, Israel — and not confuse them with other nations whose importance to the United States is a second- or a third-order priority. The post-Vietnam experience suggests, according to this view, that the domino theory was incorrect: the ASEAN nations and Japan, South Korea and Taiwan are as prosperous and as stable today as at any time in the last twenty years. Moreover, the Vietnam experience demonstrated the limitations of counterinsurgency techniques, strategic bombing and coercive diplomacy. The United States must never again become embroiled in a conflict in which there is an asymmetry of incentives, with the United States having less at stake than its opponent. The principal threat to the United States is Soviet expansion, and this threat can be checked by enlisting the support of our allies and those nations in local areas threatened directly by such expansion.

The paradigm deniers argue that nothing is needed to replace containment, that the world is simply too complex and too unpredictable to formulate any useful set of general guidelines for American foreign policy that are applicable across both functional issues and regional areas. The one lesson that should be learned from the Vietnam experience is that international politics is not science, and that it is both foolish and dangerous to believe in and try to implement any general guideline — no matter what its character — to problems of foreign policy. There are no universal norms in international affairs. The Vietnam war was *sui generis,* as have been all wars throughout human history. Those who seek patterns in international conflict are doomed to find them and to be misled by them. Instead, the United States should be guided by specific interests in particular regions that are subject to constant reexamination and redefinition. If the Soviet Union, or any other nation, seeks to implement its foreign policy based on a set of universal norms, it too will suffer a fate similar to the Amerian experience in Vietnam.

It is likely that the American wounds from Vietnam will remain sufficiently sore as to preclude the adoption of the thesis of the paradigm defenders. Similarly, the American penchant to address global problems, and the desire to introduce theory and concept into policy, make it unlikely that the paradigm deniers will have their way. Rather, it is most probable that containment will be adjusted, refined and re-labelled and, in its modified form, will become the new paradigm. The Vietnam experience will be the dominant memory that will shape this paradigm — whether we wish this to be the case or not.

Notes

1. Graham Greene, *The Quiet American* (New York: Bantam Books, 1957), pp. 86-87.

2. Robert Jervis has been particularly active in this field. See *The Logic of Images in International Relations* (Princeton: Princeton University Press, 1970); and *Perception and Misperception in International Politics* (Princeton: Princeton University Press, 1976). But despite his subtle use of theoretical models and historical examples, Jervis also fails to construct a conceptual framework that has wide-ranging applicability.

3. See Thomas Kuhn, *The Structure of Scientific Revolutions,* 2nd ed. (Chicago: University of Chicago Press, 1970); and Leon Festinger, *The Theory of Cognitive Dissonance* (Evanston, Illinois: Row, Peterson & Co., 1957). Kuhn's work has been the subject of great debate and criticism; see particularly Imre Lakatos and Alan Musgrave, eds., *Criticism and the Growth of Knowledge* (London: Cambridge University Press, 1970). And Festinger has been criticized by several of his colleagues in social psychology. But for purposes of explaining aspects of international politics especially relevant to American policy in Vietnam, Kuhn and Festinger have far more to tell us than their critics.

4. "Mr. X," "The Sources of Soviet Conduct," *Foreign Affairs,* July 1947, pp. 566-582. At the time Kennan was Director of the Policy Planing Staff in the Department of State.

5. This abbreviated interpretation of the highly complex immediate postwar period that led to the cold war obviously rejects revisionist interpretations of the origin of the conflict which stress as the cause either American aggressiveness or a process of mutual misperception.

6. Kennan has in recent years claimed that containment was misunderstood and misapplied, and a debate has arisen over whether his criticism is justified. See John Lewis Gaddis, "Containment: A Reassessment," *Foreign Affairs,* July 1977, pp. 873-887; and Eduard Mark, "The Question of Containment: A Reply to John Lewis Gaddis," *Foreign Affairs,* October 1977, pp. 430-441.

7. *A Report to the National Security Council by the Executive Secretary on United States Objectives and Programs for National Security,* April 14, 1950, p. 63. Known as "NSC 68," this important document was declassified in February 1975.

8. Truman claimed in his memoirs that this doctrine was "the turning point in America's foreign policy, which now declared that wherever aggression, direct or indirect, threatened the peace, the security of the United States was involved. . . . It must be the policy of the United States to support free peoples who are resisting subjugation by armed minorities or by outside pressures." See Harry S. Truman, *Years of Trial and Hope, Volume II* (New York: Signet Books, 1965), p. 129.

9. *Department of State Bulletin,* February 6, 1961, pp. 175-176.

10. Note, for example, that David Halberstam, who subsequently became one of the most outspoken critics of containment and of American policy in Vietnam, wrote in 1963 that "Americans have given their solemn word that they will stay to win here |Vietnam|. If they fail, the word will be out that Americans are paper tigers" (quoted in Henry Fairlie, "We Knew What We Were Doing When We Went Into Vietnam," *The Washington Monthly,* May 1973, p. 21). One of the few noted scholars who argued consistently that containment could not be applied successfully in Asia was Hans Morgenthau. But his views were not taken very seriously by Washington policy-makers.

11. It is now clear that massive retaliation was adopted not only because it was the choice of Eisenhower and Dulles on strategic grounds, but because it would provide a rationale for reducing the defense budget which was in keeping with Republican Party preferences at the time.

12. Among the most important works that made these points were William Kaufmann's *The Requirements of Deterrence,* Memorandum No. 7 (Princeton: Center of International Studies, 1954); and Robert Osgood's *Limited War: The Challenge to American Strategy* (Chicago: University of Chicago Press, 1957).

13. Maxwell D. Taylor, *The Uncertain Trumpet* (New York: Harper and Brothers, 1959), p. 6. Taylor and Mathew B. Ridgeway, each formerly U.S. Army Chief of Staff, as well as James N. Gavin, former U.S. Army Deputy Chief of Staff for Plans and Research, called for the acquisition of such capabilities as Kennedy took office.

14. Schelling must be credited with all these insights except the notion of controlled escalation. His work, *The Strategy of Conflict* (London: Oxford University Press, 1960), was based in part on articles published in the *Journal of Conflict Resolution* and several journals of economics between 1956 and 1959. A later work, *Arms and Influence* (New Haven: Yale University Press, 1966), in which the distinction between deterrence and compellence was set forth, to some extent drew on articles published by Schelling in journals in the early 1960s. Kahn's views on controlled escalation were presented in *On Escalation: Metaphors and Scenarios* (Baltimore: Penguin Books, 1966). He offered his views to several high-level civilian and military audiences prior to the book's publication.

15. Among the officials familiar with these concepts were McGeorge Bundy, William Bundy, Roger Hilsman, Robert Kennedy, Robert McNamara, John McNaughton, and Walt Rostow. Language and concepts strikingly familiar to that of Schelling and Kahn may be found at several points in *The Pentagon Papers.* Note, for example, the following items cited in *The Pentagon Papers: The Senator Gravel Edition,* vol. III (Boston: Beacon Press, 1971), pp. 119-120, 124, 694-702, and 632, respectively.

   1. An interagency study group under the Department of State's Vietnam Committee produced an interim report on March 1, 1964, entitled "Alternatives for the Imposition of Measured Pressure Against North Vietnam." The objectives were to force North Vietnam to cease support of the Viet Cong; to strengthen the morale of the government

of South Vietnam while reducing Viet Cong morale; and to prove to the world U.S. determination to oppose communist expansion.

2. A draft presidential memorandum was completed on May 23, 1964, that spelled out a thirty-day scenario of graduated political and military pressures against the north. However, it was never adopted.

3. In March 1965 John McNaughton developed an elaborate plan of controlled military escalation against North Vietnam. The purpose of the proposed escalation was to demonstrate that the U.S. has "kept promises, been tough, taken risks, gotten bloodied, and hurt the enemy very badly. We must avoid harmful appearances which will affect judgments by, and provide pretexts to, other nations regarding how the U.S. will behave in future cases of particular interest to those nations — regarding U.S. policy, power, resolve and competence to deal with their problems."

4. In a memorandum to Secretary McNamara dated November 16, 1964, on "military dispositions and political signals," Walt Rostow made the following points:

> "Following on our conversation of last night I am concerned that too much thought is being given to the actual damage we do in the North, not enough thought to the signal we wish to send. The signal consists of three parts: a) damage to the North is now to be inflicted because they are violating the 1954 and 1962 Accords; b) we are ready and able to go much further than our initial act of damage; c) we are ready and able to meet any level of escalation they might mount in response, if they are so minded."

It cannot be stated unequivocally, however, that the writings of Schelling or Kahn or both inspired these proposals and evaluations.

16. See N.S. Khrushchev, "For New Victories for the World Communist Movement," *World Marxist Review*, January 1961, pp. 3-28.

17. Arthur Schlesinger, Jr., *A Thousand Days* (Boston: Houghton Mifflin Company, 1965), p. 304.

18. Franklin Osanka, ed., *Modern Guerrilla Warfare* (New York: The Free Press of Glencoe, 1962), pp. xvi, xxi.

19. These words were part of a speech Johnson delivered at Syracuse University the day after the passage of the Gulf of Tonkin resolution. See Lyndon Baines Johnson, *The Vantage Point: Perspectives of the Presidency, 1963-1969* (New York: Holt, Rinehart and Winston, 1971), pp. 112-114.

20. South Vietnam was not a party to the treaty. But a protocol to the treaty specified that the parties unanimously designated Cambodia, Laos and "the free territory under the jurisdiction of the State of Vietnam" as states and territory to which provisions of the treaty concerning collective defense and economic assistance were applicable.

21. Ball was originally appointed Undersecretary of State for Economic Affairs in the Kennedy administration. In late 1961 he was promoted to Undersecretary of State, the number-two position in the department. He held this post until 1966.

22. In his memoirs Johnson described Ball as playing the role of devil's advocate on Vietnam policy (see *The Vantage Point*, p. 147). Perhaps Johnson was unaware that the definition of the term "devil's advocate" is "a person who upholds the wrong side, perversely or for argument's sake."

23. Alastair Buchan, "Questions About Vietnam," *Encounter*, January 1968, p. 3.

Alternate Sources of Middle East Conflict

Thomas C. Schelling

In America we have been concerned so long with the hostility between Israel and neighboring Arab countries, and with the unreconciled if not unreconcilable conflict of claims between organized Palestinians and the State of Israel, that we may too readily believe that a lasting and credible settlement of those issues could be described as "peace in the Middle East." That there can be no peace without such a settlement is easily confused with the expectation that with a settlement there would be peace. If we believe that, or if knowing better we get the habit of working with the assumption that the settlement of Israel's outstanding conflicts is sufficient as well as necessary for peace in the Middle East, as I think we often do; and if that assumption is wrong, as I think it is, then our strategy will be misconceived.

It may be misconceived in two respects. We may exaggerate the value of an Arab-Israeli settlement — not the value to Israel, but the value in relation to the broader foreign policy objectives of the United States. And we shall be unprepared for the disappointment that succeeds a settlement, and find that we had incurred some commitments, or abandoned some, on expectations that fail us.

The Arab-Israel conflict shines like a floodlight and keeps us from seeing what ought to be visible. The Arab-Israel hostility so epitomizes strife and conflict in the Middle East that, like a well-diagnosed ailment, it invites the belief that all the other symptoms stem from the same cause.

It is easier to rehearse the reasons why the Arab-Israel conflict is *not* the only source (or necessarily the main source) of conflict in that part of the world; it is harder to draw inferences for policy. One inference I draw is that the *American* interest in a decent resolution of the Arab-Israel or Palestinian-Israel conflict should not be thought to differ much from *Israel's* interest. We can differ, among ourselves and with Israelis, as Israelis differ among themselves, about the likelihood or the character of a settlement or the process by which it might be reached. But we should not suppose that Israel, in searching for and perhaps holding out for arrangements compatible with its own

206

security, is holding up the prompt achievement of a wider peace. If we think that much more is at stake than the security of Israel and its Arab neighboring countries against the outbreak of another war, and if we think that, in the interest of some wider Middle East peace, Israel should make sacrifices and not merely incur prudent risks, then there may be a fallacy in the reasoning. There may be a greater belief in an ensuing quiescence than is justified by current fact and recent history.

All I can do is to remind us of what I think we know. The Soviet Union probably has no strong or lasting interest, one way or the other, in Israel itself. However one formulates the nature of the Soviet interest in Middle East affairs, that interest is strategic and multifarious, involving the Mediterranean, the Black Sea and the Indian Ocean, North and East Africa, relations with Turkey and Greece, naval bases, oil, rivalry with China, and especially its simultaneous détente and confrontation with the United States. If the Israel-Arab conflict subsided for good, there would be substantial tactical readjustments in Soviet policy; but it is hard to see why Soviet-American or Soviet-Chinese relations, or Soviet interests in Iran or Ethiopia, should be thought of as stemming from the Arab-Israel conflict.

Few countries are more tragically caught in a possibly hopeless battle against poverty, urban unrest, and potential military disaffection, than is Egypt. Just across the Red Sea is wealth on a scale that the ancient Pharaohs could never have dreamed of. And just a little farther, in and around the Persian Gulf, still within the family united by Arab nationalism, is more wealth, and the richest people who ever populated a country. It is so nearly unbelievable that maybe only fiction can do justice to the potential for bitterness, outrage, and mischief. What an extraordinary balance of power it is that, for the time being, upholds those property rights and such historically suspect sovereignties. Can the people who claim to be so united — by religion, language and heritage — endure disparities in wealth unmatched in any country in the world?

As modern land warfare, nothing in history rivals the great tank, artillery and rocket battles of the October 1973 War. But measured in terms of the dead or of duration, it is in Lebanon that the violence and the hatred have seemed most intractable. It is even in Lebanon that military occupation by a neighboring country, measured either in square miles or in people, is most extensive. People more knowledgeable than I may have reason to expect that peace between Israel and its neighbors would eliminate the hostilities, if not the hostility, in Lebanon; but a cautious expectation is not a certainty.

Recently the Cubans have been receiving new attention in the United States, and people of my age, who thought that the "Horn of Africa" was the famous Trader Horn of the silent film by the same name, have learned better in the last year or two. A whole new desert region is now known to most of us by its proper name. There are those who see Afghanistan, Turkey, Ethiopia, and the Soviet naval forces east of Suez as an ominous enveloping pattern. Whether they see more than is there, or read more purpose into what they see than there really is, or impute to the line of dominoes more relatedness and more instability than events will ultimately bear out — peace between Israel and its neighbors will not relieve their anxieties, nor should it.

Just to continue this catalog of troubles, recall that Libyan and Egyptian ground forces had a non-accidental military engagement only last year. At the time Syria intervened in Lebanon, a few years ago, concern was voiced that Iraqi armored units were poised in a manner that menaced, or were intended to look as though they could menace, Syria's eastern frontier. Palestinian commandos "occupying" a corner of Jordan were forcibly expelled, and the bitterness of the occasion is evidently not forgotten nor forgiven. And it may be only in fiction that the rivalry between the Shah of Iran and the royal family of Saudi Arabia motivates their common demand for high-performance military aircraft, but the basis for Saudi Arabian insecurity is quite tangible. It is not clear just where militant Palestinian warriors will turn their attention in the event of an Arab-Israel settlement; but should they be more peaceful towards Israel after such a settlement, they are not without targets, or altogether without bridgeheads, to the east of them.

The relation of Israel to Arab oil is a strange one. Before 1973 the idea of an Arab oil embargo — at least one not imposed by terror and sabotage — was often dismissed with the reflection that oil-supplying countries could not long survive without oil proceeds. In particular, no single oil-supplying country could harm any customer more than it harmed itself by refusing to sell oil while its neighbors made up the difference. Two things happened in 1973. One was that the circumstances of the October War generated the political infrastructure for an unprecedented and unexpected collaboration among the Arab members of OPEC. And the second was the discovery of the "demand curve." What many of us had neglected to remember was that half an embargo is much better than a whole one. With control over half or more of the world's supply of exportable oil, and faced with an inelastic demand, *refusing* to sell may be suicide; but *restricting* exports is the way fortunes are made. What might have appeared in prospect to be a heroic act of sacrifice and solidarity, cutting back the very production off which a country lived, was in retrospect splendid business.

My interpretation of the market for Arab oil is something like the following. Prior to 1973 there was not a "free market" in oil, because there were no secure property rights to Middle East oil in the ground. Sovereign nations had proven that any rights they might sell to foreigners could also be rescinded. One might "bank" 10 billion barrels of oil in Texas and become instantly rich on its anticipated earnings, but nobody could bank in that fashion the vast reserves of oil beneath the sands surrounding the Persian Gulf. Nobody could guarantee to be still in possession in the future, or to be financially responsible in the face of temptation. Oil was therefore pumped at a price at which it might have been a wiser investment to let it appreciate in the ground. But if your lease is short and you can't take it with you, what you pump today is yours and what you save may not be. Furthermore, a country that is poor and illiquid needs the proceeds fast. Now that many of those governments have more liquid and semi-liquid assets than they have any desperately urgent use for, they can at least contemplate the alternative of selling oil in the future at prices that may be higher by more than the rate of inflation, higher by as much as the deflated rate of return on whatever investments they would buy with oil proceeds. In a few short years what might have been a "cartel" unsustainable for lack of discipline has so changed the terms on which Middle East oil is owned, and so changed the financial status of its owners, that perhaps what we see today is not far different from what a "market price" would be. (If a large part of that oil were in Alaska, it is not clear that its owners would pump it as fast as they could; it is not even clear that wise government policy would encourage them to.)

So what began as embargo became business. What began as countries substantially incapable of measuring out their oil has become a set of governments with "investments" in oil. The connection with Israel is mainly just that five years ago Israel was in a war in which oil appeared to be a weapon to which Israel's supplier, America, was vulnerable. That connection served a somewhat more commercial purpose and is mainly history now.

Lebanon had no oil. I have speculated before on how the course of events during the Lebanese civil war might have been different had it been known that Lebanon had, in assembled form, a few nuclear weapons or enough weapons-grade plutonium, whether from power reactors or from research reactors, to fabricate several weapons. What commandos from other countries might have rushed in to capture the stuff, if only to keep it from falling into the wrong hands? Disorder in Lebanon was neither much of a temptation to invasion by any country nor enough of a threat to require pacification.

Sustained disorder in an oil-rich country would pose a different set of temptations and suspicions. Where Syria was allowed to elect itself the benign occupier of Lebanon, no country, large or small, near or far, could quite so innocently move into a land of petroleum wealth.

These reflections and observations do not lead me to any immediate conclusions, especially not with respect to Arab-Israel relations. They appear to me neither to enhance the urgency of a settlement in any obvious way, nor to reduce the value of a settlement; nor do they help in discerning the kind of settlement that might be achievable and then sustainable. They do suggest the possibility of drastic change in the Middle East. They suggest that the character of the region may be enormously changed during the coming decade. They remind us that events could occur in the Middle East that would so preoccupy the major nations of the world that the floodlight centered on Israel, which made it hard to see the rest of the conflict in the region, may itself appear to grow pale. Except for the United States, most of the world's interest *in* Israel is not *about* Israel.

The Middle East:
The View from Washington

Robert W. Tucker

I

The history of America's Middle East policy since 1973 is marked by an apparent paradox. When measured by the scope of its aims and the degree of its
involvement, this policy plainly seems more ambitious than ever. It also appears more successful than ever, when judged by America's present role as
mediator over the Arab-Israeli conflict. Yet there has been no proportionate
increase in the power at the disposal of policy. Instead, a policy that has
grown in ambition has been attended by the relative decline of American
power. How far this decline has progressed over the past five years is a matter
of controversy and uncertainty. What is not uncertain is that the relative
power of the United States in the region has diminished since the October
1973 war, and this despite America's displacement of Soviet influence in the
principal Arab state. For that displacement cannot be seen in isolation from
other developments. It did not result in the reduction of Russian influence in a
number of other Arab countries, or in the reduction of Soviet military power in
the region. According to the estimates of most expert observers in these matters, Moscow's military power here—as elsewhere—has increased relative to
that of the U.S. Where these observers differ is over the degree and
significance of this increase.

The loss of American power in the Middle East must also, and perhaps even
primarily, be measured in relation to the principal Arab oil producers. Within
the span of a few years, changes in power relationships have occurred that are
almost without precedent. States that had once been the objects of American,
and of European, power have come to enjoy a leverage with the great industrial consumers of Middle East petroleum that would have been dismissed
as incredible only a decade ago. In the years that have followed this
astonishing assertion of power — astonishing because it was made virtually
without serious challenge — a considerable effort has been devoted to

minimizing the loss of power suffered by the West — in particular by America. What has happened, it is argued, is that a once dependent relationship has now become a relationship of interdependence. To this is generally added the point that the Arab oil producers — and above all Saudi Arabia — can be expected to act with moderation and restraint because it is in their interests to do so. The argument provides cold comfort. In this context, interdependence is no more than a euphemism for the loss of power formerly enjoyed, a loss attended by the hope — it can be no more — that those who now control access to an indispensable source of the world's energy will conform to Western views of prudence and self-interest.

It is against this general background that America's Middle East policy since 1973 must be seen. And against this background the conclusion forces itself that an apparently more ambitious policy is not rooted in the assurance that comes from a stable, let alone an ascending, position of power, but in the anxiety that results from an awareness of growing vulnerability. This awareness forms the principal motivation that has prompted a deepened American involvement in the Middle East. The same awareness accounts for the changing character of that involvement. A growing vulnerability must find its compensation in a policy designed, above all, to avoid the one contingency that is feared might suddenly reveal the full dimensions of the decline in American power. Thus another war in the Middle East is commonly found to hold out greater potential for superpower confrontation than did the 1973 war, itself seen as a sobering lesson in the dangers of permitting the Arab-Israeli conflict to erupt into armed hostilities. Such confrontation might arise independently of an Arab oil embargo. More likely, it would arise as a result of an embargo. For an embargo — and certainly a serious one — would confront the United States with an agonizing choice of passivity or intervention. The risks of remaining passive could prove very considerable. Yet the risks of intervention could also prove very considerable, not least of all because of the prospect that intervention would be actively opposed by the Soviet Union. Even when this prospect is largely discounted, the continued reluctance to seriously consider American intervention in response to another embargo, or to the functional equivalent of an embargo, is a matter of record.

Given these considerations and apprehensions, the determination of American governments to establish the United States as the mediator of the Arab-Israeli conflict becomes entirely understandable. The principal lesson of the October war, and of developments related to the war, is that the United States must henceforth extend its full efforts to ensuring the stability of the region. A further lesson, however, has been that stability cannot be ensured by a policy that emphasizes the special relationship with Israel, that supports Israeli military predominance, and that refrains from bringing pressure to bear on Israel to give up any of the occupied territories in the absence of Arab willingness directly to seek peace with the victor of the 1967 war. This had been, in substance, American policy in the aftermath of the 1967 war and, the abortive Rogers plan apart, it more or less remained American policy until 1973.

The October war marked the beginning of a new policy whose general implications are clear only in retrospect. The prime desideratum of this policy is stability. But the promise of stability is incompatible with the maintenance of the post-1967 status quo. Israel can maintain this status quo only by the continued willingness to risk war on its behalf. In the circumstances of the past five years, however, war has been seen to threaten American interests as never before. Accordingly, the avoidance of a further round of hostilities cannot be left to the unaided and unguided will of the parties. Its avoidance must be sought through such alteration of the status quo as will satisfy the demands of those who in the absence of change may once again resort to war, who in desperation may once again turn to the Russians, and who in the last resort may once again make use of the oil weapon. To avoid these prospects, America must now preside over the process that effects the necessary change in the status quo. It can do so by virtue of the special relationship it has with Israel.

In the past, this relationship had regularly placed the Arab confrontation states at odds with Washington. There was no intrinsic reason, though, why the relationship could not be transformed so as to constitute in Arab eyes an American asset rather than a liability. All would depend upon how it was now to be exploited by Washington. Properly exploited, it could win Arab support and place Washington in a position of great advantage over the Russians. What the Arabs wanted, Moscow could help them get only through war. But Washington could help them get what they wanted — or what, at least, they now increasingly said they wanted — through far less dangerous methods. The myth of the 1973 Arab "victory" — a myth of crucial significance — might thus be preserved. With the sense of inferiority and humiliation now in part erased by a war that could be seen as a victory and by control over a resource that brought sudden wealth and deference, the Arab confrontation states and their principal supporters might at long last move in a direction of greater moderation. If so, the stage would be set for Washington to play the ambitious role it now cast for itself and which, indeed, it felt compelled to play because of its declining power and rising vulnerability.

II

These considerations point to a logic in America's Middle East policy over the past five years that transcends the particular custodians of policy as well as their distinctive diplomatic methods and tactics of implementation. To say this is not to dismiss the latter as being without significance. It is only to insist that the starting point of inquiry and understanding must be what have been commonly seen since 1973 as the great imperatives of policy. These imperatives held quite as much for Henry Kissinger as they now hold for his successors. Indeed, it was Kissinger who first articulated them and who gave essential form to the new diplomatic design that emerged in the wake of the October war. Neither were the changed imperatives of policy merely articulated by the then secretary of state; he also played no small role in creating them. It was Kissinger who sought to demonstrate the very great dangers of any further resort to arms, not only for the parties to the Middle East conflict but, in the potential for superpower confrontation, for the world. Equally, it was Kissinger who remained passive before the challenge mounted by the oil producers and who, through his failure to respond, relinquished American interests and power to an extent we cannot accurately gauge even today. The twin threats posed by superpower confrontation and the oil weapon have since formed the principal constraints on American policy. They are the imperatives to which the new policy has responded.

Even so, the response has not been uniform. Although Kissinger's apologists have made too much of the differences presumably separating his policy from that of his successors, there are differences and they are significant. In part they reflect a contrasting outlook. Kissinger entertained a more profound view of the conflict than those who have followed him. He appreciated its deep-rooted character and the great obstacles in the way of its resolution. By contrast, his successors have often shown an optimism over the prospects of resolving the conflict that betrays little awareness of its almost intractable sources. Then, too, Kissinger was innately cautious, again in marked contrast to at least his self-chosen epigone. It was this combination of skeptical outlook and innate caution that led the former secretary of state to a diplomatic design that held out only such apparently modest results.

The diplomacy of step-by-step put forth no grand design for resolving the Arab-Israeli conflict. It deliberately avoided even the suggestion of what the eventual shape of an overall settlement might be. Instead, step-by-step sought to maintain a minimum stability, a stability to be achieved through a series of limited agreements that left ambiguous the shape of the ultimate outcome. Its premise was that where the parties to a conflict are unable to agree upon the outlines of a general settlement, limited agreements are possible only by leaving the greater issues in abeyance. What adversaries will not accept when presented with as a whole, they may accept when unfolded over a period of time in increments, or steps. Limited agreements might serve progressively to narrow the initially profound differences separating adversaries, while slowly establishing an increasing measure of trust and confidence.

This was the well-known rationale of step-by-step diplomacy. From the Israeli viewpoint, Kissinger's policy was not objectionable because it failed to set forth the general outlines of a settlement. Nor was it that step-by-step demanded too much from Israel even when measured against the American promise of greatly increased economic and military aid, though this complaint was frequently voiced. Instead, the principal objection centered on American willingness to mediate under Arab pressure and to do so without insisting upon Arab concessions in return for Israeli concessions. The pattern established by Kissinger relieved the Arabs of negotiating directly with the Israelis for the return of territory. At the same time, it served to transmit Arab pressure through the American mediator to Israel. The effectiveness and credibility of step-by-step diplomacy depended on the Arabs retaining confidence in the ability of the American government to show "progress," that is, to demonstrate that it could bring sufficient pressure to bear on the Israelis to make concessions. Thus progress and minimum stability depended on American ability and willingness to hold out to Israel a compelling mixture of sanctions and rewards. Kissinger resorted to both, though he understandably preferred the latter. In either case, the effectiveness of step-by-step was necessarily a function of Israel's degree of dependence on the United States, a dependence the 1973 war had increased and that American policy served to increase further.

Did Kissinger's diplomacy contain the seeds of the diplomacy that succeeded him? Is it fair to say that those who followed Kissinger have simply carried his policy to its logical conclusion? If the questions are pertinent, they are also difficult to answer with any assurance. Quite possibly, Kissinger would have resisted doing what his successors have done. After all, it may be argued that policies are often perverted precisely by virtue of carrying them to their logical conclusion. The line separating compromise from appeasement, or firmness from intransigence, depends on not pushing too far, on not carrying a policy to its logical conclusion. In the case at hand, there is the added consideration that the architect of policy apparently did not intend pushing beyond a certain point. This explains why he was content to leave the Geneva option stillborn and why he paid no more than lip service to the notion of a comprehensive settlement. It also explains his reluctance even to acknowledge, let alone seriously address his attention to, the Palestinian problem.

On the other hand, it is quite plausible to argue that had Kissinger remained in office he would have moved well beyond his initial design. For this design relieved only immediate pressures, and then only at a not inconsiderable cost. It did not, and probably could not, adequately respond to the dangers that Kissinger was as intent on avoiding as are those who have followed him. Once the great imperatives of American policy had been defined as they were defined in 1973, there was very little alternative to moving beyond the seemingly modest objectives of step-by-step diplomacy. Kissinger admitted as much at the time in acknowledging that step-by-step had probably run its course after the conclusion of the September 1975 Sinai agreement. Yet if this were true, what assurance could there be that minimum stability would be maintained? In what manner could the United States satisfactorily respond to rising Arab demands for Israeli withdrawal from the occupied territories and for the creation of a Palestinian state? In the final year of his period in office, Kissinger had no ready answers to these questions. But his successors did.

III

The Carter administration came to power determined to remedy the shortcomings in America's Middle East policy. What Kissinger had seen as the virtues of his policy, his successors had seen as serious defects. The new presidential assistant for national security, Zbigniew Brzezinski, had on more than one occasion in earlier years criticized the Kissinger diplomacy for its ambiguity. The policy of step-by-step, Brzezinski had urged, placed Israel in the unfortunate dilemma of either appearing intransigent or running considerable risks. By refusing to agree to a particular step without knowing where it might ultimately lead, Israel appeared intransigent. Yet by agreeing to a particular step without knowing where it might lead, Israel ran considerable risk. On the Arab side, Brzezinski argued, the step-by-step approach sowed the distrust that had been evident between Egypt and Syria in the aftermath of the 1975 Sinai agreement. Committed to partial settlements, to separate deals, the Kissinger policy worked to divide the Arab states through encouraging agreements that would be seen by at least some of the Arabs as a betrayal of their common cause. This consequence alone was seen as a fatal defect, since it was taken as axiomatic then, as it is still taken today, that just as the major Arab regimes could only make war together, they also could only make peace together. A strategy that either sought to divide these regimes or had the effect of doing so was held as inimical to American interests.

The more general criticism of step-by-step, whether by Brzezinski or by others, was that it amounted to little more than a sophisticated macawberism. Beneath its rather pretentious verbal trappings, Kissinger's diplomacy merely served to buy time in the hope that something might turn up. But little, if anything, was considered likely to turn up. Instead, time would be bought for reasons and in ways that would only exacerbate tensions already high.

Kissinger's soon-to-be successors did not differ with his general conception of the "problem" in achieving a Middle East settlement. The dilemma of such settlement, Kissinger had often declared, "is to balance physical security against legitimacy." How was the balance to be struck in practice? The former secretary of state was careful not to commit himself. Perhaps he had never resolved the dilemma in his own mind. Others had. Brzezinski, never one to be daunted by dilemmas, immediately struck the balance that had eluded Kissinger. "How does a nation become 'legitimate' to its neighbors?" he asked. His reply, of more than historical interest, was this:

> Only with an arrangement that gives Israel security, and also gives it to its neighbors, with borders that are mutually acceptable and hence have not been imposed by one side or the other, can the reality of coexistence be translated by history into 'legitimate acceptance.' In other words, the sequence cannot be... from recognition of legitimacy to a territorial settlement, resolving along the way the future of the Palestinians, but the other way around. By creating a situation in which both sides become secure, and hereby find it more possible to coexist with each other, the basis for 'legitimacy' will be laid.[1]

This brief statement reveals, and with great clarity, an outlook on the Arab-Israeli conflict that goes far in explaining the subsequent policy of the Carter administration. What Brzezinski is saying is that Israel's illegitimacy in Arab eyes is not of her "being" but of her "doing," that is, of her continued occupation of Arab territories and of her treatment of the Palestinians. Let her return the occupied territories and agree to self-determination for the Palestinians and she will create the basis for her legitimacy. Brzezinski was of course aware of the fact that the issue of Israel's legitimacy did not arise in the years after the 1967 war. If he nevertheless argued that legitimacy would result through undoing the consequences of that war (plus permitting the creation of a Palestinian state), it could only be because he assumed by 1975 that the Arabs had already changed, that in the main they had already become moderate in their view of the conflict, and that what stood in the way of this moderation finding concrete expression was Israel's refusal to give back what she had taken in 1967.

In contrast to step-by-step diplomacy, the critics of Kissinger argued that the only viable approach to the Middle East conflict was one that sought a comprehensive settlement. The concessions such settlement would require of Israel were, from the outset, quite clear. By contrast, the concessions that would be required of the Arab states were considerably less than clear. Although Kissinger had been reproached for the risks he had pressured the Israelis to take without knowing where these risks might lead, the risks had in fact been of limited character. Given their incremental character, they could be compensated for, if the need arose, and even reversed. This was a saving virtue of Kissinger's policy. The policy advocated by his critics did not consist of limited steps but of one giant step that, once taken, could be reversed only with great difficulty, if at all. This irreversibility of a comprehensive settlement was and remains in their eyes a virtue. Yet it was undeniable that it also raised a considerable difficulty. Unless Israel could be assured that her legitimacy *and* security were placed beyond serious question by a comprehensive settlement, the charge made against Kissinger could also be made, and with far greater justice, against those criticizing him in the name of such settlement. This was all the more true if a comprehensive settlement was not in fact comprehensive, as the early proposals were not, in that the issue of legitimacy, with its concomitant of the normalization of relations, was expected only to follow from a settlement.

Finally, even if the issue of legitimacy were to be resolved, there would remain the issue of security. Legitimacy is not the perennial concern of states, security is. A legitimate Israel could not be equated with a secure Israel. Legitimacy was undoubtedly a significant part of Israel's security problem, but it was not and could not be the whole of it. History affords any number of examples of states that have been regarded as legitimate by their neighbors and yet were insecure. In many cases, they were insecure though they held no territories taken in war or to which their neighbors could otherwise lay rightful claim. Neither were they insecure because they perceived themselves to be insecure. In some instances they were insecure simply because they faced neighbors who, for any number of reasons, were potentially hostile and against whom they had little, if any, strategic depth for defense.

These remarks are sufficiently banal that it is almost embarrassing to make them. They are made only because, in the context of the never-ending dialogue on the Arab-Israeli conflict, the distinction they point to is regularly either overlooked, or confused, or — not infrequently — simply dismissed. Kissinger certainly appreciated the distinction though, by his ponderous formulations of the Middle East problem, he often confused others. Kissinger's principal critics and eventual successors have also appreciated the distinction. Although they have consistently maintained that the Israeli concern for security verges on the obsessive, they have denied neither that the concern is real nor that in some measure at least it is just. From the outset, their response to this concern has been the proposal of a guarantee — ultimately an American guarantee. Whether implicit or explicit, the guarantee has been, throughout, the means that is expected to remove the ultimate obstacle to a comprehensive settlement. It is, without exaggeration, the key to virtually all the proposals for a comprehensive settlement and without which such proposals have always been vulnerable to the criticism that they would, if acted upon, place Israel in a position where — even though legitimacy had been once obtained — she might well be unable to defend herself.

The need for a guarantee to attend a comprehensive settlement was acknowledged in the December 1975 report of the Brookings study group bearing the title "Toward Peace in the Middle East." The Brookings study group included members destined to occupy critical positions in the Carter administration (Brzezinski, William Quandt, Robert Bowie). The report was represented as a compromise position of a group whose members otherwise entertained quite diverse views towards the Arab-Israeli conflict (discretely termed a "dispute"). It was "essential," the report declared, that a comprehensive settlement "be promptly found." The failure to find such settlement presented the threat of renewed hostilities, with all the incalculable consequences war might now bring. The theme of urgency suffuses the report. So does the insistence that the choice is one of peace (genuine peace) or war. While insistent on the great dangers held out by war, the report is optimistic on the prospects of peace. The parties are seen as disposed to negotiate a permanent settlement. What they lack is a viable plan, a satisfactory framework for negotiations, and the proper encouragement.

The Brookings proposals are indeed comprehensive. They call not only for the establishment of mutually acceptable boundaries (defined essentially as the pre-1967 lines), the acceptance of a Palestinian right of self-determination (together with resettlement of Palestinian refugees in a new-formed Palestinian entity), and something approaching the internationalization of Jerusalem, but also for a peace that comprises the normalization of relations (though full normalization is made a long-term objective of peace). The settlement is to be implemented in stages that are to be spelled out explicitly. These stages, the report reads, "will require considerable time, probably several years, for full implementation." Either side is entitled to suspend its own implementation if it believes the other side has not complied with the agreement, though who will ultimately determine whether the agreement is being carried out in good faith is left unclear. Face-to-face negotiations between the parties is called for, though within a more general framework that should include the United States and the Soviet Union. The parties "will need help," the report emphasizes, and this can best come from the great powers who should also be prepared to guarantee the settlement reached.

What is significant in the Brookings report is not so much the specific content of the settlement it prescribes as its assumptions and general tone. This is not to say that the content is without interest. The report may not provide a precise blueprint for the policy subsequently pursued by the Carter administration, as some have argued, but the many points of congruity are surely apparent. Still, it is the assumptions and tone of the report that bear striking resemblance to the assumptions and tone of the present administration. The assumptions that there is no viable alternative to a comprehensive settlement, that the parties — particularly the Arabs — are ready for such settlement, that without it a war disastrous to American interests is inevitable and imminent, and that a comprehensive settlement can be negotiated and implemented in no more than several years — these are the evident assumptions of the Carter administration. So too the insistent tone that the great powers — particularly the United States — can, and if necessary will, do for the parties — particularly Israel — what unaided they may be unable to do for themselves is the authentic tone of the Carter administration.

* * *

Much has been made of the mystery that is Jimmy Carter. What is he really committed to? The question has been endlessly asked. Did he mean what he said in his campaign speeches about his commitment to Israel? If he did, how does one reconcile his statements before becoming president with his actions as president? Nor is the difficulty merely one of reconciling campaign speeches with presidential actions. As late as May 1978, on the occasion of Israel's thirtieth anniversary, Mr. Carter reaffirmed in emotional terms and "without reservation" the nation's ties with Israel. The United States, the president declared, "will never waver from our deep friendship and partnership with Israel; our total absolute commitment to Israel's security." Yet at the moment Mr. Carter was making this vow to the Israeli prime minister, his administration was pressing hard for congressional approval of a measure — the sale of planes to Israel, Egypt and Saudi Arabia — that appeared to strike at the core of the special relationship that had once largely defined American policy towards Israel.

Are we to conclude that the president has been insincere, that he would not have acted as he has over the past year and a half if he meant what he has often said? Not necessarily. It may be that he has been quite sincere and that his very sincerity affords a guide to his action. Mr. Carter may well believe that all his actions have been in the best interests of Israel, even if the Israelis and their supporters often have not had the detachment to appreciate this. He would not be the first to so believe. On more than one occasion, a man far more skeptical than Mr. Carter of men's sincerity, his own included, was known to complain indignantly about those who questioned the sincerity of his assertions that he had only acted in the best interests of Israel. And if Henry Kissinger, then why not Jimmy Carter?

It is the president's sincerity, then, that may provide a clue to the apparent equanimity with which he views his actions. His conviction that he is committed to act only in Israel's best interests enables him to dismiss the charges that he has acted, or at least may have acted, otherwise. Mr. Carter's sincerity permits very little self-doubt. Neither is his assurance disturbed by the recognition that his first duty, after all, is to pursue this nation's interests in the Middle East, not Israel's. He appears persuaded that the interests of the two countries, if properly seen, are congruent, and that what is good for the United States is also good for Israel. In this, one must note, he is as one with many of Israel's ardent supporters who differ only in that they would reverse the intended equation.

On occasion, it is true, the president's more sophisticated advisers have been known to acknowledge the disparity of interests between the two countries. They have rarely done so openly. And even when they have so expressed themselves off the record, they have added that the disparity would be reduced to marginal significance if only Israel were to take a more detached and clearer view of her real interests. To pressure her into doing so they have seen as unavoidable. The outlook that has characterized the Carter administration, from the outset, is perhaps best expressed in the title of a well-known essay by George Ball: "How to Save Israel in Spite of Herself."[2] Mr. Ball, an outsider, voices the same aggressively well-meaning concern over Israel's security and well-being as do a number of the president's advisers. Writing in the early months of the Carter administration, he also expressed most of the central assumptions of this administration's policy while anticipating much of the strategy it would follow.

It is imperative, Ball wrote, that the stalemate in the Middle East be broken. If it is not, the likelihood is that the present moderate leadership in the Arab front-line states — and Saudi Arabia — will be replaced by radical leadership. Should this once happen, the stage will be set for war, with all the dangers another war must hold out for superpower confrontation and the Arab use of the oil weapon. Even without war, the absence of substantial progress toward resolving the conflict may lead the Arabs to the use of this weapon. But the kind of progress needed can no longer be achieved through partial solutions. Nothing less than a comprehensive settlement can ward off the otherwise imminent prospects of instability and war.

The difficulty, Ball argued, is that neither side is willing or able to break the stalemate with a compromise solution the other side can accept. This being the case, the United States had little alternative but to pursue an "assertive" diplomacy that would do for the parties what they were unable to do for themselves. It was not a matter of imposing a settlement, but merely of insisting that both sides carry out the "straightforward trade-off" envisaged by United Nations Security Council Resolution 242. The trade-off, as Ball saw it, was on most points similar to the Brookings proposals. He dissented from the earlier proposals only in doubting the desirability of implementing a comprehensive settlement by stages. Moreover, in his proposal the Arabs would be required not only to recognize a sovereign Jewish state, but to commit themselves at once as part of the settlement to full normalization of relations.

Although the Ball scheme went well beyond what the Carter administration considered at the time politically feasible, he accurately reflected the administration in his insistence on a comprehensive settlement, in his fears for the future if a breakthrough were not soon made, in his assessment of Arab moderation together with his anxiety over warding off the threat of Arab radicalism, and in his conviction that — given the sources of Arab strength — "time is clearly not working on Israel's side." Thus American and Israeli interests, properly perceived, compelled the grand solution Ball outlined. If the Israelis and their American supporters could not be brought to understand this through reason, they would have to be pressured into doing so. Ball did not hesitate to point to the means whereby the American government might bring the Israelis to reason. By contrast, he was remarkably silent about the pressures that might be brought to bear on the Arabs. His essay left the clear impression that these pressures did not exist and that, if anything, it was the Arabs who might more effectively bring pressure to bear on America.

The Ball effort had illuminated the policy landscape, but the light was too bright for the new administration. Political realities required a strategy of indirection, one less overt and more subtle than Ball had proposed. The assumptions Ball accepted and the imperatives he responded to were the assumptions and imperatives of the Carter administration. Accordingly, the settlement he sought was substantially the settlement the administration sought. The problem was how to get from where the administration found itself to where it wanted to go. As long as the special relationship with Israel remained more or less intact, this would prove to be no easy task. Kissinger, it is true, had used the relationship to establish America as the mediator in the Middle East. In doing so he had already altered its character, since the new role required greater American pressure on Israel. Still, there were limits to the pressures the Kissinger policy dictated, if only because the concrete concessions he demanded of Israel also remained quite circumscribed. The fabric of the special relationship began to show distinct signs of wear at the edges, but it was not yet badly torn.

The policy of the Carter administration clearly necessitated more drastic measures. If Israel opposed the comprehensive settlement the administration had determined to achieve, which it could be expected to do, the special relationship would have to be ended. Indeed, it would have to be drastically changed in any event, since the requirements of the comprehensive settlement the administration envisaged — requirements that reflected what were now the settled imperatives of American policy — could scarcely be reconciled with the character the special relationship had previously taken. The "new" special relationship, if there were to be one, would have to be expressed in the form of a guarantee to Israel, a guarantee that would attend the comprehensive settlement. In the meantime, however, the old relationship stood in the way of such settlement and would have to be broken. George Ball had not minced words about this. The administration, he warned, would have to take the bit in its teeth and confront both Israel and its supporters in this country. Ball recalled President Eisenhower's action of twenty years ago in forcing Israel to withdraw from the Sinai and held this up as an example to be emulated. But the Carter administration, beginning with the president, was not given to the kind of resolute action Ball urged, and the circumstances of 1977 were not those of 1956. Besides, the president had committed himself both before and after his election not to use American military and economic aid to pressure Israel. Mr. Carter had repeatedly criticized Henry Kissinger for having done just this. In politics, commitments are always at a discount, but a decent interval must at least be observed before they are discounted. Caution was required, particularly in the period before the Israeli elections. And there were indications that with the prime minister, Yitzhak Rabin, out of the way, Washington anticipated greater flexibility from his designated successor, Shimon Peres. Instead, the Carter administration was confronted with Menahem Begin.

There is no evidence that the Begin victory affected the essential outlines of American policy. It did not influence the determination to push toward a comprehensive settlement within a reconstituted Geneva framework in which all the parties to the conflict — hence to the settlement — were represented. So too the insistence that such settlement include both Israeli withdrawal from all the occupied territories (minor modifications of the borders apart) and the creation of a Palestinian entity with the substance, if not the forms, of independence did not hinge on political developments in Israel. And too the overall tactics to be employed in working toward those goals were independent of the particular government in Israel. These tactics may best be described by the metaphor that described the Kissinger policy. In moving to Geneva and in creating the negotiating framework for Geneva, the administration would proceed step-by-step. Thus the meaning of U.N. Resolution 242 would be "clarified" through a series of interpretations that, in their cumulative effect, would enable satisfactory representation of the Palestinians at Geneva and, in broad outline, shape the desired terms of settlement. In the meantime, Israel and its American supporters could also be dealt with in steps, but here according to the formula of Lenin's famous pamphlet: "Two steps forward, One step backward." Confrontations were not to be avoided, since their avoidance was impossible. Once brought on, however, the administration would eventually back a step away. But the retreat would leave the special relationship on a changed, and lower, plateau. The advantages of this tactic are apparent. The element of risk involved in one grand confrontation was avoided. At the same time, the administration would appear to be bending over backward to accommodate Israel and its supporters while the latter would appear, as ever, inflexible.

The advent of the Begin government did not result in an alteration of tactics, but simply made the tactics already chosen a good deal easier to apply. Given Begin's record, and particularly his well-known position towards the West Bank, the administration seemed to have found an adversary made to order for its tactics. In fact, the practical differences separating the new Israeli prime minister and his predecessors were easily exaggerated. The Rabin government — and very likely a Peres government — was no more ready to negotiate Washington's comprehensive settlement than was Mr. Begin. This had been demonstrated on a number of occasions, one being the coolness with which that government had reacted to the comprehensive plan of settlement put forward unofficially by its own foreign minister, Yigal Allon. The policy of the Rabin government was to sit tight and to wait — for what? The difference was that in the case of the Rabin government, sitting tight, particularly in the West Bank and Gaza, was justified in terms of security; in the new government it was justified in terms of historic claims and security. In theory, the one policy was provisional, the other permanent — a difference not unimportant for opinion in America. In practice, though, the difference was marginal.

Throughout the summer and early autumn of 1977 the Carter administration addressed its efforts to setting the stage for Geneva. At almost every turn, these efforts were to bring the administration into conflict with the Israeli government, though only on rare occasions with Arab governments. Yet the formal record shows that Washington was asking for concessions from the Arabs as well as from the Israelis. As a June 27 statement of the State Department insisted: "We are not asking for one-sided concessions from anyone." Why, then, did this even-handedness lead to one-sided conflicts?

In part, the answer may be found not so much in what Washington was asking but in the manner in which it was asking. In the June 27 statement, for example, the Arab states were told they "will have to agree to implement a kind of peace which produces confidence in its desirability," but that "also involves steps toward the normalization of relations with Israel." Israel was told that it "clearly should withdraw from occupied territories" and that "no territories, including the West Bank, are automatically excluded from the items to be negotiated. . . . to exclude any territories strikes us as contradictory to the principle of negotiations without preconditions."

The statement — in the manner of similar statements of the period — was evidently directed primarily to Israel and not to the Arab states. Its intent was to admonish the Begin government, to warn it of the consequences it might expect unless it became more flexible. Thus the specificity of what was required of Israel and the emphasis with which the requirements were expressed, in contrast to the general, even vague, concessions required of the Arab states.

In large part, however, the conflicts between Washington and Jerusalem were simply the result of the Carter administration's determination to do precisely what it disavowed doing. Although insistent on the principle of negotiations without preconditions, Washington was slowly but surely setting a number of preconditions. The process of doing so had not started with the coming to power of the Begin government; it had been initiated some months before. There was, moreover, an apparently reasonable ground for doing so — namely, United Nations Security Council Resolution 242. For the text of that resolution, taken literally, did not support the principle of negotiations without preconditions. At least, it did not do so in the sense that it abstained from laying down principles that were to guide the course and, indeed, broadly determine the outcome of negotiations. On the contrary, in this sense 242 laid down a substantial number of such principles. Nor did it matter that these principles could be and were interpreted in a number of different and quite conflicting ways. In the years since the resolution had been passed there had never been agreement upon what it required. A huge literature, almost theological in flavor, had sprung up devoted to what 242 required, in what order its requirements were to be met, and the character of the negotiating process by which these requirements were to be met. The text of 242 was a delight for the exegetically minded. Not only were there ever-flourishing disagreements over what resolution 242 *said*, there were disagreements even over what it *was*. In the statement of the State Department noted above, 242 is variously referred to as a "starting point" for a negotiated peace, a "process of negotiations," and a "framework for negotiations."

The many meanings and faces of 242 were of course no accident. The resolution was the product of the parties involved, directly and indirectly, in the Middle East conflict. To be acceptable to them, it had to respond to their disparate interests and, on the whole, has done so with marked success. The Carter administration found in 242 a ready and useful instrument for advancing its design of a comprehensive peace and, more immediately, for prodding Israel. The Israelis were reminded that every administration since 1967 had "consistently supported" the resolution. This was literally the case. What was not, was the implication that every administration had given the same nuanced interpretation of and general policy significance to resolution 242. In the hands of the present administration its "territorial" emphasis reflected the change in policy that had taken place. The beauty of 242 was that it helped to obscure the shift under the guise of a consistent devotion to principles.

Even where the famous resolution might have appeared as an obstacle to American policy, it was not. The resolution gave no status to the Palestinians. It did not even speak of Palestinians, let alone of their right to self-determination, but only affirmed the need to "achieve a just settlement of the refugee problem."[3] Given this wording and the circumstances in which it was agreed upon, the most reasonable interpretation of the resolution in this respect was that it assumed a solution of the Palestinian problem within something approaching the old — that is, pre-1967 — territorial framework. The Arab states had made it clear, however, that there must be self-determination for the Palestinians, and that there would be no Geneva conference without their representation. Before this demand, the administration was not disposed to literalness in interpreting resolution 242. The spirit, not the form, of the resolution was the essential thing. And the spirit called for a comprehensive peace, a peace that could not be achieved without satisfactorily addressing the Palestinian issue, by now seen as the very heart of the conflict. The difficulty was that representation meant for the Arab states the PLO; and on this Israel was adamant, since consent to such representation would have been tantamount to recognition.

In the early autumn, the Carter administration made a heroic effort to bridge the gap. Although the Arabs had to be satisfied, on this issue the Israelis could not be openly abandoned. The device of a unified Arab delegation, presumably the result of the September talks between Secretary Vance and Foreign Minister Dayan, might, if liberally interpreted, have satisfied the several parties. That device already came very close to covert recognition of the PLO. In the interpretation Dayan himself subsequently was alleged to have made, the Israelis would not look too closely into the credentials of those representing the Palestinians. The Begin government had moved, but Washington sought to move it still further, now through the Russians. In October a joint Soviet-American statement on the Middle East went beyond any previous American position. A resolution of the Palestinian question, the statement read, must include "insuring the legitimate rights of the Palestinian people" within a Geneva peace conference "with participation in its work of the representatives of all parties involved in the conflict including those of the

Palestinian people..." The Soviet-American statement did not 'introduce" the Russians into the administration's plan for a Middle East settlement. They had never been excluded from that plan. The American action did convey the message that Washington would not hesitate to pay for Soviet support, though the ultimate price might be charged to Israel.

Thus by early November the Carter administration had gone quite far along the road leading to Geneva. Whether the conference would have convened by the year's end, as the American plan called for, remained doubtful at the time since the critical issue of Palestinian representation was still unresolved. Whether, if it had convened, it would have marked any real progress is even more doubtful given the differences among the Arabs themselves. Though the administration had put forth its best effort, there were still distinct limits to the pressure that could be brought to bear on Israel. These limits could not easily be breached so long as the position of the Arab countries — particularly the major Arab country — remained substantially unchanged. It was not enough to argue that the Arab confrontation states had moved toward a more moderate position and that they now accepted Israel as a fact. So long as they insisted that they would not recognize Israel, that they would not acknowledge her legitimacy, and that the prospects for normalization of relations were virtually non-existent, the Carter administration had to contend with forces at home that continued to place sharp constraints on its policy. The events of November were to change these constraints.

IV

There is little reason to assume that Washington had any foreknowledge of the Sadat initiative. The astonishment with which the Carter administration received the news did not seem feigned. As late as forty-eight hours before the Sadat departure for Jerusalem, more than one high American official had been heard to dismiss the Egyptian's bid as a "public relations stunt." If Washington officialdom was acting, it had seldom before given so dazzling a performance. Was the Israeli government equally taken by surprise? The story persists that it was not, and that although it may not have known the manner in which Sadat would make his initiative, it did know that an initiative would be forthcoming. During the preceding months Egypt and Israel had conducted negotiations through third parties. They had even agreed on the approximate terms of a peace settlement, a separate peace. Egypt would regain the Sinai, and without the conditions Israel was subsequently to attach. In turn, Cairo would be content with a very general declaration of principle on the disposition of the other territories. Once made, Egypt's duty towards its Arab brothers would be considered fulfilled.

Although dismissed by the involved parties, as might be expected, and treated with skepticism by most Middle East experts, the story is not on the face of it implausible. It is not ruled out simply by pointing to Sadat's insistence that his aim was a comprehensive peace, and one based on the principles he laid down in addressing the Israeli Knesset. Any other position would have exposed him to still greater hostility than he was already certain to risk by going to Jerusalem and accepting Israel's legitimacy and sovereign independence as a nation state. Moreover, Sadat could scarcely have thought that in breaking from the other Arab confrontation states he could exact concessions from Israel that the Arabs were unable to exact while maintaining at least a semblance of unity. Unless the Egyptian president really believed that 70 percent of the conflict is psychological, and that this element was — or should have been — erased by his pilgrimage to Jerusalem, his intent in making his initiative was either to conclude a separate peace or to alter world, and particularly American, opinion by demonstrating that Israel was not after security but after Arab land. Of course, the two aims are not mutually exclusive. Sadat might have entertained both, hoping to achieve the first but ready, if it failed, to fall back on the second.

Amidst these uncertainties, one conclusion may be safely drawn. It was not only Jerusalem that was unhappy with the Carter administration's Geneva-bound policy. Cairo was also unhappy, though for different reasons. Washington's ignorance of the impending Sadat initiative was as indicative of this dissatisfaction as the initiative itself. The administration's Geneva vision held out no visible benefits to Egypt. Instead, it promised to advertise her declining influence in Arab councils and her growing inability to exercise any real initiative. Caught between a Syrian-Palestinian bloc — supported by the Soviet Union — and the Begin government, Sadat would have little if any room for maneuver. Even if Israel, under American pressure, made concessions, they would further strengthen the Syrian — and Palestinian — position, not Egypt's. If Israel resisted making any concessions, Egypt would be no better off. Geneva presented Sadat with the choice either of appearing impotent or, if he sided with the Syrians and the PLO, intransigent. In the latter case, his prospects of receiving the American support he desired — particularly arms — might well diminish further.[4]

229

In going to Jerusalem, then, Sadat sought to restore a declining position in the Arab world and to recover an independence of action. He had undertaken his dramatic move not only from a sense of growing frustration, but also from a sense of growing weakness. But if a growing weakness had largely driven him to make his initiative, the same weakness placed constraints on his ability to carry it out. To sustain it, to follow through with a separate peace, he needed all the help and cooperation he could get from Israel and the United States. Indeed, it is arguable that Washington's support was in the last analysis even more critical than Israel's. Of course, Jerusalem also had to play the game; and this required, at a minimum, demonstrating by word and deed that Egypt would regain, without conditions, what she had lost in the 1967 war. In the event, Israel did not play the game as she might have, and should have, done. The Begin government did not offer to return the Sinai without condition. Neither did it make the dramatic gesture it might have of immediately beginning a thinning-out of forces in the Sinai. Instead, it permitted the momentum necessary for concluding a separate peace to falter by setting conditions on its offer to return the Sinai and by spurning the dramatic gesture. To make matters worse, Mr. Begin came to Washington to seek approval of his plan for administrative autonomy in the West Bank and Gaza. In taking this initiative, President Sadat had suddenly placed the United States on the sidelines. For the immediate period, the play would be confined to the two parties. Once they had set the terms of play, America could re-enter and give the necessary support against others who would wish to put the game to an end. But the Israeli prime minister did not play the game in this manner. Not only did his initial move (on the Sinai) fall short of the move he might have made, he also moved to bring in the party that for the time being was to be left out.

We can only speculate why Mr. Begin took the actions he did. It does not seem unreasonable to assume, however, that the conditions attached to giving back the Sinai were made in response to what Jerusalem saw as a rising Egyptian price on the West Bank. If so, Begin was using the Sinai as leverage to moderate this rising price. Any other interpretation must assume that the Israeli government was from the outset unwilling to consider the Sinai as the necessary price for peace with Egypt, that to detach Egypt from the conflict, and thereby to transform its character, was not worth abandoning the settlements and the military bases in the Rafiah salient. But this assumption must disregard what for two decades had been the cherished vision of Israeli governments, and one that Mr. Begin had shared with his political opponents.

The criticism that the Israeli prime minister should have refrained from using the Sinai as a bargaining counter once he felt the Egyptians were raising their price on the West Bank, that he should have ignored this move and driven ahead on the Sinai, is very different from the charge that he was simply unwilling to yield on the issue of the Rafiah salient.

The former criticism is serious enough; the latter charge suggests an obduracy and incompleteness of an entirely different — and, indeed, implausible — order.

Equally and perhaps even more important is the question: why did Mr. Begin run to Washington with his plan for the West Bank and Gaza? Why did he thus effectively deal Washington back in and seek its approval, the same Washington that had been leaning so heavily on him in the preceding months and that had clearly established the patterns of judging Israeli concessions by the test of their acceptability to the Arab states? Why, indeed, did Begin even need a plan at this point? It will not do simply to argue that he felt he had to make an adequate response to the Sadat move and that the plan was his response. If Egypt could not be satisfied with the Sinai and a very broad statement of principles, acceptable even by Mr. Begin's standards, she could hardly be satisfied with his plan. For the plan, whatever its real merits as a first step toward a resolution of the Palestinian problem — and they were not inconsiderable — could still only have the effect of reaffirming the position that, for the forseeable future, Israel was prepared to consider self-determination for the Palestinians. Why did this Israeli determination need to be given such specific form, a form that could only embarrass Sadat and make his position more difficult?

One answer to these questions is that Sadat's price on the West Bank and Gaza had been impossibly high from the very start, that he had indeed meant what he said in the Knesset, and that Begin, appreciating this, had devised his plan and taken it to Washington for the purpose of countering the effects of Sadat's initiative. For reasons elaborate elsewhere,[5] this answer seems implausible in its interpretation of the Sadat move. But even if it is accepted for the sake of argument, the Begin response was woefully inadequate. The Israeli government could not in this manner counter the effects of so apparently grand a gesture as Sadat had made, and to suppose that it believed otherwise is to impute to it an extraordinary naiveté. Whether Sadat was sincere in putting forth his *stated* terms of settlement or whether his entire move had been mere grand-standing for the Americans, a very different response was required. By responding as he did, however, Begin gave every indication that he

231

was not engaging in mere counter-posture. Its introduction and the attempt to elicit Washington's approval of it may have been mistakes. Still, these actions appear as a serious response to what Begin saw at the time as a new and imposing obstacle in the way of a separate peace with Egypt.

The obstacle, of course, was the Palestinian issue. Had it always been there or had Washington, after its initial surprise and confusion, been instrumental in reintroducing it? Certainly, this issue had always been apparent in the sense that any Egyptian-Israeli agreement would have to deal *in some manner* with the Palestinians. But in what manner the issue might be dealt with would evidently depend largely on the position taken by the United States. With strong American support it might be kept to a modest role in the negotiations. Without such support, this would prove supremely difficult to do. For then Sadat would be fully exposed to his erstwhile allies. Their opposition might be sustained; but the opposition of Saudi Arabia was a different matter, given Egypt's continued dependence on Saudi financial support. The Saudis, however, could not be expected to endorse a separate peace that would be seen throughout much of the Arab world as a betrayal of the Palestinians. Their mounting claim to a pre-eminent leadership position in this world alone precluded such endorsement (not to speak of their need to placate — or bribe the more radical Arab forces in order to ensure the survival of the medieval the Saudi dynasty). The Saudi leadership might be expected to adjust to, and even eventually to support, a separate peace if confronted by a *fait accompli* that clearly enjoyed American support, but not otherwise.

It is for these reasons that the position taken by Washington was probably critical in determining the course of events after Sadat's trip to Jerusalem. And while there is no way of detailing with assurance what this position was, its broad outlines are well enough established by this time. Having once recovered from its initial shock, the Carter administration picked up essentially where it had left off in the weeks preceding the dramatic events of November. Although the goal of Geneva obviously had to be abandoned, Washington continued to insist on a comprehensive peace, or what now was its revised version of such a peace. Accordingly, the Sadat initiative would have to be "broadened" in order to enjoy American support, broadened both with respect to the issues addressed in the ensuing negotiations and to the parties involved. The Palestinian problem could not be dealt with merely by a vague statement of principles. A viable plan would have to be developed for West Bank and Gaza that ensured the legitimate rights of the Palestinians by permitting them to participate in the determination of their future. To this end, Jordan must soon be brought into the negotiations. Beyond Jordan, it was desirable, even necessary, to elicit the support of other parties as well — and above all Saudi Arabia. American support, the Egyptians were led to understand, was contingent on meeting these conditions. In meeting them, however, whatever prospects there may have been for a separate peace were virtually doomed.

It was in this manner that Washington intervened to support the Sadat initiative. One immediate effect of the intervention was to cause Sadat to raise his effective price for peace with Israel. After all, he could hardly be placed in the position of asking less from Israel than the Carter administration was asking for him. Another effect was to lead Begin to put forward his plan for the West Bank and Gaza and to seek Washington's approval of it. The response of the Carter administration was one of tentative and cautious encouragement. Begin was advised to "repackage" his plan and offer it to Cairo. But Sadat was merely embarrassed by it. The Begin proposal could only have the opposite effect of that intended by its author. It would be seen by the Arab world as the open abandonment of their sacred cause. Its rejection by the Arab states whose support the administration considered essential was guaranteed. Riyadh could have no use for a plan whose acceptance would open the Saudis to the charge of betraying the Palestinians. Hussein ridiculed it as a step backward and declared he had no intention of joining the negotiations. Jordan's king was not interested in Begin's plan. His terms for negotiating an agreement with Israel were essentially the terms he had offered the Israelis almost four years earlier. He would take back the West Bank, but without conditions.

Whether a separate peace between Egypt and Israel had ever been a solid prospect remains unclear. One thing is reasonably clear, however, and that is the effects of Washington's intervention. At a critical juncture, the Carter administration had acted as it might have been expected to act. Given the assumptions it entertained, and the policy to which it was strongly committed, it could have no confidence in the Sadat initiative, if the intended outcome of that initiative was a separate peace. Administration spokesmen had little reluctance in saying as much at the time. Nor was Washington prepared to pressure any of the third parties whose support was needed to maintain the momentum created by the trip to Jerusalem. Of these parties, Saudi Arabia was by far the most important. But Riyadh viewed the proceedings in Jerusalem and Cairo with thinly veiled hostility; and Washington, respectful as always of the country now considered an American ally and a great force for moderation in the Middle East, applied no pressure. If anything, what pressure there was appeared to operate in the opposite direction.

In the period since middle January that followed the breakdown of negotiations, a period in which there was little if any real movement, an all too familiar pattern again emerged. Washington was fully restored to its former position as mediator between the parties. (Sadat insisted that the United States is more than a mediator, that it must be considered a "full partner" in the negotiations. The administration was not disposed to disagree.) The initial promise of direct negotiations was abandoned by Sadat in favor of the familiar pattern of dealing through the Americans, a pattern that effectively meant transmitting pressure to Israel through the Americans. Despite occasional pro forma appeals to the parties to renew direct negotiations, the Carter administration clearly was not unhappy in assuming its former role. Direct negotiations threaten the loss of control. They raise the specter of a settlement that, in Washington's view, may give rise to even greater instability in the region. That specter arose momentarily in November 1977. It must not be allowed to arise again.

In other respects as well, the pattern of a recent past is apparent. The one-sided conflicts with Israel have once again followed from Washington's determination to set a number of pre-conditions for negotiations while nevertheless insisting on the principle of negotiations without preconditions. And here again resolution 242 has provided an apparently reasonable basis for doing so, a basis the Begin government made no small contribution to by insisting for a time that the requirement of withdrawal from occupied territories did not of necessity apply to the West Bank and Gaza. That gratuitous, though momentary, insistence apart, the position of Israel is that it is "prepared to negotiate peace treaties in fulfillment of all the principles of the U.N. Security Council Resolution 242" and that these principles "will serve as the basis for negotiations between Israel and all the neighboring states." It is not with this commitment that Washington disagrees but with the Israeli government's continued refusal — in the absence of direct negotiations — to go beyond its offer of December 1977.

The point is significant and worth emphasis. On the general principles that are to govern both negotiations and an eventual peace, there remained very little difference between the two sides. At least this was the case if the statement agreed to by Presidents Sadat and Carter at Aswan in January is taken as the model of such principles. The one point in this statement the Begin government clearly had not as yet agreed to is that "there must be a resolution of the

Palestinian problem in all its aspects." But surely it was not beyond the wit of the parties, if they wished to reach an agreement in principle, to resolve this difference.[6]

The real difference that continues to separate Egypt (together with the United States) and Israel is not one of general principles. It is not the Sinai either, since the Israelis let it be known that they would not allow the settlements and air bases in the Sinai to stand in the way of an agreement. Instead, it is the insistence — Egyptian and American — that Israel go beyond the Begin plan and that she do so as a condition to the renewal of negotiations. How much more? The answer remains obscure. Its exploration is not important in this context. What is important is how "more" will be determined by Washington to be sufficient. Here, at least, the answer seems reasonably clear. The adequacy of Israeli concessions will be determined by the Egyptian response to them. And to the extent the Egyptian response is in turn shaped by others, the adequacy of Israeli concessions rests with whose who give vital financial support to Egypt and whose moderation and good will Washington too remains as anxious as ever to ensure.

V

The point was made at the outset that over the past five years the ever-deepening involvement of America in the Middle East has its roots in a declining power and rising vulnerability. An involvement that has seemed to grow with each passing year has not reflected a corresponding growth in power. Quite the contrary, a heightened involvement has sought to compensate for a relative decline of power. Involvement has responded to the perceived imperatives of policy, but these imperatives have been formed not from a sense of strength but weakness.

These considerations are crucial to the understanding of America's Middle East policy since 1973. They explain the fate of the once special relationship with Israel. Before the October war, this relationship expressed the one-sided support the American government was prepared to accord Israel. In Henry Kissinger's hands, the special relationship took on a new dimension that altered its meaning. Now it was used as a means to win Arab confidence and influence by extracting largely unreciprocated concessions from an Israel that had become ever more dependent on this country. Still, in the Kissinger period the support given Israel retained a special significance while the concessions asked from her remained limited. In the period after Kissinger, the special significance of the support given Israel has virtually disappeared, while the concessions asked from her no longer have readily discernible limits. The Carter administration has effectively ended the special relationship. This is the clear meaning of the recent arms package for Israel, Egypt and Saudi Arabia. It is also the meaning of the care the president has taken to characterize each of these states (and Jordan as well) as America's "ally and friend." The transformation in policy begun by Henry Kissinger has thus been carried very far.

This is not to say that American policy will be carried full circle and that Israel will once again have a special relationship, only now one that bears obverse significance to the relationship of the recent past and is instead reminiscent of the early Dulles years. Then, American policy was that Israel should surrender territory but get little, if anything in return. Yet it would be rash to rule out this prospect. However misplaced one may consider the present imperatives of America's Middle East policy, these imperatives are firmly held and may over time pave the way for a policy carried full circle. The consequences to date of the Sadat initiative add further weight to this prospect, for they have given unexpected and widespread attractiveness to Washington's simple "withdrawal for peace" formulation. Israel's security dilemma, which is scarcely resolved by this formula, is at best difficult to grasp. The Israelis themselves have made the task still more difficult by having so often given the impression that their security was equated with their legitimacy. By granting the latter, Sadat has made the former appear still more elusive and, perhaps, still more difficult to defend. There have been greater ironies in history.

Notes

1. "An Exchange on the Mideast," *Foreign Policy* 21 (Winter 1975–76): 217. The statement was made in reply to Shlomo Avineri's criticism of Brzezinski and others for "overlooking the fact that the real issue for Israel, in the long run, is not security but legitimacy, and that everything in the Middle East revolves around this."
2. *Foreign Affairs*, April 1977, pp. 453–471.
3. The "refugees," it should be recalled, included not only the Arabs who had formerly lived in what was now Israel, together with those who had left the West Bank in 1967, but the Jews who had left Arab lands in the late 1940s and early 1950s and emigrated to Israel.
4. To this extent, at least, Sadat may well have thought that in warding off Geneva he was saving the Carter administration from itself.
5. See the author's article, "The Middle East: For a Separate Peace," *Commentary*, March 1978.

6. The Israelis have agreed that the Palestinians "will have the right to participate in the determination of their future through talks to take place among Egypt, Israel, Jordan, and the representatives of the Palestinian Arabs." Save for stipulating the parties, this statement of the Begin government parallels the Aswan statement. It is true that the Aswan statement also reads that a resolution of the Palestinian problem "must recognize the legitimate rights of the Palestinian people." But unless these legitimate rights encompass — which was expressly denied by the American government — an unrestricted right to self-determination, then the most significant of these rights is precisely that of "enabling the Palestinians to participate in the determination of their future."

An Image: Israel as the "Holder" of the Regional Balance

Nissan Oren

Thinking about the more remote political future has never been part of our ethos. In many ways this has been our strength and the mainstay of our success. Had the founders of political Zionism contemplated the possibility that it might be up to us to become the sole balancers of the multitude of Arab peoples in the area, they may well have lost their messianic fervor before starting out on the road to national resurgence.

Ours is not altogether a unique case. Unlike political managers, political revolutionaries — and this is what our founding fathers were — are single-minded in their thinking and temperament, rather than well-rounded individuals sensitive to all possible contingencies and pitfalls that may arise on the way.

This then is the basic question implicit in the present essay: has our revolution come to an end, do we want to see managers as the captains of our foreign policy, and what is the course of action leading to a port of safety? What, in other words, can we reasonably envisage as a livable political habitat in this part of the world to which our next generation can aspire, a habitat that occupies the middle ground between the utopia of the incorruptible liberals and the inferno of the romantic chauvinists on both sides of the battle divide?

Since we are dealing with an image of the future proceeding from what we believe to be the reality of the present, and in view of the fact that this essay will, among other things, deal with prescriptive recommendations, inevitably we will have to rely on a whole set of assumptions. Needless to say, it is in the very nature of assumptions that they are contestable, as they should be if we are not to go astray from the outset.

The dilemma facing Middle East analyses resembles the ordeal of cold war scholarship in the decade following the end of the Second World War. The needs of statesmen to deal with bipolarity — a rare political structure — were passed on to the academic strategy assessors who undertook an analysis before an adequate account of Soviet Russia's foreign policy experience had been worked out. It was only in the 1960s that the two pursuits began to converge. In the case of the Middle East the sequence is likewise uneven. In the face of a volatile conflict-in-being, the requisites of the moment are to provide answers before offering comprehensive explanations. The historians have lost touch with the academic strategists, who are already offering policy prescriptions. The latter have neither the time nor the inclination to await the arrival of the rear guard carrying the factual inventory. At the same time, events will not await the process of data collecting. In the light of this, one is inadvertently inclined to accept the suggestion to the student of politics who is instructed to get more light from the "strategic beam" and not work only by the "inventory beam," where he is forever stepping into shadows. Ideally, the pointing of the two beams should be accomplished in the context of continuous readjustment and mutual verification of the very sources from which they emanate.

How we perceive ourselves, how our rivals perceive us, and what we believe our rivals' perception of us to be constitute the perennial triangular syndrome on which the formulation of rational foreign policy depends. To say that there exists a great discrepancy between these three perceptions and the three sets of realities is to indulge in truisms. Statecraft can probably never quite succeed in closing the gaps, though statesmen are expected to do all in their capabilities in order to narrow down the margins between the imaginary and the concrete. Much has already been written about perceptions and misperceptions in the Middle East conflict, and much more is yet to be done in the future. Since the confines of this essay are modest and the policy goals limited, all that will be done here is to form a list of five diagnostic observations and close with a proposed scheme for the future.

Our first observation has to do with ourselves as a state. In the very nature of things, the Israelis are and will remain an esoteric political case, which is to say that the magnitude of our self-misperception is easily comprehensible — though not excusable — in view of our very complex political realities. At one and the same time, we are audacious and desperate in the extreme. We speak of our uncertain political survival and our undoubted military invincibility almost in the same breath.

The sense of bipolarity in our destiny is undeniable. Within the span of a single decade we lost one-third of our people in the Holocaust and gained a sovereign nation-state which, after all, we possessed only very briefly in remote antiquity. Starting from zero, as it were, we now generate a gross national product as large as that of Egypt, the most potent Arab state.

Perceptually, our capabilities and our susceptibilities represent an inexplicable mess: our leaders, even the most responsible and judicious among them, can and do say — sometimes in a single sentence — that tomorrow we can take Cairo in a storm if need be, but also lose Netanya in an instant. The juxtapositions of extreme divergencies of these kinds can be arranged in an almost endless string. In a very real sense, there are ingredients of great-power capabilities in the Israeli arsenal, together with ingredients of fragility bordering on utter weakness. We can mobilize world public opinion on behalf of Soviet Jews the way no superpower can; no less importantly, we can exercise an immense influence on the U.S. Congress (somewhat diminished as of late) the way no other foreign country has ever been able to do. At the same time, we can hardly take casualties and each war fatality as a cause for national mourning. What are we then? Are we a great power because of our influence in Washington and influence by remote control in Moscow? Are we a pocket superpower in the region because we can take Cairo and, if need be, Damascus at the same time? Or, are we just a mini-state because we cannot even contemplate the possibility of absorbing even ten conventional missile charges on our cities?

There is no denying that the distance between the various poles within the realm of our realities is long indeed. What is contested here is our conviction that this distance is in fact as long as we think it is. We must start educating ourselves to be less audacious and more hopeful as to the long run. Our political survival is not in doubt; what is in doubt is what will become of us as a society while surviving. Remaining militarily invincible does not mean that we cannot afford losing one battle, or two or three. We must not forget the Holocaust, but we must not go on being obsessed with each and every war fatality of ours because of the oceans of Jewish blood spilled by the Hitlerites.

Unless we can revitalize our economy and revert back to a rate of growth to which we were accustomed during the first twenty-five years of our sovereign existence, it is doubtful whether we can maintain a GNP equal to that of Egypt for long. The fact that we can take Cairo if necessary does not mean that we can hold it longer than a few days. If indeed we can take Cairo militarily and also lose Netanya, as the "realists" say, we must in the future so reapportion our military capability as to minimize the danger of losing Netanya even if this means diminishing the chances of occupying Egypt's largest city.

Even though we have done marvels in cracking the Soviet shield, thus enabling 173,000 Jews to find their way to safety, we should not assume that in the coming generation we will succeed in reuniting with the Jewish diaspora in Soviet Russia. We must educate ourselves to accept the fact that in a future war we may have to absorb not ten conventional missile charges but two hundred and more, and still not succumb. We are, therefore, not a great power, nor are we a regional pocket superpower. We are a very resourceful and impressive small state with extensive influence in the Western world, one that stands a very good chance of withstanding various physical assaults of different power combinations but not of all possible alignments. Unless we begin by curing ourselves of propensities to elation, euphoria, depression and masochism in their acutest national forms, and unless we succeed in aligning our collective image of ourselves with reality, we will not be able to formulate a rational political strategy and an intelligent diplomacy to go with it.

Our second diagnostic observation has to with the divergent views we hold of our assessment of the past and of the national goals ahead. The problem here is largely one of hopes, values and aspirations. On the one side are those who point to the fact that we in Israel are only one-fifth of the Jewish people and that the very *raison d'être* of the state is to assure the ingathering of most, if not all, of our people around the world; we are therefore, from this aspect, an unfinished political product, and, as custodians of the future of the nation, we must perceive the present as being no more than the beginning of the national resurgence. Any limitations we take upon ourselves, political or physical in nature, are, in that view, not only wrong but immoral because they foreclose future options. Once such premises are set down, a complete political outlook follows automatically.

On the other extreme there are those for whom the State of Israel long ago came to fulfill its function by providing shelter to those willing and able to come. The general outlook emanating from this stand is directed not so much at the Jewish dispersion as it is toward the non-Jewish people of the region, with whom we should coalesce politically, culturally and ideologically.

These are, to be sure, the two extremes on the spectrum. What they had in common is a certain mutual restrictiveness which has to do with quantities, physical measurements and masses. Yet the questions implied in the two positions are important and must be dealt with even if their pointers may well be misdirected.

The contention we choose to expound on here is that essentially the revolution fostered and carried out by the founders came to an end long ago. More than that, the view expounded here is that the period of socio-political *innovation* came to an end by the mid-1930s, by which time the institutional design of the new society was all but completed. We are presently in the midst of an *imitative* stage, and have been for the last forty years. Statehood, the establishment of the Israeli army and the construction of the fifteen or so townships where the bulk of the Jewish immigrants from the Arab East were settled, the three most significant developments in the post-revolutionary era, did not greatly alter the foundations laid down during the period of innovations. Essentially, the perimeters of our physical settlement were fixed during the period of innovation (except for the Negev which was sparsely populated by Arabs).

What is significant in the above analysis is that, though we multiplied six-fold during the entire imitative period, we did so without impairing or altering the contours of the design handed down from the revolutionary period. We have demonstratively proved that growth depends on motivation and capital rather than on space. Even if the impossible were to occur in the foreseeable future and half of the Soviet Jews were to come to us, in addition to half a million Jews from the Argentinian diaspora, we could absorb them fully and harmoniously; the same cannot be said of the more than one million Palestinian Arabs residing within our military domain.

The conclusions to be drawn from the above premises are as follows: strategic considerations notwithstanding, the national ideals can be fully pursued within the physical confines of the nation-state we acquired together with our sovereignty. Unless we ourselves are so reassured, we will not succeed in reassuring our neighbors, and this, after all, is of the essence if we are to make progress in the international politics of the region. It is worthwhile noting at this stage that the dichotomy between the period of innovation and the period of imitation on the socio-political plane of our development has no equivalent in the realm of our foreign policy, where we have essentially been imitative all throughout.

Our third diagnostic observation is based on hard facts and can be thus stated briefly. Though generously endowed in terms of space, peoples and capital assets, the Arab world has been most cruelly treated by history in that the apportionment between space and people, on the one hand, and capital assets, on the other, has been unequal in the extreme. With the exception of Algeria and Iraq, one can say that those Arab lands possessing an adequate socio-political infrastructure suffer from extreme lack of capital, while the abundantly rich possess but a meager social potential for development. Since no Arab country can muster enough might to impose a hegemony by means of which the capital assets can be redistributed more adequately, and since it is safe to assume that such a redistribution of wealth will not be brought about by voluntary means, the conclusion is that the Arab region is destined to linger on in a state of turmoil, intra-Arab strife and interstate conflict. If anything, the conflict between the Arabs and the Israelis has tended to mitigate intra-Arab conflicts rather than aggravate them. Essentially, however, the juxtaposition of money on the one side and people on the other is a permanent fixture unrelated to the conflict we have in mind, a constant potential source of conflict.

Our fourth diagnostic observation is of great significance by itself and of crucial importance to the general theme of this paper. Let it be said at the outset that the observations are contestable largely because of limited time and insufficient empirical evidence. Putting forward our premises in a blunt and somewhat oversimplified fashion, the contention expounded here is that, in the "battle" between the forces of great Arab nationalism and those of Arab national particularism, it is the latter that have proved to be stronger and that are likely to become more so in the future.

The two forces, of course, are not mutually exclusive. Indeed, they overlap in large measure. Everybody in the Arab world is a great Arab nationalist. Pan-Arabism is a potent force that is not about to wither away. What is of significance for our present prognosis is the strength and future dynamism of the elements that reinforce the cohesiveness of the state units within the Arab world. Such intra-unital characteristics correspond to Western-inspired particularistic modern nationalism, whose outstanding example is modern Egyptian nationalism before the coming of Nasser.

Arab nationalist particularism requires little amplification beyond the Western model it emulates. Even though it contains important elements of Islamic appeal, it capitalizes on and rationalizes the common historical experience of a national heritage and a national myth, with a special emphasis on a more or less identifiable ethnicity. Particularistic nationalism is introspective and introverted, fostering a sense of pride common to all, with accompanying elements of xenophobia as the inevitable derivative of recently acquired political sovereignty. Nationalist particularism relates to the true or idealized social mores of a people in the context of a definable geographic setting. Translated into political terms, national particularism fosters the evolution of the modern nation-state, providing it with the behavioral ingredient of political egotism, which sets the operational rules in the state's interaction with its outer environment. Particularistic nationalism tends to reinforce the process whereby the society and the state become coexistential. Its political instrumentalities vary according to historical circumstances and the levels of social development.

A native dynasty, an administrative bureaucracy, a rising bourgeoisie, an army and a political movement of mass appeal may — all or some of them — contribute to the formation of such primary national allegiances. More than that, it is in the interest of a financial elite, of the administrative bureaucracy, the intellectual elite, the military hierarchy, and the like to maintain and perpetuate the acquired social advantages, rather than see themselves dissolved in the larger pond of any one of the federative or confederative designs of pan-Arabism.

If one were to apply a metaphor on top of a metaphor, one could well say that the cluster of present-day Arab states resembles an unstable molecule on the verge of breaking up into its component parts, and that because the centripetal forces (pan-Arabism) are rapidly being exceeded by the potency of the centrifugal forces (national particularism).

Our fifth and last diagnostic observation stretches into the span of the future generation. Cutting into the fog of the future is admittedly a hazardous undertaking in all cases. Still, this is what we have undertaken to do, basing ourselves on the above-made assumptions and adding a few.

If we were to stretch the development curves of the recent past on into the future, must we not assume that Israel will not long succeed in maintaining itself as the sole balancer of the adjacent and neighboring Arab states as it has done for the past thirty years? Though the rich Arab states have not willingly parted with their capital assets in order to enhance the economic development of the poor, they have been much more generous when the question was one of increasing their military potential. If the conventional regional balance of forces becomes irrevocably disrupted, one of three things is bound to happen. Let us spell out all three consecutively, arranging the variants in a sequence from bad to worse.

1. Our dependency on the United States will spiral upward until the U.S. Congress rather than the Knesset will, in effect, come to legislate and formulate our security and foreign policy doctrine; this will most probably be done in the context of a treaty of guarantee, which may or may not provide for an American base on Israeli territory to serve as a combination of a live trigger mechanism, a hostage and a symbol aimed at defusing Arab motivation to do us in. It is interesting and significant to note that, rather than creating a precedent, if such a base were indeed to be established on Israeli territory, the act would, in fact, be a gesture of parity, because an American physical presence of immense magnitude — military as well as civilian — has for some time

now existed on the territory of at least one major Arab country, namely, Saudi Arabia. What would an American treaty of guarantee do to our national ethos? Will the formal underwriting of our national security not impair our perception of ourselves irreparably? And finally, are treaties of guarantee between unequals of lasting validity, even if we were to assume, as we do, lasting goodwill on the part of the majority of the American people as well as a fairly good record on the part of American governments to abide by treaty obligations?

2. When the regional balance of forces becomes irrevocably disrupted in our disfavor, how long will it take for our generals to suggest, for our politicians to accept, and for the national consensus to confirm a doctrine of defensive counter-strikes, as they are elegantly termed, or, more bluntly, preventive wars, as such things should properly be called? The consequences of such a strategy need not be explicated here. It is not inconceivable, from the stifling state of isolation in which we find ourselves today, that the international community will insist that we be placed under political quarantine.

3. The bomb, embraced by us and by our rivals in the region in a mad endeavor to reproduce on the local plane the global balance of terror, is of course the worst scenario for a situation in which the conventional balance of force has become irrevocably altered. This is not a moralistic judgment but a practical assessment. The physical size, the state of socio-economic development, the political cultures of the peoples in the region and the civilizational plateau on which all of us in this part of the world subsist would tend to foreclose political stability by means of the mutual ultimate threat to life.

Is there a middle road that stretches between the near certainty of a regional balance disrupted to our disfavor within the foreseeable future, on the one hand, and the three scenarios spelled out above, on the other? A suggestion of this middle way is contained in the title of this paper. However, precisely because titles should be brief, we must beware of misrepresentations and misunderstandings at the outset. The "holder of the balance" concept is borrowed from the somewhat archaic past of political history. Even in the classic period of international relations very few states succeeded in attaining the enviable position of being the holder of the balance. Venice did so for a time, and of course England for a much longer period. It is clear that the past cannot be grafted onto the twentieth century. Moreover, the idea of the holder of the balance is relevant to international contexts larger than the regional context of concern here. Finally, states that in the past aspired to the desirable role of the holder did so largely because of economic considerations: it is plainly more economical to maintain a fleet — as Great Britain did — large enough to constitute an effective balance to the combined total of the might of the two largest fleets of the other side, than to maintain a naval establishment capable of matching the mights of all fleets on earth. For us the problem is not merely one of economy but of necessity.

The idea of the holder of the balance in the classic sense is as simple as it is splendid in its perception. The holder does not enter into permanent alignments and is not a participant in the balance system. It is for the "others" to construct and maintain a balance system. The holder intervenes only when each perceives the beginning of a disruption in the balance, tilting its weight on the side of the weaker party. By definition, the diplomacy of the holder is an-ideological. The moral implication of such a commitment is severe indeed. It means that at any given point — so our image prescribes — we may have to ally ourselves with Qaddafi against Sadat, with the Muslims in Lebanon against the Christians of Lebanon, with Syria against Jordan (or rather "Palestine," as the Hashimite Kingdom would have become by that time) or with their future equivalents. Such alignments will always remain temporary and in effect only as long as we become satisfied that the inter-Arab regional balance remains intact. Let us in all cases remind ourselves that though amoral by definition, such strategy is bound to be the strategy of the higher ethics as compared to the utter immorality implied in the three options spelled out above, namely, the plan that forces us to "embrace the bomb," the one that leads toward a future where we become debilitated as a people because of the utter dependence on others, or else the necessity of launching repeated preventive wars.

What is the hope of our ever attaining such a position within the region, a position, may we add, desirable and of lasting advantage with or without a comprehensive settlement of the Mideast conflict? Can Israel reasonably hope to remove itself from the perennial position of serving as the lightning rod of intra-Arab quarrels? The conflict between us and the existing Arab states is gradually becoming de-ideologized as well as de-emotionalized, or so at least it seems to us. The process must and possibly will go on. The legitimacy we so long asked for has in a large measure been given to us, at least by Egypt. Was England under Henry VIII, when the stance of the holder began to be effectuated, less of a pariah state in the eyes of the Catholic states of Europe than we are in the eyes of the Arab states of the region? The very doubtful value of such parallels notwithstanding, it is still worthwhile noting that the game of the balance and the balancer was played out successfully and uninterruptedly with the rise and fall of temporary alignments between Protestant princes and Catholic kings. Are the things spelled out here merely utterances based on wishful thinking? We do not really know because the future remains inpenetrable to a very large extent. All that is stated here is that the endeavor is worthwhile and that the pursuit of such a goal should be launched forthwith. It should be made clear that we are not presenting a model or providing statecraft with a timetable. Certainly, our ability to directly affect the development of political processes in the Arab states is meager, if not nil. What is absolutely essential — and this is the major prescriptive recommendation in this essay — is that we do not interfere with such processes in the Arab world which, as we said above, are characterized by two central features, namely, an inherent political contradiction within the Arab cluster because of the mild distribution of political assets, as well as the general movement away from pan-Arabism and to the direction of the strengthening of the Arab nation-state.

What are some of the elements in the operational code we must adopt in pursuing an objective of the kind recommended here? It is, of course, absolutely necessary that we decide very soon what our state frontiers are going to be (with or without an overall settlement) and proceed to reshape our army (if that is necessary) in such a manner as to make it an effective guardian of precisely those boundaries. For all practical purposes, Jordan of today is already Palestine; why must we hamper that very process? If we are to travel the road leading to our becoming the regional holder of the balance, we must at the very least first regain the regional status held by us for a long period until the Six-Day War. Until that fateful event, we did in many ways — passively, to be sure — play the role of the holder of the balance: the Republic of Lebanon was tacitly our protectorate, as was in many ways the Kingdom of Jordan, both of which would have become truncated if not for our presence in the region. If not for us, it is not improbable that Nasser may well have tried to make war on the Saudis directly in order to acquire possession of those assets Egypt requires so badly. These were admittedly tacit situations, and there were many more in addition. We must first regain both things we unwittingly lost in the last decade, and from that point on proceed to make overt and explicit those things which start out as tacit.

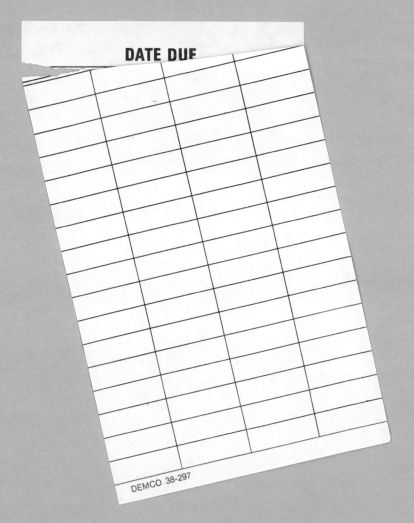

DATE DUE

DEMCO 38-297